# The Policy of Payment by Results in Irish Primary Schools, 1871–1900

# The Policy of Payment by Results in Irish Primary Schools, 1871–1900

## rancour and discord

**Tony Lyons**

PETER LANG
Oxford - Berlin - Bruxelles - Chennai - Lausanne - New York

Bibliographic information published by the Deutsche Nationalbibliothek. The German National Library lists this publication in the German National Bibliography; detailed bibliographic data is available on the Internet at http://dnb.d-nb.de.

A catalogue record for this book is available from the British Library.

Library of Congress Cataloging-in-Publication Data

Names: Lyons, Tony, 1957- author.
Title: The policy of payment by results in Irish primary schools, 1871-1900 : rancour and discord / Tony Lyons.
Description: Oxford; New York: Peter Lang, 2024. | Includes bibliographical references and index.
Identifiers: LCCN 2023036863 (print) | LCCN 2023036864 (ebook) | ISBN 9781803741796 (paperback) | ISBN 9781803741802 (ebook) | ISBN 9781803741819 (epub)
Subjects: LCSH: Teachers--Salaries, etc.--Ireland--History--19th century. | Educational evaluation--Ireland--History--19th century. | Public schools--Ireland--History--19th century. | Education and state--Ireland--History--19th century.
Classification: LCC LB2844.I73 L96 2024 (print) | LCC LB2844.I73 (ebook) | DDC 371.1009417--dc23/eng/20231017
LC record available at https://lccn.loc.gov/2023036863
LC ebook record available at https://lccn.loc.gov/2023036864

Cover design by Peter Lang Group AG

ISBN 978-1-80374-179-6 (print)
ISBN 978-1-80374-180-2 (ePDF)
ISBN 978-1-80374-181-9 (ePub)
DOI 10.3726/ b20833


Published by Peter Lang Ltd, Oxford, United Kingdom
info@peterlang.com – www.peterlang.com



This publication has been peer reviewed.

# Contents

# Tables

# Acknowledgements

My thanks to the Library staff of Mary Immaculate College, University of Limerick, for their unstinting level of service, in particular Ms. Elizabeth Brosnahan.

Gratitude is also extended to the wonderful staff of the National Library of Ireland, Kildare St., Dublin.

An especial thanks goes to my wife Sadhbh, for her support and patience.

# Prelude

Education: a debt due from present to future generations.

– George Peabody

A Payment by Results system was introduced in England by Robert Lowe in 1862, and roughly a decade later it was introduced in Ireland by Patrick Keenan. At first, it was introduced to the Model Schools alone, but in 1872 the results system expanded into all national schools in the country. The results regime, in both England and Ireland had two fundamental objectives – to ensure that teachers would be more accountable for the progress of their pupils, and as well as that, to expedite progress towards children's acquisition of the three Rs. The emphasis on gaining some prowess in the three Rs caused the curriculum to be very bookish, and this turned out to be one of the cesspits of the system which eventually led to its demise at century's end. The results programme fostered a constricted approach to the curriculum, and a methodology which was unyielding and implacable. Exact programmes were laid down for each class level in the schools. There was no deviation from the content of each syllabus. There was no space allowed for a teacher's individuality. The methodology was hard and fast, and bound to the criteria laid down. Inspectors were at hand to ensure there was no deviation; the worth of the teacher was determined by the results each pupil received at the annual examination. There were many flaws in the system, which will be discussed throughout the book.

The following chapters discuss the germination of the payment by results regime at an international level (chapter one); the adoption of the results programme within the national school system in Ireland is dealt with in chapter two; chapter three tackles the nuts and bolts of the system within primary education in Ireland; the ebbing and demise of the scheme is discussed in chapter four; the concluding chapter deals with a synthesis and an analysis of the programme.

Though the scheme was introduced at intermediate level in Ireland, this aspect is not the remit of this book.

Payment by Results was an English phenomenon in the nineteenth century. In due course it spread to Scotland, Wales, Ireland and to some other countries within the British Empire, such as Malta and Trinidad and Tobago. It stemmed from the fact that education was a costly business, and increasing as such, so much so that governments felt it necessary to curtail as much expenditure as possible in schools that were becoming increasingly associated with the state. The Treasury was one of the key supporters with a vested interest in such a regime.

Most historians interpret England's attitude towards education provision during the nineteenth century as one of *laissez-faire.* This policy fostered a market economy in which the law of supply and demand was to be the self-adjusting mechanism in human affairs. Adam Smith's *The Wealth of Nations* (1776) was one of the great bedrock texts of *laissez-faire* economics. Smith urged the state to concern itself with providing the poor with 'the most essential parts of education, to read, write, and account'. Smith exhorted that in order to ensure value for money the teacher should be kept dependent on private fees for the great part of his enrolment.[1] Smith hoped that such a system would provide a more useful industrial workforce and biddable citizens who are 'more disposed to respect superiors and lawful authority'.[2] This market-led economics played a fundamental role in establishing a Payment by Results system of education in England, and later in other countries of the United Kingdom. This current book explores the political, economic, social and educational circumstances of this particular education system in Ireland and to a lesser extent in Britain. It is the book's intention to elucidate and clarify the interlocking web of factors which came to surround the operation of the scheme. The book examines the actual operation of the scheme in the concrete educational circumstances of the schools of the period in which exposition, analysis and evaluation are interwoven. The programmes of examination are studied as are the prevailing teaching methods, the condition of the schools, the pupil

1 Ed. Cannan, ed., *Wealth of Nations*, vol. 2 (London: Methuen, 1904), 270.
2 Cannan, ed., *Wealth of Nations*, 273.

success rates and attendance patterns, teacher remuneration and conditions of employment, textbooks, equipment, and so forth, in an effort to get an inside look at the school systems in operation under the results policy. Reactions of key interests and personnel towards the policy are explored. Further insights emerge from close study of pertinent official commissions of inquiry which affected the payment by results policy.

The beginning of state support for education in England and Scotland was a feature of the nineteenth century. Payment by Results came to the rescue, with the costly Crimean War as a backdrop, in the latter half of the century when state subvention was burdened by rising costs. Payment by Results, with its annual examination of pupils, made it possible for the state's endeavours to ensure that value for money was a welcome outcome.

It was Adam Smith's ideas on teaching and the proper mode for its remuneration which were to be the greatest consequence for the later policy of Payment by Results. Basing his view on the utilitarian maxim of self-interest he set down the following:

> In every profession the exertion of the greater part of those who exercise it is always in proportion to the necessity they are under of making that exertion. This necessity is greatest with those to whom the emoluments of their profession are the only source from whence they expect their fortune, or even their ordinary revenue or subsistence. In order to acquire this subsistence, they must in the course of a year execute a certain quantity of work of a known value, and where the competition is free, the rivalry of competitors who are all endeavouring to jostle one another out of employment, obliges every man to execute his work with a certain degree of exactness .... It is in the interest of every man to live as much at his ease as he can, and if his emoluments are to be precisely the same whether he does or does not perform some very laborious duty, it is certainly his interest, at least as vulgarly understood either to neglect it altogether, or if he is subject to some authority which will not suffer him to do this, to perform it in as careless and slovenly a manner as that authority will permit.[3]

In line with utilitarian ideology on state support for education John Stuart Mill extolled such a philosophy when he expressed support for state support in this instance because it was not one of the cases in which 'the tender of help perpetuates the state of things which renders help

3 Cannan, ed., *Wealth of Nations*, 249–250.

necessary'. Mill did not favour allowing the state have a free hand over education – there should be limits. He wished for diversity within the population – if the state had unlimited control over education a scenario might ensue where universal moulding could take place. Supporting individuality, for Mill, would be conducive to progress. State support for education should be confined to the elementary level, and only in voluntary schools.[4]

In 1859 Darwin's historic *Origin of the Species* leapt upon the scene and was to have resounding echoes on nineteenth-century thought. On opposing sides of the fence were the theologians and the scientists, and on occasions participants were thrust into learned, and sometimes, agonizing controversy. At the same time, the general public, who for the most part did not have any first-hand acquaintance with Darwin's thesis, were nevertheless very affected by it:

> The effect of 'Darwinism' upon the non-scientific world in England was immediate and profound.[5]

With *Origin of the Species* came the message which became popular, 'the survival of the fittest' and it strongly endorsed an atmosphere of thought in line with stark and rugged individualism and it validated the confidence in continuing progress which was widely shared.

To infer that no opposition to the above outlined values existed in the second half of the nineteenth century, would be an exercise in deception, as there were many writers and social commentators like Coleridge, Carlyle, Ruskin, Newman, Arnold, and we can include Dickens as well, who were very critical of such a regime.[6] They all challenged Utilitarianism, and they favoured a more humanistic ideal, while eschewing the mechanistic methods of the Doctrine of Utility. As a counter aim, they did not see people as objects of raw socialization, and in short, they wished that human

4 See R. L. Archer, *Secondary Education in the Nineteenth Century* (Cambridge: Cambridge University Press, 1921), 147–149.

5 D. C. Somervell, *Nineteenth-Century Thought* (London: Methuen, 1964), 137.

6 See for defined treatment, Raymond Williams, *Culture and Society, 1780–1950* (London: Pelican, 1971).

motivation would be formed on a higher level than that of self-interest. They were opposed to the philistinism which was inherent in self-interest and self-reliance, and 'in the hardness and vulgarity of middle-class liberalism'.[7]

One person to embrace the philosophy of Payments by Results was Robert Lowe. He had also taken a liking to *Origin of the Species*, stating that he was 'completely fascinated by it'.[8] The year 1859 also witnessed the publication of Samuel Smile's *Self-Help*, a book which proved a great popular success, selling over 250,000 copies by the end of the century. The title of this book, along with another three by Smiles speak for themselves – *Character* (1871), *Thrift* (1875), and *Duty* (1887). His books encouraged the Victorian values of self-reliance; application and diligence; the value of patience, obedience and so on. The language of Smiles was simple and could be understood by the ordinary person, enabling that person to grasp the vicissitudes in the doctrines of the more philosophical or economic language of the theorists.

Educationists have condemned Robert Lowe, and some have gone so far as to apply the epithets 'knave' and 'tyrant'.[9] One of the chief weaknesses of the English system was poor and irregular pupil and student attendances. The Newcastle Commission reported in 1861 that, of 2,213,694 children at school, 38.81 per cent attended for less than a year.[10] Lowe introduced Payment by Results with the catch-all cry, 'if it is not cheap, it shall be efficient; if it is not efficient, it shall be cheap.'[11]

The abiding attraction of such a system was its value for money – teachers received extra payment if their pupils passed the annual

7 Mathew Arnold, *Culture and Anarchy* in G. Sutherland, ed., *Arnold on Education* (London: Pelican, 1973), 164–269.

8 A. Patchett Martin, *Life and Letters of Viscount Sherbrooke*, vol. 2 (London: Longmans, Green, 1893), 202.

9 See K. Richmond, *Education in England* (London: Penguin, 1945), 7, 154.

10 Cited in H. C. Barnard, *A History of English Education from 1760* (London: University of London Press, 1969, 1st ed., 1947), 112. Lowe was the chief national administrator of education in England. He had taken up the mantle on the retirement of Kay-Shuttleworth in 1849.

11 Speech, 13 February 1862, H.C., vol. 165, 229. Cited in Barnard, 112. Payment by Results, when introduced to British schools in 1862 came in under the title of the Revised Code.

examination. Extra payment was the chief inducement for the teachers. Inevitably, teachers knew how to butter their bread, and teaching towards the examination day became part and parcel of their daily routine. This new system would be the answer to all their prayers. It is salutary to reflect upon the commissioners' views on the character and personality of the teachers employed to educate the children. They felt that a significant proportion of the children were not satisfactorily taught what they had come to school to learn; in some districts some pupils could not read or write:

> They work sums, but they learn their arithmetic in such a way as to be of little practical use in common life. Their religious instruction is unintelligent, and to a great extent confined to exercises of merely verbal memory …[12]

The introduction of the results scheme in England coincided with *laissez-faire* government policy. The scheme was deemed to, at least, ensure that schools would become more efficient, and this should satisfy the denizens of Westminster who held the purse strings. It lasted for forty years, with some modifications. And, so it did impress those very denizens: In 1861 the education grant was £813,441; this fell to £636,806 in 1865. The Revised Code, as it was termed, also brought with it increased average attendances. In 1862, the average was 888,923; in 1866, 1,048,493. The examination for Payment by Results was practically based on everyday circumstances; for reading, it meant reading a newspaper story; for writing, it meant taking down some dictation and for arithmetic, adding up bills of parcels.[13]

All political, social and economic evolutions have a starting-point, or, at least a spot in history which can highlight some particular event which gives rise to a particular movement, or, in this case a policy injection.

In Ireland, although the vital change in Primary Education following the Powis Report of 1870 was the adoption of the system of Payment by Results, the educational scene was also bound up with the Disestablishment Act of 1869, which removed the Church of Ireland from its status as the 'established church'. This meant that the Church of Ireland could no longer

12 Quoted in Ivor Morrish, *Education since 1800* (London: Allen and Unwin, 1973), 16.

13 Figures in H. C. Barnard, 112.

claim to control education in Ireland. The passing of the Disestablishment Act also meant there was an abundance of monies available to the government to spend as it saw fit. The national system of education was one area interested in such a surplus of funds, especially with the introduction of the Results programme in 1871.

When the Results Plan was introduced, the number of pupils attending schools was decreasing, owing to the prevalence of epidemics, resulting in a high mortality rate. Schools had to be closed frequently. This was the atmosphere into which the new regime was immersed in the early 1870s.

In Ireland, the policy of Payment by Results was introduced, tentatively at first, in 1871 and in the following year the policy became more widespread. It was customary that trends in education policy in England had a knock-on effect on policy in Ireland during the latter half of the nineteenth century. Ireland's national school system embraced Payment by Results fully from 1872 to 1900.[14]

The policy in Ireland became closely associated with denominational affairs and tensions. Many political conflicts also attended the inception and operation of the results programme in Ireland. This study makes an effort to explicate and clarify the many interlocking aspects which came to encircle the operation of the system. At first glance, the policy could be perceived to be an administrative device for the remuneration of teachers on set criteria. Upon further examination, the scheme had profound effects on the school curriculum and on the teaching methodologies used in schools. The system interpenetrated many features of education practice and policy at the time.

Between 1871 and 1900 Irish primary schools gained significant experience from the application of Payment by Results. Its introduction was accompanied by denominational squabbles, which had been a recurring problem for several decades prior to this. At first, some individuals felt that this new system would be good for education, but it had intense consequences on what was being taught in schools, and, also on the relationship between teacher and pupil.

14 See *Sixty-Seventh Report of the Commissioners of National Education in Ireland, for the Year 1900*. Pub. In 1901; 37.

The pages of this book examine the operation of Payment by Results at the coalface in which critique, investigation and appraisal are blended. There were many reactions to the results policy, and these are explored. Emerging insights from official commissions' reports are taken on board on how the results policy was performing.

Payment by Results was a unique phenomenon, and aspects of its philosophy and worth are very liable to surface at different times, especially when a country's economy is under stress.

The *Belmore Commission on Manual and Practical Instruction* reported in 1898, and as a result of this report, Payment by Results came to a close and was replaced by the *Revised Programme* in 1900.

The two decades prior to the establishment of the Irish Free State in 1922 was an eventful era in Irish education policy and administration. Two major efforts were made by the state to introduce a radical revamping of education. Attempts were made to achieve reform in primary, intermediate and technical levels of education. The climate of thought had shifted from one of the promotion of self-interest to one of an all-encompassing nature, in which the pupil took on a central role.

Sources used for this work are a mixture of primary and secondary ones, for example, the *Annual Report of the Society for Promoting the Education of the Poor in Ireland, 1813;* Mr Keenan's *Memorandum in Parliamentary Papers* H.C. 1870, XXVIII, Pt III; *Circular to Inspectors (including programme),* 24 Oct. 1871; *Appendix to Rules and Regulations of the Commissioners,* Oct. 1874; *Annual Report of the Gaelic League,* 1897; the *Irish Teachers' Journal.* See the Bibliography at the end of the book for a comprehensive list.

CHAPTER 1

# The Germination of Payment by Results

'Education is too important to be left solely to the educators.'

– Francis Keppel

## Introduction and Backdrop

In England, education was among many themes that exercised the political state between the introduction of the Reform Bill of 1832 and the death of Sir Robert Peel in 1850. That period of time witnessed extraordinary alteration in British life; and as D. G. Paz, so eloquently comments, 'it was as if the dyke erected at Waterloo could no longer hold against the liberal ideas of 1789.'[1] The twin social aspects of the Industrial Revolution and the consequent increase in population created unforeseen problems and exaggerated the old ones; there was a new order after 1830 which provided the means and language of reform. This new order urged the likes of Thomas Wyse to consider an education scheme which would respond to the requirements of the newly created circumstances. While he was absent from the House of Commons, he studied both British and Irish society, and their necessary requirements, and in 1836 he published a monumental treatise, *Education Reform*. In the book he came to the conclusion that technological changes had transformed the nature

1 D. G. Paz, *The Politics of Working-Class Education in Britain, 1830–1850* (Manchester: Manchester University Press, 1980), 7.

of society, producing severe disruptions in the relationships of the classes. The answer to these problems was education reform. In the short run, it would prevent revolution, and in the long run, it would enable the lower orders to take their place in the governing of society.[2]

And, when the *Central Society of Education* was formed in 1837, it was in fact the brainchild of Wyse supported by Duppa. Its ideas paralleled those elucidated in *Education Reform.* This Society was a lobbying body, its main function being to publish papers on current ideas in teaching methods, and child psychology, and on foreign educational systems. It attacked the monitorial system, and asked for its abandonment. The Society, unlike the Utilitarians,[3] favoured state intervention in education provision, and the religious problem could be resolved by separating religious from secular education based on the Irish model.[4] The form of government intervention should also follow the Irish model.[5]

Wyse toured industrial and commercial centres, including Liverpool, Sheffield, Manchester and Leeds, in 1837, promoting the Irish solution. In Parliament, Wyse asked for a select committee to be appointed to oversee the administration of the school grant. The ensuing debates found favour with this proposal, but there was very strong opposition as well. The Treasury rejected Wyse's proposal, and Lord John Russell defended the Treasury on the basis that the existing body in charge, the Treasury, should get more funds rather than crating a split between two organizations. He agreed with Wyse, however, that not enough children were being educated.

Wyse's motion failed: Radicals and Irish supported the motion; Whigs and Tories opposed. This failure also spelled the end of the *Central Society of Education,* its last edition being in 1839. The Radicals, too, never again mounted a formidable challenge.[6]

2 Paz, *The Politics of Working-Class Education in Britain*, 7–10.
3 Paz, *The Politics of Working-Class Education in Britain*, Chapter 1.
4 B. F. Duppa, 'Objects of the Society', *First Publication* (1837), 14; Central Society of Education, *Schools for the Industrious Classes; or, The Present State of education Among the Working People of England* (London, 1837), 6–30, 53–54.
5 Paz, *The Politics of Working-Class Education in Britain*, 70.
6 Paz, *The Politics of Working-Class Education in Britain*, 72.

Whatever happens in educational developments is forever in the context of social, political, economic, and often demographic circumstances prevailing at the time.[7] One needs to countenance and appreciate all these contingencies when one is dealing with changes to education provision, or when dealing with changes in policy formation. And, as Brian Simon puts it: '[T]he history of education is full of incident and interest, touching on all sides of life, on the outlook and interests of all classes of society.'[8]

Governments, by and large, are more influenced by social, political, economic and demographic considerations when dealing with modifications to education provision than they are by educational hypotheses. Society's values and requirements alter from epoch to epoch, and the changed circumstances are reflected in the educational provision associated with any particular era. To that extent, the study of the type of education provision in its schools and curricula and the manner in which its youth usually reflects greatly on society as a whole.

Payment by Results is associated with the nineteenth century, at a time when certain levels of education were sub-vented by the state. This is particularly true of the second half of the century when we witness state support for elementary schooling in England and Scotland. To counteract the costs involved it was thought necessary to adjust education provision in such a way as to make it more accountable and more effectual. The answer resulted in a Payment by Results policy. With its introduction came the realization that the state needed to ensure that value was given, and seen to be given, for the public expenditure involved. 'The state's attitude and involvement in education at the time was part of a complex interwoven web of societal factors,'[9] and as S. E. Maltby maintains:

7 T. G. Cook, ed., *The History of Education in Europe* (London: Methuen, 1974), viii.

8 Brian Simon, *The Two Nations and the Educational Structure, 1780–1870* (London: Lawrence and Wishart, 1974), 13.

9 John Coolahan, *The Origins of the Payment by Results Policy in Education and the Experience of It in the National and Intermediate Schools of Ireland* (M.Ed. thesis submitted to Trinity College, Dublin, 1975), 1–2.

> To understand the long failure of Parliament to establish universal education in England is to understand a very large portion of life of England in the nineteenth century.[10]

The same Maltby had more to say on the monies emanating from the Great Exhibition,[11] along with further grants from Parliament, thus, enabling the purchase of three estates in South Kensington to be purchased and here the Board of Trade established a Department of Practical Art in 1853, with Henry Cole, reputed originator of the Christmas card, as secretary, and a Department of Science in 1854 with Lyon Playfair as secretary.[12] When the Education Department was established at Whitehall in 1856, the two departments at South Kensington were merged to form the Department of Science and Art.

Payments by results, as part of the fully operational Revised Code, became operative in Scotland from 1873 and continued in that form until 1890. From 1890 it operated only in a modified form based on the performance of classes rather than individuals, and, in 1899, it was dropped altogether as the basis of financial support for schools.[13]

## Social, Political and Economic Forces

One of these factors was economic necessity. The Science and Art Department set the pattern. However, its initial attempts to promote science classes were poor. By 1859, only four 'science' schools existed. Now,

10 S. E. Maltby, *Manchester and the Movement for National Elementary Education, 1800–1870* (Manchester University Press, 1918), V.

11 The Great Exhibition, or the Crystal Palace Exhibition, was an international exposition of culture and industry that took place in Hyde Park, London, in 1851. It was attended by Charles Darwin, Karl Marx, Michael Faraday, Charlotte Brontë, Charles Dickens, Lewis Carroll, George Eliot (AE), Alfred Lord Tennyson and William Makepeace Thackery.

12 Maltby, V.

13 S. Leslie Hunter, *The Scottish Education System* (Oxford: Pergamon Press, 1972), 19.

Henry Cole who was appointed secretary of the whole department, promoted a scheme for paying teachers on the results of their pupils' success in examinations set by the Department each May.

One hundred and four candidates presented themselves in 1860, 1000 in 1861, 34,000 in 1870, and by 1895 there were 202,868 candidates presenting.[14]

Political and societal changes in Britain often transferred to Ireland in one shape or another. Occupational expansion in post-Famine Ireland occurred mainly in the public service, in teaching and nursing, and in the Catholic Church. What distinguished these occupations from others was the requirement of some prerequisites for entry. In that sense educational requirements introduced some performance criteria. However, education remained primarily functional in its purpose as a means to an end, not of knowledge, but of security of tenure. Traditional society had difficulty grasping any concept of education except the provision of security for the educated.

Education held an ambiguous pressure over the performance ethic. The post-Famine educational system has been criticized for allegedly inculcating rigidity of perspective, lack of imagination, lack of entrepreneurial initiative. Patrick Pearse's memorable criticism of the system in 'The Murder Machine' made many telling points. More recently, Ivor Kenny has noted that 'conservatism, authoritarianism – are lessons learned young … children are encouraged to think about what they want to be, not what they want to do'.[15]

The teacher training colleges, which attracted the academically brighter children of 'the medium and small-sized farms in the south and west, were in many ways, and far more than the universities, seminaries of a new work ethic.[16] Significant numbers of teachers, instead of opting for a quiet life, tended to embrace a high-powered vocational conviction and instil in their

14 W. H. G. Armytage, *Four Hundred Years of English Education* (Cambridge: Cambridge University Press, 1965), 120.

15 Ivor Kenny, *Government and Enterprise in Ireland* (Dublin: Gill and Macmillan, 1984), 73.

16 Joe Lee, *Ireland 1912–1985: Politics and Society* (Cambridge: Cambridge University Press, 1989), 394.

pupils a credo that performance could lift them out of the ancestral furrow of humdrum existence. During the last three decades of the nineteenth century, teachers in Irish primary schools found an avenue of expression for the foregoing qualities, an avenue which expressly fitted in with the wishes of the denizens of the Payment by Results regime. An intimation of such an attitude is evident in many of the Inspectors' Reports for the years 1872–1899. One such Report, by an inspector, visiting a Co. Mayo national school in 1892 states, 'the Senior Classes should have been much better prepared. In these classes the following subjects are very defective – Spelling, Grammar and Agriculture in Sixth.'[17] In the same school, two years later, the same inspector found that Agriculture in Fourth, Fifth, and Sixth Classes is extremely bad, the inspector was disappointed that only 43 pupils qualified for the examination, when he expected two or three times that number in a school that size.[18]

In the same school, in 1897, we find a more sympathetic Mr Newell (Schools' Inspector) acknowledging the circumstances under which the teacher worked. He wrote:

> It is impossible for any One Teacher to do full justice to such a large number of grown and highly classed pupils. There has for a long period been an average [sic] for an Assistant. The failure to appoint one is much to be regretted.
>
> Mr. McGowan has evidently been doing a reasonable amount of work. Single-handed, however, it is very difficult for him to impart efficient instruction to so many pupils in even the ordinary subjects. He has also taken up Book-keeping and Drawing. A larger staff would enable other desirable branches to be taught.[19]

As Agriculture was one of the subjects achieving low grades during the results era, it might be worthwhile to put this in context. 'Relevance' is a word often applied to curricula, but in the circumstances of the late nineteenth century it should be borne in mind that 'traditional' society had difficulty accepting some subjects on the school curriculum. Agricultural

17 J. O'Riordan, *Report of a Results Examination of Swinford Male National School*, 15 January 1892.

18 O'Riordan.

19 Mr C. Newell, *Report of a Results Examination of Swinford Male NS*, 28/31 May 1897.

education appeared incomprehensible to most farmers, and to their offspring. We have stated that education was for security, but, as security on the land was not a consequence of education, the idea of agricultural education was almost tautologous for the vast majority of farmers.[20]

The late eighteenth-century reformers found that their ideas and policies were expressed in England as that country moved into the age of the Industrial Revolution, an epoch which produced a rising industrial middle class. The early portion of the nineteenth century witnessed unprecedented changes in economic, social and demographic aspects of English civilization. The population grew from eleven millions in 1801 to twenty-one millions in 1851. This shift in population gave an already advancing episode of movement from rural to urban dwelling an impetus that few could be prepared for. Vast numbers swelled cities like Manchester and Birmingham, with their already large conurbations resulting from the first Industrial Age. Imperial outlets for their produce meant that affluence flourished in English cities with their mines and factories, raw materials and markets: thus, the Great Exhibition of 1851 was an emblematic representation of all that was good and redolent of an age conspicuously associated with the 'great engine of progress'.

While being a period of great self-belief and prosperity, social inequality and exploitation saw the rise of movements for political, social and humanitarian reform. Electoral reform was one area in which franchise acts which led to the abolition of some of the worst abuses of the patronage and rotten borough system and led to a more democratically controlled political system. Some of the more serious forms of oppression inherited from an earlier age were terminated with the abolition of the slave trade and the ending of the penal legislation against Catholics and Dissenters. It was also an epoch in which efforts were mounted by means of the Factory Acts to curb inhuman working conditions for women and children in the mines and factories of industrial entrepreneurs. With the introduction of a Bill in 1833, the manufacturers secured the appointment of a Royal Commission to clear themselves of charges of exploitation. The subsequent 1833 Factory Act ensured that children could no longer be employed in two

20 See Lee, *Ireland 1912–1985*, 394.

different factories on the same day. Also, it was stipulated that children under 9 were not employed, and inspectors were appointed to ensure that this was the case. They also had to ensure that 9- to 13-year-olds attended school each day for two hours, six days a week.

It was a period when reforms came about in a polished manner, without any major revolutionary upheavals, and they were confined to the constitutional framework which absorbed much of the difficulties. There were periods of social tension such as Peterloo, but it never threatened the workings of government.[21]

Perhaps, it is timely to bind together the political, social, economic and demographic elements into a manageable whole so that we can make an affirmation regarding the position education played in English affairs in the first half of the nineteenth century. Why Payment by Results? Did the unimaginable societal changes in English society lead to a policy change in English schools? Raymond Williams may have one of the answers:

> It is not only that the way in which education is organised can be seen to express, consciously and unconsciously, the wider organisation of a culture and society, so that what has been thought of as simple distribution is in fact an active shaping to particular social ends. It is also that the content of education, which is subject to great historical variation, again expresses, again both consciously and unconsciously, certain basic elements in the culture, what is thought of as "an educated being" is in fact a particular selection, a particular set of emphases and omissions ... the cultural choices involved in the selection of content have an organic relationship to the social choices involved in the practical organisations.[22]

For much of the nineteenth century in England, the prevailing philosophy was Utilitarianism. So John Plamenatz confirms:

> For a period of over a hundred years Utilitarianism was the dominant political and moral theory in England.[23]

21 There were many Factory Acts throughout the nineteenth century: 1802; 1819; 1833; 1843; 1844; 1864; 1867; 1874; 1878.

22 Raymond Williams, *The Long Revolution* (London: Chatto and Windus, 1961), 125.

23 John Plamenatz, *The English Utilitarians* (Oxford: Blackwell, 1966), 45.

'The greatest happiness of the greatest number,' a phrase, which became his mantra, was Bentham's discovery in a book by Joseph Priestley. The resulting consequences of this discovery, and no doubt many others, was that Bentham 'taught his age the importance of rational criticism and systematic reform'.[24] The morality of human action was dependent on the pleasure-pain principle; engage in pleasurable acts and avoid ones that cause pain. Bentham went on to define 'utility as that property in an object whereby it tends to produce benefit, advantage, pleasure, good or happiness'. In Bentham's theory, an action conforming to the doctrine of utility is right or at least not wrong; for Bentham, rights and duties have legal connotations, linked with the notions of command and sanction. What is called moral duties and rights would require a moral legislator. Natural rights and duties suggests a law without a legislator, and was condemned by Bentham. Likewise, he also found fault in the belief in natural rights on the grounds that it inspired violence and bloodshed, as witnessed in the excesses of the French Revolution. Bentham believed that with a gradual improvement in levels of education in society, people would be more likely to vote on the basis of rational thinking of what would be for their long-term benefit, and individual rational decision-making would in turn lead to a greater general happiness in society.[25]

The objective of education, wrote James Mill,[26] 'is to render the individual, as much as possible, an instrument of happiness, first to himself, and next to other beings'.[27] These premises had serious consequences for social policy. Utilitarianism did not welcome government involvement in people's affairs, especially commerce and social conditions. The utilitarians campaigned for the abolition of protective trading barriers and bounties

24 Cited in Harold Silver, *English Education and the Radicals 1780–1850* (London: Routledge and Kegan Paul, 1975), 25.

25 See Thomas Mautner, ed., *The Penguin Dictionary of Philosophy*, 2nd ed. (2005).

26 James Mill, 1773–1836, was a Scottish historian, economist, political theorist and philosopher. His son, John Stuart Mill, was a philosopher, political economist, Member of Parliament and civil servant.

27 James Mill, 'education', in *Supplement to the Encyclopaedia Britannica* (1818).

and strongly advocated free trade. Their success meant that free trade became the prevailing commercial philosophy of the age.[28]

No one took up the system of *laissez-faire* (or 'donothingism' as Thomas Carlyle satirized it) more enthusiastically than Bentham and the utilitarians. That is, Bentham and his utilitarians embraced the notion that everything was quantifiable and everything should be made practicable, including education, both teaching and learning. Jeremy Bentham (1748–1832)[29] worked for the organization of practicable – therefore cheap – universal education. He embarked on a survey of the whole field of human knowledge, including the most recent advances in science and technology; this he systematized and set down in tabular form – an 'encyclopaedic table'.[30] He then proceeded to reduce the various fields of knowledge to a logical order, or priorities, the order in which they are most advantageously taught.[31] This was determined by the two principles of utility and facility. Those subjects which had the clearest application 'to several purposes of common life' should be included. 'The educational process must, above all, be systematic,'[32] the body of knowledge 'is imposed by the educator,' and knowledge is arranged in a certain order. John Stuart Mill, in his *Principles of Political Economy* (1848), took up the mantle and reiterated the oft-enunciated axiom of the classical economists:

28 Asa Briggs, *Victorian People: A Reassessment of Persons and Themes, 1851–1867* (Chicago: University of Chicago Press, 1970), 2.

29 He is widely regarded as the founder of modern utilitarianism, which remains an important theme in contemporary moral and political philosophy. His theory of democracy has replaced that found in James Mill's *Essay on Government* and John Stuart Mill's *Consideration on Representative Government.* See E. O' Carroll, *William Thompson, 1775–1833, and the Radical Tradition in Education* (M.Ed., Thesis submitted to Mary Immaculate College, University of Limerick, 2007).

30 In the eighteenth century encyclopedism came into vogue in many countries as a response to the rapidly growing corpus of knowledge. The purpose of Encyclopedism was to bring knowledge into an ordered structure of proper relationships. See James Bowen, *A History of Western Education: The Modern West, Europe and the New World* (London: Methuen, 1985), 81–82.

31 Brian Simon, *Studies in the History of Education* (London: Lawrence and Wishart, 1960), 79.

32 Simon, *Studies in the History of Education*, 79.

> *Laissez-faire,* in short, should be the general practice: every departure from it, unless required by some great good, is a certain evil.[33]

Bentham excluded imaginative literature from his corpus of knowledge, seeing it as having no practical utility. In his *Chrestomathia*[34] (1816) and *Public Education* (1822), he set forth his curriculum which was heavily dominated by a range of scientific, technical and applied subjects.[35] These subjects could be conveyed in 'short lessons containing an account of those objects and of the facts relating to them, and may be repeated over and over again until they are learned perfectly.'[36] The children 'never deviate from a steady and regular course: whence the habit is founded on doing everything in its proper hour and place'. The instrumental philosophy of this type of education is emphasized by Bentham's colleague James Mill:

> There is a vast treasure of facts which the observation and experience of mankind have accumulated: it is the business of education to communicate a knowledge of these facts.[37]

Bentham and Mill were not original in their attitude toward education. Locke, one of the great fathers of the age of reason, charged that the 'key concern of the educator should be the early conditioning of good habits and when the rational faculties were capable of it the early shaping of the rational, organised, well-regulated person.'[38] Bentham in one of his works which dealt with education, *Chrestomathia* (1816) intimated that the aim of education was to teach what was most useful to know and what was most conducive for happiness to do. He suggested

33 John Stuart Mill, *Principles of Political Economy* (ed., D. Wench) (Harmondsworth: Penguin, 1970), 314.

34 This word derives from two Greek words, meaning 'conducive to useful learning'. *Chrestos* = useful, *mathos* =learning or knowledge.

35 J. Coolahan, 'Fear of the Imagination: Roots of the Tradition.' Paper read at the European Conference on Reading in St. Patrick's College, Drumcondra, Dublin, 15 July 1985, 3.

36 *Westminster Review*, no. 1 (1824), 64.

37 *Westminster Review*, 43.

38 Coolahan, 'Fear of the Imagination', 3.

that schooling should communicate a knowledge of the facts which the experience of mankind had accumulated.[39] As well as the three Rs, Bentham enumerated the subjects in a curriculum of his choice – English, French, Mineralogy, Botany, Zoology, Geography, History, Chronology, Mechanics, along with Magnetism, Electricity, Galvanism, Ballistics, Mining, Geology, Land-surveying, Architecture, Husbandry, Physical Economics, Hydraulics, Music and the higher branches of Mathematics and Astronomy. Perusing this list, it is very clear that Bentham was revolting against the traditional grammar schools, and he wished the curriculum to have a more scientific platform. He eschewed the classics and religion.

Many criticized this approach to educating the youth of the country: conceivably, a world without Shakespeare, Coleridge, theatre, song, artistic endeavours would leave a void in the experience of many generations. And, in Ireland, where would the world be without Yeats and Goldsmith? Science is of course very important, and essential as part of the school experience. However, the Benthamites were willing to exclude many valuable aspects of essential school experiences.

Dickens scorned this attitude toward the imaginative faculties in the dramatic opening paragraph of *Hard Times*, in which he satirizes the 'facts' of Mr Gradgrind and McChoakumchild[40]:

> Now, what I want is, Facts. Teach these boys and girls nothing but Facts. Facts alone are wanted in life. Plant nothing else, and root out everything else. You can only form the minds of reasoning animals upon Facts: nothing else will ever be of any service to them. This is the principle on which I bring up my own children, and this is the principle on which I bring up these children. Stick to Facts, Sir![41]

It was the concern of the utilitarians to cultivate the rational man. They sought the inculcation of useful knowledge,[42] facts and certitude. They

39 *Westminster Review*, vol. 1 (1824), 43–79.

40 The teacher who has been trained to choke the imagination out of his students, leaving them only with facts and figures.

41 Charles Dickens, *Hard Times* (London: Everyman's Library), 1.

42 The idea of 'usefulness' abounded in the writings of a number of people, among them William Thompson (1775–1833). Many of these writers urged reform in

held a mechanical concept of external nature the knowledge of which could be set out as facts. Tales of the imaginative adventure, mystery, terror, fantasy, folk tales or nonsense rhymes were regarded as subversive of the solid good sense which it was necessary to develop in young people. They were influenced by the classical economists, such as Adam Smith, who were anxious that the laws of orthodox political economy explaining the social stratification of society whereby the rich were rich, and entitled to be, and the poor were poor as God intended, should be inculcated among the poorer classes. The ubiquitous presence of the monitorial system in the early part of the nineteenth century made this process one of mechanical drill and repetition.[43] Utilitarian emphasis on facts and useful knowledge was very much part and parcel of many people's thoughts. Their suspicions of the imaginative, the fantastical and the aesthetic were shared by the Evangelical movement:

> Laissez-faire in politics and Evangelical piety in religion were contemporaries in their rise, their climax and their decline.[44]

Herbert Spencer published a trenchant attack on the classical grammar schools and their tradition, and he was reminiscent of *Chrestomathia* in his placing of science at the centre of the curriculum.[45]

Victorian values such as self-reliance, thrift, moral virtues, application and diligence, and the value of patience were all part of everyday affairs. Samuel Smiles's *Self-Help* book of 1859 proved to be a very popular, selling 250,000 copies by the end of the century. His other book titles do not need any explanations: *Character* (1871), *Thrift* (1875) and *Duty* (1887), each exemplifying the values of the age.

---

British education as a response to increased industrialization and as a backlash at the 'useless' education afforded to the aristocracy and moneyed elites. See Brian Simon, *Studies in the History of Education 1780–1870* (London: Lawrence and Wishart, 1960), chapters 2, 3 and 4.

43 Coolahan, 'Fear of the Imagination', 14–18.

44 D. C. Somervill, *English Thought in the Nineteenth Century* (London: Methuen, 1957), 102.

45 Asa Briggs, *The Age of Improvement, 1783–1867* (London: Longmans, 1959), 402.

## The Rationalists

Richard Lovell Edgeworth, along with his daughter Maria, also had some leanings towards utilitarianism, though for *pater familias* the concept was in the future.

On the question of poetry the Edgeworths take a Lockian stand – that poetry is 'an agreeable amusement',[46] but should be permitted only now and again because 'the inventive and reasoning faculties must be injured by the repetitions of vague and of exaggerated description with which most poetry abounds'.[47] Richard Edgeworth acknowledged a useful role for the imagination but he was careful that it needed 'to be judiciously managed'.[48] In the various collections of moral tales for children produced by Maria, there was never any danger of confusing right and wrong. 'We should be able to ascertain the boundaries of right and wrong with geometrical precision.'[49]

> Like other rationalists of the age Edgeworth feared the effects of 'enthusiasm' and the 'wise preceptor' was cautioned to control the sensations of highly emotional and suggestive children. At the other end of the scale, reverie was highly suspect and Edgeworth joined with Locke in arguing that it should not be indulged.[50]

Richard Lovell Edgeworth was one of the earliest proponents of Payment by Results as well as a fixed salary for teachers in a Bill prepared by him for the last year of Grattan's Parliament, 1799.[51] Both Bentham and Mill eschewed the Arts or any aesthetic subjects on their curriculum.

The philosophy extolled by Bentham and Mill is mindful of Plato's custodianship and another Platonic stricture is that children's books should be censored, and that over-emotional stories and novels should be banned.

46 S. J. Curtis and M. E. A. Boultwood, *An Introductory History of English Education since 1800* (London: University Tutorial Press, 1970), 109.
47 Coolahan, 'Fear of the Imagination', 6.
48 Coolahan, 'Fear of the Imagination', 6.
49 R. L. and M. Edgeworth, *Practical Education* (London: Johnson, 1798), 322.
50 Coolahan, 'Fear of the imagination', 7.
51 D. H. Akenson, *The Irish Education Experiment: The National System of Education in the Nineteenth Century* (London: Routledge and Kegan Paul, 1970), 74–75.

*Robinson Crusoe,* for instance, is deemed too stimulating for lively boys unless they are intended for the armed forces.[52]

The qualities of self-reliance and self-help, two nineteenth-century precepts, were admired by the utilitarians; individuals should not rely on state aid, and there was no place in their thinking for the welfare state. On the other hand, they favoured the abolition of political patronage and forms of privilege, as it led to inefficiency and wastage of resources.

The desire to reduce things to certainty and to rational analysis and explanation can also be attributed to Richard Lovell Edgeworth, a friend of Bentham and James Mill. Education, as the great engine of progress, remained a central concern for him.

The Benthamites were not always wearing utilitarianism on their sleeves, but it has been observed that:

> ... the systematic social views of the Benthamites and the unexpressed and perhaps unreflective attitudes of some of the leading politicians and of their followers reinforce one another .... As a consequence, it would be difficult to overstate the importance of the achievements of Benthamism in England.[53]

Utilitarian deliberation stemmed from Bentham to James Mill to John Stuart Mill and was copper-fastened by the classical economists Adam Smith, Malthus and Ricardo, who themselves were utilitarians.[54] When these minds met at a confluence of intellectual pursuits, the resulting outcome could not avoid influencing and shaping any emerging public policies: a climate of thought was formed embracing one another's ideas and thus enabling such policies which often reflected one or other or all of these thinkers.

Utilitarianism was very concerned with social reform, but for the sake of efficiency and economy, rather than any egalitarian efforts at legislation to enhance the circumstances of the poor in society. In fact, the

52 Curtis and Boultwood, *An Introductory History of English Education*, 109.

53 W. Harrison, ed., Jeremy Bentham, *A Fragment on Government and Introduction to the Principles of Moral Legislation* (Oxford: Blackwell, 1948), xiii.

54 John Plamenatz, *The English Utilitarians* (Oxford: Blackwell, 1948), III. See Leslie Stephen, *The English Utilitarians*, 3 vols (New York: Peter Smith, 1950). Pub. Online by Cambridge University Press, 2013.

utilitarians and the classical economists championed and espoused the policy of *laissez-faire*:

> The negative aspects of Benthamism are imposingly displayed in the work of the 'classical school' of political economists. British political economy had its roots in Adam Smith and not in Bentham, for Bentham was no economist. But James Mill was an economist as well as a Benthamite, and the classical economic doctrines may be regarded as a specialized and technical application of the Benthamite principle of individualism or laissez faire.[55]

And, as John Coolahan writes:

> The cross-fertilization and inter-penetration of ideas between the Utilitarians and the Classical Economists made their thought a formidable moulding agency of nineteenth century political and social thought.[56]

Utilitarianism, no doubt, can safely be associated with the concept of free-enterprise entrepreneurism upon which the Industrial Revolution was based. Not all of the tycoons and entrepreneurs of industry were well-versed in utilitarian ideology, but, nevertheless, they were influenced by the general climate of thought and opinion which had its inspiration in them. R. D. Altick's comment on utilitarianism may well be a succinct interpretation:

One aspect of social affairs was education, and to the Benthamites, this meant reform, and one of the principal aspects of this reform was the achievement of mass education; for one reason people needed to be educated if there is any hope of an ordered society.

Though the utilitarians looked askance at state intervention in social affairs, one exception was allowed for in a few areas, education being one. The fact that allowances were made for state intervention to some degree, circumspection still played a significant role in what degree to which governments became involved. Elementary education was the only aspect of all the levels involved where state support was acceptable. This applied to the poorer classes and to those where voluntary effort was not obtainable.

55 Somervell, *English Thought in the Nineteenth Century*, 52.

56 Coolahan, *The Origins of the Payment by Results in Education*, 5.

Due diligence was paid in the case where families contributed a token amount for the schooling of their child that this practice should not be infringed upon.

Perhaps, it would be worth our while looking at Eric Hobsbawn's succinct, but caustic, comments on the utilitarian project, and its blind-spots:

> Arithmetic was the fundamental tool of the Industrial Revolution. Its makers saw it as a series of sums of addition and subtraction: the difference in cost between buying in the cheapest market and selling in the dearest, between cost of production and sale price, between investment and return. For Jeremy Bentham and his followers, the most consistent champions of this type of rationality, even morals and politics came under these simple calculations. Happiness was the object of policy. Every man's pleasure could be expressed (at least in theory) as a quantity and so could his pain. Add the happiness of all men and deduct the unhappiness, and that government which secured the greatest happiness of the greatest number was the best. The accountancy of humanity would produce its debit and credit balances, like that of business.[57]

The greatest-happiness principle, despite any appearance to the contrary, was, in fact, as Sylvester comments, a 'deeply individualistic doctrine'.[58] For Bentham, assuming that pleasure and pain were the ultimate motivating forces in life, and pleasure the ultimate value, came to the conclusion that since these could only be experienced by individual men and women it was by reference to them that the value of laws and governments should be assessed. Reform is the end result if the laws and government fail to satisfy human needs.[59]

If Lowe had not applied payment by results to elementary education, then it seems that someone else would have done so. In this sense Lowe was merely an agent of his times.[60]

One of the great foundation texts of *laissez-faire* economics was Adam Smith's *The Wealth of Nations* (1776). A substantial quotation from Smith's

57 Eric J. Hobsbawn, *Industry and Empire: From 1750 to the Present Day* (Hammondsworth: Penguin, 1987; First publication, 1968), 23.

58 D. W. Sylvester, *Robert Lowe and Education* (Cambridge: Cambridge University Press, 2010; First published 1974), 15.

59 Sylvester, *Robert Lowe and Education*, 15.

60 Sylvester, *Robert Lowe and Education*, 58.

book elucidates the connection between *laissez-faire* economics and education provision:

> But though the common people cannot, in any civilised society, be so well instructed as people of some rank and fortune, the most essential parts of education, however, to read, write, and account, can be acquired at so early a period of life, that the greater part even of those who are bred to the lowest occupations, have time to acquire to acquire them before they can be employed in those occupations. For a small expense can facilitate, can encourage, and can even impose upon almost the whole body of the people, the necessity of acquiring these most essential parts of education. The public can facilitate this acquisition by establishing in every parish or district a little school, where that even a common labourer may afford it; the maser being partly, but not wholly paid by the public; because if he was wholly, or even principally paid by it, he would soon learn to neglect his duties.[61]

Clearly, a class-based education matrix was the order of the day in Smith's mind; the poor would receive a basic schooling in the three Rs, and before they 'can' be properly employed. All this leads to basic education or schooling providing better workers, more intelligent use of machinery should ensue, waste might decrease while productivity should increase. Perhaps, education may well play a role in forming compliant and biddable citizens, and Smith was very cognisant of such a scenario:

> The State, however, derives no inconsiderable advantage from their instruction. The more they are instructed the less liable they are to the delusions of enthusiasm and superstition, which, among ignorant nations, frequently occasion the most dreadful disorders. An instructed and intelligent people, besides, are always more decent and orderly than an ignorant or stupid one ... they are more disposed to respect superiors ... and lawful authority.[62]

Smith may well be correct in his estimations. However, history is full of scenarios involving risings and revolutions in which the leadership, at

61 Edwin Cannan, ed., (Adam Smith), *An Inquiry into the Nature and Causes of the Wealth of Nations* (London: Methuen, 1904), vol. 2, 270. The detail in this comment by Adam Smith is not too dissimilar from what constituted the National System of Education as established in 1831.

62 Cannan, ed., *An Inquiry into the Nature and Causes of the Wealth of Nations*, 273.

least, were well-educated. A case in point is the 1916 Rising in Dublin, whose leaders were poets and members of the intelligentsia.

The purpose of Payment by Results in English schools was to reduce expenditure at elementary level, and in this it was successful.[63] A second aim was to concentrate the efforts of teachers on the three Rs, and in this it was partially successful, but only at the cost of forcing entirely mechanical drill methods of teaching on the teachers.[64] This aspect of the Revised Code (Payment by Results), introduced by Robert Lowe, a pivotal conservative spokesman in 1862, was criticized so strongly by such commentators as Kay-Shuttleworth, who believed that the Code was accused of promoting rote learning, with an over-emphasis on the three Rs, and seeking to reduce expenditure on education. W. B. Stephens, in his *Education in Britain, 1750–1914,* takes a different approach in stating that the Revised Code brought to an end a system under which the government was faced with an open-ended, ever-expanding obligation to fund schools over whose standards of instruction it had limited control. 'Instead government proposed to pay out to schools which were already doing their job of providing a solid basic elementary education.'[65] Stephens goes on to observe that the Code did much to increase literacy; in fact it gave a 'crash course in literacy', raising standards in the 'basic subjects', and curtailing an over-emphasis on religious instruction, improving attendance and ensuring that all pupils were given proper attention. And, when standards in the basic subjects had improved financial aid was gradually transferred to achievement in other subjects.[66] Stephens does admit that despite such developments, however, the voluntary system had considerable flaws: the provision and quality of education

63 The Treasury grant to elementary schools fell from £813,441 in 1861 to £636,806 in 1865. Source: Brian Simon, *Education and the Labour Market, 1870–1920* (London: Lawrence and Wishart, 1965), 115, fn. 3.

64 Simon, *Education and the Labour Market,* 115.

65 W. B. Stephens, *Education in Britain, 1750–1914* (London: Macmillan Press, 1998), 7.

66 See J. S. Hurt, *Education in Evolution: Church, State, Society and Popular Education, 1800–1870* (London: A. Hart-Davis, 1971), 221; R. D. Anderson, *Education and the Scottish People, 1750–1918* (Oxford: Oxford University Press, 1995), 57–59; Sylvester, *Robert Lowe and Education,* 84–93.

provided varied geographically, and until schooling became compulsory in the wake of the 1870 Education Act, levels of attendance varied greatly from place to place and among different social groups.

Perhaps, T. L. Jarman offers a more realistic interpretation on the success or otherwise of the Revised Code when he states:

> The system lasted, with modifications, for about forty years, and with all its shortcomings was probably a good enough rough and ready method of achieving a degree of efficiency in elementary education.[67]

Kay-Shuttleworth, on the other hand, offers a rather picturesque image of elementary education in some parts of England. Arguing that a test in reading, writing and arithmetic was far too limited and not a fair assessment of the socializing elements that exists in a typical elementary school. In the schools of northern England there 'are floated a constant supply of an immigrant semi-savage population, bred on the moors of the Pennine Chain'. Those children had 'to be taught to stand upright – to walk without a slouching gait – to sit without crouching like a sheepdog. They have to learn some decency in their skin, hair and dress.' From the thieving of the London streets and the most squalid slums, 'children have of late years been netted in shoals – got into schools, have been won, tamed, and in some degree taught'.[68]

However, this approach, a survival from the days of Bentham and James Mill, was no longer popular and carried little weight, so that a fundamentally restrictive system persisted for another thirty years.

Perhaps, Ivor Morrish encapsulates the problems associated with Lowe's Revised Code of 1862 when it was instituted as 'payment by results' and had 'deleterious effects upon the pupil teacher system as well as upon training colleges'.[69]

He expounds further:

67 T. L. Jarman, *Landmarks in the History of Education: English Education as part of the European Tradition* (London: John Murray, 1970), 263.

68 J. Kay-Shuttleworth, *Four Periods of Public Education as Reviewed in 1832, 1839, 1846, 1862* (London: Longman Green, Longman Roberts, 1862), 580–587.

69 Morrish, *Education since 1800*, 132.

> The narrow application of study to those subjects which alone would be taught in the schools, and the somewhat nervous desire to satisfy the inspectorate with the 'right answers' to inevitable questions, led to a pressurized system of rote-learning of required material. The defects of the teacher-training system were, in fact, a reflection of the defects of the educational system at large, and a certain reluctance to enter the profession resulted, as well as a growing apathy amongst those ahead in the profession towards true and liberal learning.[70]

Within the payment by results ideology, the teacher could be expected only to work when his payment directly depends on some method by which his work rate could be accurately assessed.

Adam Smith set forth a results-based criterion so as to measure a teacher's worth. In economic terms this was no or no less than free market for teachers. And, Smith, in supporting his argument extols the ancient Greeks and Romans when 'the emulation which an unrestrained competition never fails to excite, appears to have brought that talent to a very high degree of perfection'.[71]

The doctrine of innate ideas did not sit comfortably with the utilitarians; their understanding was that differences in humans were the result of education. James Mill fell closely within the realm of Helvetius's 'L'education peut tout' when he declared:

> This much at any rate, is ascertained, that all the difference which exists, or can ever be made to exist, between one class of men and another, is wholly owing to education.[72]

Bentham and James Mill latched onto the teaching methodology of Lancaster and Bell, known as the monitorial system. This was a system which became popular in many European countries. For example, the monitorial system of England attracted much attention in France. One of its most enthusiastic supporters was La Rochefoucauld, an influential member of the nobility. In 1814 two other distinguished Frenchmen, Jomard and the Abbe Gaultier, visited England to study the system. The result of such interest in the mutual system, as it was called in France, was

70 Morrish, *Education since 1800*, 132.

71 Adam Smith, *The Wealth of Nations*, 265.

72 James Mill, *On Education* (Cambridge: Cambridge University Press, 1969), 71.

that the Society for Elementary Education announced in 1815 that it was to achieve its objective of spreading amongst the lower classes the kind of intellectual and moral training most appropriate to their needs, by means of the mutual system.[73] Within a year fifteen hundred monitorial schools were created.[74] 'During the next two decades they were to achieve such popularity that eventually they became the chief means by which French youth was educated.'[75]

## Monitorial Schools

Joseph Lancaster, a nonconformist, and Andrew Bell associated themselves with the idea of a system of education. Lancaster boasted that, under his plan, it was possible for one master to teach a thousand pupils.[76] The keynote of the Monitorial system, as developed by Lancaster and Bell, was cheapness and efficiency.

Mill desired that education be extended to the many, but that it would be cheap and, as far as possible, based on voluntary contributions is borne out in the following remarks:

> At last an individual arose, who, having proved by his own experience that the most useful branches of education might be taught to the poor at a wonderfully small expense, at an expense so small that even the strength of private contributions might rise equal to the demand for the whole nation, conceived the glorious design of extending the benefits of education to every member of the community.[77]

73 H. M. Pollard, *Pioneers of Popular Education, 1760–1850* (London: John Murray, 1956), 103.
74 Pollard, 103.
75 Pollard, 104.
76 Curtis and Boultwood, *An Introductory History of English Education*, 10.
77 Mill, *On Education*, 123.

When one views the historical context of *laissez-faire* 'ism', one has to acknowledge certain inherent problems encountered by the move toward mass education. There was a lack of qualified teachers, and good textbooks and adequate buildings were scarce if not entirely non-existent. Thus Lancaster's monitorial system seemed to be a major breakthrough to reformers.

Lancaster hit upon the idea of having the older, better pupils teach the younger ones. 'This device is the crux of the monitorial system for which [he] became famous.'[78]

As well as economy of expenses, the Lancastrian system boasted several features: efficiency of instruction, discipline by routine, motivation by competition, and neutrality in religion.[79] The extreme mechanical notion of teaching envisaged by this system can be understood when one considers that the master confined his operations to instructing the monitors (the older pupils) and exercising supervision over the whole; he making only indirect contact with the children. By its very nature the pupils as well as the monitors could only exact their respective duties in a formal fashion embodying strict conformity to pattern and routine. The Lancastrian school included several machine-like inventions. 'Commands were given by "telegraph", at the front of the room [stood] a wooden frame with several message panels ... signifying that the students were to clean slates.'[80] Monitors themselves were somewhat like machines: the questions and answers they were to pose were all prescribed in keys, and Lancaster once declared that any boy who could read could teach.[81]

Lancaster thought that the personality and individual talents of teachers as well as monitors could be rendered irrelevant:

> ... when the pupils, as well as the schoolmaster, understood how to act and learn on this system, the system, not the master's vague, discretionary, uncertain judgement, will be in practice ... in a school properly regulated and conducted on my plan, when

78 Carl F. Kaestle, *Joseph Lancaster and the Monitorial School Movement: A Documentary History* (London: Teachers' College Press, 1973), 3.

79 Kaestle, 4.

80 Kaestle, 12–13.

81 Kaestle, 13.

> the master leaves the school, the business will go on as well in his absence as in his presence, because the authority is not personal.[82]

Lancaster's words speak for themselves.

The monitorial system was governed by the stimulus of keen emulation and the award of decorations, or of degrading punishments, as the cases demanded. A silver medal, suspended from the neck by a plaited chain, distinguished the most proficient in teaching or in study; culprits wore labels or crowns of tin or paper.[83]

The schools were designed to teach discipline and maintain order among huge numbers of pupils by means of hierarchical perks and an impersonal system of commands, rewards and punishments:[84]

> Nothing is so impressive, said Lancaster, as the sight of all the children making precisely the same motion at the same time. Military discipline, like factory discipline, would train the children of the poor how to act inside and outside of school. The promptness, obedience, and other character traits that the system would inculcate were deemed beneficial to the child as well as society.[85]

Bell and Lancaster were not of the one mind, however, concerning educational practices. Bell expected his masters to take an active part in the teaching; Lancaster looked to his merely to supervise and watch an almost automatic working of the system.[86] In the teaching of reading Bell made use of books, whilst Lancaster resorted to sheets of printed paper pinned on the walls:[87]

> None the less, though their systems were not identical, these bitter antagonists had more in common than they suspected, and subsequent generations of Englishmen

82 J. D. G. de Montmorency, *State Intervention in English Education* (Cambridge: Cambridge University Press, 1902), 284.

83 J. W. Adamson, *A Short History of Education* (Cambridge: Cambridge University Press, 1930), 247.

84 Kaestle, 16.

85 Kaestle, 17.

86 Pollard, *Pioneers of Popular Education, 1760–1850*, 102.

87 Pollard, 102.

> … reconciled all points of divergence by hyphenating their names and referring to their respective establishments as the Bell-Lancaster schools.[88]

Educational provision under the monitorial system was largely confined to the three R's, in most cases inadequately administered by monitors, a technique which not only reduced costs but replicated the basic forms of regimentation:[89]

> In other words, elementary education constituted a new form of social discipline, attuned to industrialisation, replacing time-honoured methods of subordination which were seen to be ineffectual.[90]

Images of the machine and of the military pervade the writings of monitorial school enthusiasts. 'The Lancastrian system of education was more than simply a recommendation to use student monitors; it was an elaborate set of rules, routines, and pedagogical inventions for implementing such a system.'[91]

The system was a response to technological advance, the growth of bureaucracy and a desire for order in an effort to counteract the threat of chaos in the lives of the working classes. Lancaster's themes of monitorial teaching, constant activity, strict order and emulation, gave his ideas the coherence of a complete system, capable of being extended in standard form throughout the nation and the world:[92]

> No matter how many poor children there were, and no matter how many nations were to be educated, the solution lay in providing more standardised schools and uniformly trained teachers who would in turn produce uniformly reliable workers.[93]

The content of this quotation bears some further reflection. The context of the time is an important consideration when industrialization had

88 Pollard, 102.
89 N. Rogers, 'Class and Popular Education in Nineteenth-Century Britain', *History of Education Quarterly, Spring (1979), 478.*
90 Rogers, 478.
91 Kaestle, 4.
92 Kaestle, 9.
93 Kaestle, 14.

moved forward in leaps and bounds but yet the mechanisms for social control were in their infancy. There seemed to have been an inbuilt fear on the part of those who controlled the social forces of the ever-recurring need to establish a stable population which was also increasing at unprecedented rates. It is apparent that the influence of the effects of the French Revolution was not something that could easily be ignored or forgotten.

The idea of a uniform system is consonant with the developing technological ideology of the nineteenth century, which applied not only to material production but to social organization as well. Lancaster's ideas were well received because of the:

> [e]nlightenment view that man was perfectible, institutions were remediable, and the solutions rational. The English utilitarians also fostered the notion that society operated according to general laws which could provide the basis for social reform.[94]

The doctrine of utility included a preoccupation with useful knowledge, and hence with education. The utilitarians were anxious to educate the different social classes for their different social roles – the poor to work and the middle classes to govern. Both Bell and Lancaster were hailed as 'inventors of a piece of social machinery that was both simple and economical, an instrument suited to the needs and outlook of the times'.[95]

Critics saw monitorial schooling as incompatible with newer educational ideas. Pestalozzi's emphasis on one-to-one relationships was becoming popular. The infant school movement, 'which fostered Pestalozzian ideas, was a challenge to monitorial teaching because regimentation and memory drill didn't work very well with younger children'.[96] But, utilitarianism, with monitorialism as one of its pillars held a secular theory, and this applied to many of the early nineteenth-century reformers. It was not only simple and inexpensive, quite an important consideration with rising populations, it was sufficient and the main defence of the system was that

94 Kaestle, 9.
95 J. Lawson and H. Silver, *A Social History of Education in England* (London: Methuen, 1973), 241.
96 Kaestle, 43.

it provided a modicum of education, in a way that no other system could have done at the time. However,

> the ethic of efficiency and uniformity that developed in education in this period may strike us today as distasteful, perhaps outrageous, because our attitude toward technology has taken a pendulum swing.[97]

The nineteenth-century Irish novelist William Carleton drew attention to the rigid discipline and inflexibility of approach which was a feature of the schools conducted under Lancastrian principles. This, he claimed, had a detrimental effect upon the mind of the child. Under Lancaster's methods, when the child became the passive recipient of knowledge, when rigorous mental discipline and mechanical processes and drill formed the basis of instruction in a system taken from 'the maturity of human intellect', then the psychological dangers became apparent.

## Concluding Remarks

In the nineteenth century, political, social, economic and demographic forces formed the foundation stones upon which educational movements were laid. One such movement, though not very long-lasting, was the Payment by Results policy. In its day it matched expectations of the time, as society had become associated with ideas such as self-help and prudence. There was also a belief in free trade from a commercial point of view. Generally, this philosophy stemmed from nineteenth-century positivistic theory.

Something like education became an entity which could be measured and packaged – in a word, it became tangible. Imaginative literature, in one sense could be easily accounted for, while in another, it became useless. A generation or two earlier R. L. Edgeworth had extolled such perceptions. The curriculum became hard and useful under the results regime, with

97 Kaestle, 15.

a strong leaning towards scientific principles. If 'imagination' were to be part of the school curriculum, it should be managed and controlled. Ideas such as these were at the philosophical behest of the Utilitarians and the Rationalists. Their expression found its way into the Monitorial system.

When the utilitarians and the classical economists found common ground, their theories made a mammoth moulding agency of nineteenth-century political and social thought.

In nineteenth-century England it was considered acceptable, but within an atmosphere of *laissez-faire* economics, that the state should assist voluntary effort in the provision of a basic elementary level of education for all citizens. However, the state's role should not interfere with any other student age group beyond the elementary level. Utilitarianism and 'cheapness' were twin bedfellows; therefore, state intervention at elementary level should take place where circumstances made it absolutely unavoidable. Allied to that, where public monies were to be deployed at elementary level efforts should be made to ensure that no wastage occurred. Coupled with that, every effort should be made to ensure that those benefitting from the intervention did not lose their self-reliance because of state support. Also, as in all areas of the economy use ought to be made of emulation and competition to act as a motive to perform to the optimum level. Society's progress depended on scope being allowed to individuals to prove their worth, and on the tolerance of variety and diversification.[98]

Payment by Results followed on from the Newcastle Commission[99] which was established in 1858 to 'inquire into the present State of Popular Education in England, and to consider and report what measures, if any, are required for the Extension of sound and cheap elementary instruction to all classes of the People'.[100] The survey included elementary schools in

98 Coolahan, *The Origins of the Payment by Results Policy*, 18.

99 The appointment of the Newcastle Commission and the subsequent institution of Payment by Results in 1862 were directly due to the expense of the Crimean War. See David Wardle, *English Popular Education 1780–1970* (Cambridge: Cambridge University Press, 1970), 35. It is worth noting that in the year 1861 the government allotted £26,000,000 for the army and navy services, but only £813,441 for education. See Coolahan, *The Origins of the Payment by Results Policy in Education*, 26.

100 Quoted in Sylvester, *Robert Lowe and Education*, 44.

Great Britain and abroad,[101] but it was principally concerned with England. A similar scheme was suggested for Scotland by the Argyll Commission. Three years later in 1861, the Commission recommended:

> ... a searching examination by competent authority of every child in every school to which grants are to be paid with the view of ascertaining whether these indispensable elements of knowledge are thoroughly acquired, and to make the prospects and position of the teacher dependent to a considerable extent on the results of the examination.[102]

There was an obvious implication in the terms of reference of the Report that costs for popular education should be kept to a minimum. Allied to this was the fact that Lowe's cabinet colleagues exerted pressure on him to keep expenditure on education to a minimum. Concurrently, Gladstone, the Chancellor of the Exchequer battled for economies from all quarters. In such circumstances, Lowe's Revised Code for elementary education would be welcomed, at least in government circles, with open arms.

The finale of the Newcastle Commission's report saw Payment by Results being introduced in 1862 in England. The mantra at the time was 'if it did not promote efficiency, it would be cheap'. Lowe's prophecy was right – for a time. Over three years the government grant fell and attendance rose. Children were inclined to remain in school for longer. However, issues began to creep in which were unwelcome in many quarters: rote learning was taking hold as a teaching methodology, or closer to the point to defeat the inspectors;[103] the presentation of sick children for the attendance grant could not be curtailed; and the 'cult of the register'.[104]

There was an increasing demand for educational facilities as the child population escalated in the industrial cities. A range of suggestions filled the air, suggestions on how to deal with rising populations. Rescue operations

101 The Parliamentary grant had risen exponentially between 1846 and 1859. Many of the schools enjoyed a state-subsidy. The Anglican Church was the predominant authority in educating elementary school children.

102 Quoted in Armytage, *Four Hundred Years of English Education*, 124.

103 The word 'inspector' is, perhaps, an unfortunate word to define a person who is really a profile of 'guide, counsellor and friend', not to mention adviser.

104 Armytage, *Four Hundred Years of English Education*, 124–125.

were floated as an idea; so too were terms of custodial care to prevent delinquency. Other suggestions included a stress on industrial development with provisions for a basic education. In order for society be blessed with peaceful, law-abiding citizens, a modicum of education could be the answer. However, taking this too far may have hidden consequences as Hodgson observed:

> The inconvenience of total darkness were more and more recognised and the advantage of at least, a sort of twilight state of mind was more and more perceived; but it may well be questioned whether the noonday blaze of knowledge was not more dreaded by the educational patrons of the lower
>
> classes than even the midnight blackness of total ignorance.[105]

The poor were encouraged to be content with the lot they were designed for and to perform the functions for which they were called with diligence, sobriety and obedience. Robert Lowe, statesman and contributor to education debate, made a telling comment regarding such providential expectations:

> The lower classes ought to be educated to discharge the duties cast upon them.
>
> They should also be educated that they may appreciate and defer to a higher cultivation when they meet it; and the higher classes ought to be educated in a very different manner, in order that they may exhibit to the lower classes that higher education to which if it were shown to them, they would bow down and defer.[106]

This publication began as an Address at the Philosophical Institute of Edinburgh, Friday, 1 November 1867. His book emphasized 'practical things' rather than 'speculative things' and argued that the study of English should be 'preparation for life'.

There is another side to the story surrounding the Revised Code (Payment by Results) and the criticism it suffered. The Revised Code

105 W. R. Hodgson, *Exaggerated Estimates of Reading and Writing as a Means of Education* (1867). Cited by H. Silver, *The Concept of Popular Education* (1st ed. 1965; Republished, Routledge, 2013), 24.

106 Robert Lowe, *Primary and Classical Education* (Edinburgh: Edmonston and Douglas, 1867), 32.

brought to an end a system under which government was faced with an open-ended, ever-expanding obligation to fund schools over whose standards of instruction it had limited control. Instead government proposed to pay out to schools which were clearly doing their job of providing a solid elementary education. The Code thus represented a 'crash course in literacy' doing much to raise standards in England and Wales in the basic subjects. It also curtailed an over-emphasis in the teaching of religion.

*The Education Bill of 1870* intimated another step in the extent to which the state was becoming involved in education provision. Forster felt that the extension of education to the poor was necessary for 'the good and safe working of our constitutional system'.[107] Allied to that was his concerns for the ongoing development of industrial competitiveness and prosperity. The involvement of the state in the education of the masses stemmed from a complex admixture of motivating factors. This admixture of motivating factors was strongly prescriptive of a system such as payment by results, which became the linchpin of British education in the second half of the nineteenth century.

An idyllic scenario did not apply to the situation in Britain regarding the payment by results system and its application to education provision. There were those, many of them very eminent, who opposed payment by results: Coleridge, Carlyle, Ruskin, Newman and Arnold[108] laid a challenge at the door of utilitarianism and its particular mechanistic cultural brand.[109] Their view of society embraced a more humanistic ideal, in which people were not seen as mere cogs in the wheel of industrialization and crude socialization. In 1886 a Royal Commission, with Sir Richard Cross as Chairman, was appointed to examine the workings of elementary education

107 Speech by Forster in J. S. Maclure, *Educational Documents in England and Wales* (London: Chapman and Hall, 1968), 104.

108 Arnold proffered a broad notion of school inspection and he was quite critical of the Revised Code introduced in England in 1862, where the 'tone' of the school was lost in inspectors' reports, in favour of the minutia of the 'code'. He did not favour this mechanistic system of inspection, but instead sought a general flavour and tone of the school. See *Vice-Regal Committee on Primary Education in Ireland* (Dill), Second Report, Appendix (Cd.7228.9).

109 Williams, *Culture and Society, 1780–1950*.

since the passing of the Education Act of 1870. Two reports were issued in 1888, a majority and a minority one; both reports, more or less agreed with one another. The Commissioners claimed that they

> are unanimously of opinion that the present system of payment by results is carried too far and is too rigidly applies, and that it ought to be modified and relaxed in the interest equally of the scholars, of the teachers, and of education itself.[110]

The Cross Committee had many concerns about the Payment by Results system, and in their report they suggest different ways of allocating money for education:

> … In reference to the Parliamentary grant, and to payment by results, we are of opinion that the best security for efficient teaching is the organisation of our school system under local representative authorities over sufficiently extensive areas, with full power of management and responsibility for maintenance, with well graduated curricula, a liberal staff of well-trained teachers, and buildings, sanitary, suitable, and well equipped with school requisites.[111]

The *Report* goes on to elaborate on the duty of the State in securing all the above conditions, and in aiding all local effort, but leaving some of the costs to local initiative. This was a step towards dispensing with the current system based on the results of an examination.

They foregoing-mentioned gentlemen were opposed to the boorish and vulgar existence which they found, or to enjoin Matthew Arnold's phrase, 'in the hardness and vulgarity of middle-class liberalism'.[112] However, this alternative view to utilitarianism did not find currency until the last quarter of the century, and its effect on education policy was delayed until the very end of the 1890s. Arnold, not only inveighed against the essence of this formula, but also what he viewed as the entirely superficially plausible reasoning behind it. He argued that the primary schools of England were being expected to 'cram into the space of two or three years the instruction

110 Cited in Barnard, *A History of English Education from 1760*, 174–175.

111 *Royal Commission on Elementary Education, Final Report*, 249, PP, 1888 (C 5485), XXXV.

112 Matthew Arnold, 'Culture and Anarchy', in G. Sutherland, ed., *Arnold on Education* (Pelican, 1973), 164–269, and 17.

which ought to occupy five or six'[113] and claimed that standards of literacy would rise if teachers concentrated on the 3Rs alone.

Arnold elaborates:

> What renders impossible the attainment by so many of a power so considerable – a power which is a real lasting acquirement for the whole life – is the utter want of care for books and knowledge in the homes from which the majority of them come forth ... in a word, the general want of civilization in themselves and in those among whom they pass their lives ... It is the advance of them and their class in civilization which will bring them nearer to the power, not the confining of them to reading lessons, not the striking out of lessons in geography or history from the course of our elementary schools. Intelligent reading ... is not very common even among the children of the rich and educated class. When children in this class possess it, they owe it not to the assiduity with which they have been taught reading and nothing but reading, but partly to natural aptitude, far more to the civilizing and refining influences, the current of older and educated people's ideas and knowledge, in the midst of which they have been brought up.[114]

Arnold was vehemently opposed to Payment by Results, but not just what it proposed to do but also the means by which it proposed to do. Arnold has been quoted at some length, not to display his singular position regarding the policy adopted in English schools in 1862, and its subsequent demise. His opposition captures

> certain continuities in English primary schooling which outlasted both the Code and elementary education: minimalism *versus* breadth; class-based assumptions and expectations about what children from particular backgrounds can or cannot do ...[115]

Arnold, one of the best-known government school inspectors, writing in 1867 left the reader in no doubt about his views on Payment by Results:

> I cannot say that the impression made upon me by the English schools at this second return to them has been a hopeful one. I find in them, in general, if I compare them

113 M. Arnold, *Democratic Education* (1862), ed. R. H. Super (Ann Arbor: University of Michigan Press, 1962), 220.

114 Arnold, *Democratic Education*, 223–224.

115 R. Alexander, *Culture and Pedagogy: International Comparisons in Primary Education* (Oxford: Blackwell, 2000), 136.

> with their former selves, a deadness, a slackness, and a discouragement which are not the signs and accomplishments of progress. If I compare them with the schools of the continent I find in them a lack of intelligent life much more striking than it was when I returned from the continent in 1859.
>
> This change is certainly to be attributed to the school legislation of 1862. That legislation ... has introduced the mode of aid which is commonly called *payment by results* (Arnold's italics), and has withdrawn from teachers all character of salaried public servants.[116]

To help counteract any minor assaults against the Revised Code of 1862, five years later the government increased the grant for certain 'specific' subjects like history, geography and grammar. Something of a war of attrition surfaced about this time, but within the big picture this amounted to a mere skirmish. Arnold, speaking from the Inspectorate point of view stated on the issue of them versus us – that the operation was 'game of mechanical contrivance in which the teachers will and must more and more learn how to beat us'.[117]

Matthew Arnold's attacks on the Revised Code were prolific, but many of the inspectorate were more positively inclined. Take, for example, the views of one, Mr Du Pont:

> ... I see daily the advantages of the New over the Old Code. In the oral lessons under the Old Code, whether in geography, history or scripture, it was very generally the fashion to allow a whole class to call out its answers altogether; hardly ever were the children pressed to answer one by one, and the evils of that system hardly need to be pointed out, they are now so patent to those who have seen the individualizing work of the New Code.[118]

Conditions in Ireland differed significantly from that which pertained to Britain, particularly with regard to industrial development and unprecedented urbanization. Nevertheless, Ireland being within the United

116 *Report of the Committee of Council on Education* [England and Wales], (1867–1868), 290–291, 295–296.

117 Cited in Armytage, *Four Hundred Years of English Education*, 125.

118 *Report of the Committee of Council on Education* [England and Wales], (1869–1870), 66–68. See also, J. M. Goldstrom, *Education: Elementary Education, 1780–1900* (Devon: David and Charles, 1972), 125–1161 – various.

Kingdom, certain similarities apply, chief among them being the *laissez-faire* policy. One example of this in the Irish context was the manner in which the Great Famine drew relatively little intervention by Westminster. Belated reaction to the Famine came with public works, but there was a reluctance to anything for nothing to 'able-bodied' people who had to earn their keep by engaging in allotted works. Classical economists opposed the extension of the Poor Laws to Ireland as they would 'weaken thrift and industry, promoting improvidence and idleness in their place'.[119]

In the first half of the nineteenth century educational provision was probably ahead of that of England. Ireland during these decades was used as an experimental workshop.[120] Later decades witnessed Ireland coming more under the wing of England in educational policy.

Mid-century witnessed the astronomical costs of the Crimean War (1854–1856), amounting to £78,000,000, it shocked contemporaries. There was also uproar over the incompetence of the officers. There was also dissatisfaction with the civil service, as promotion was influenced by a traditional system of patronage, where social contacts meant more than ability. This post-Crimean period witnessed a definite demand for the end of the 'aristocratical monopoly of power and privilege,' and gave great impetus to the re-emergence of radical attitudes. The real conduct of 'public affairs' was at issue, and people like Roebuck, Dickens and Morley, 'the rich radical wire-puller of the age,' sought full information about the civil service and the running of the army. The Foreign Office felt the brunt of the attacks. 'There must be an end put to every mystery of office,' was the cry. The call went out for greater transparency.[121]

The public mood questioned the protection of individual inefficiency, and, furthermore, it was claimed that the pool of potential talent was not being sufficiently harvested. The reformers wished to see more open competition and they sought to lay the foundations of a meritocracy of talent to replace an aristocracy of privilege.[122]

119 R. D. Collison Black, *Economic Thought and the Irish Question, 1817–1870* (Cambridge: Cambridge University Press, 1960), 91.

120 See Akenson, *The Irish Education Experiment.*

121 Asa Briggs, *The Age of Improvement 1783–1867* (London: Longman, 1959, Third impression 1977), 430–436.

122 Coolahan, *The Origins of the Payment by Results Policy in Education*, 23.

Competitive examinations, under the newly formed Civil Service Commission, were introduced to the army and civil service. This commission held its first meeting in June 1855, and within twenty years the open competition format was expanded, though the Foreign Office still held on to some privileges. Jeremy Bentham, of course, had long ago called for such a measure, while John Stuart Mill endorsed the idea with his remarks:

> ... the proposal to select candidates for the Civil Service of Government, by a competitive examination, appears to me to be one of these great public improvements, the adoption of which would form an era in history.[123]

As a result of endorsements such as the above, testing became the norm throughout the whole educational world, and it was supported by the public. Various bodies embraced the new regime with gusto: College of Preceptors; The Local Examinations of Oxford and Cambridge; London University Matriculation Examinations; the South Kensington Science and Art Department. The 'fever' for testing became so endemic that by 1875 boys leaving secondary school could choose between seventeen different examinations.[124] This system has been referred to as 'the Victorian commercial code applied to education'.[125]

The cram market benefited as short manuals, outlines and annotated texts appeared in great quantities. The manuals helped students to improve their aim, and one school inspector capitalized on this analogy by stating, 'examination is to the student what the target is to the rifleman – there can be no definite aim, no real target without it.'[126]

In the early stages of its introduction, payment by results as a new system was warmly welcomed by the majority of teachers. However, as the years passed, attitudes began to change and protests against a system

123 Cited in Fred. W. O'Connor, 'Competitive Examinations and Their Bearing on the Civil Service', *Journal of the Statistical and Social Inquiry Society Ireland* 3 (1863), 87.

124 See R. D. Altick, *The English Common Reader: A Social History of the Mass Reading Public, 1800–1900* (Chicago: University of Chicago Press, 1957), 184.

125 Referenced in R. F. Foster, *Vivid Faces: The Revolutionary Generation in Ireland, 1890–1923* (London: W. W. Norton, 2014), 33.

126 Altick, *The English Common Reader*, 184–186.

which designated schools and teaching to being no more than slaves to the ever-increasing number of examinations. In 1888, a strong protest was raised against 'the incessant frequency of examinations, the growth of the practice into a highly artificial symptom, the creation of a profession of examining, and its correlative the profession of cramming, the wholesale, mechanical and hurried way in which the examinations are held, and the subjection of teaching to examining'.[127] As well a culture of examining pervading school life, since the 1850s the Treasury gained considerable control over many government departments. A climate of accountability ensued, especially with Gladstone's appointment of Public Accounts Committee in 1861.[128] Expenditure on education came under close scrutiny, as the state's subvention escalated from £33,000 in 1833 to £837,000 in 1859.[129] As a result of this increase, expectations within government circles revolved about the concept of 'value for money'. To get some perspective on government spending and its priorities it is worth drawing attention to 1861 when the budget for the army and navy services was approximately £26,000,000 while the budget allotted for education was £813,441.[130]

The Newcastle Commission was established to

> inquire into the present state of popular education in England, and to consider and report what measures, if any, are required for the extension of sound and cheap elementary instruction to all classes of people.[131]

Reporting in 1861, it recommended the replacement of the existing grants for elementary education, and it was highly critical of attendance levels

127 Profs. Muller, Harrison and Freeman, 'The Sacrifice of education to Examinations', *Nineteenth Century Review* XXIV (1888), 617–652; 646; and XXV (1889), 286–322. This protest included the signatures of 100 MPs.

128 Coolahan, *The Origins of the Payment by Results Policy in Education*, 25.

129 Figures from Coolahan, *The Origins of the Payment by Results Policy in Education*, 26.

130 See Simon, *Education and the Labour Movement, 1870–1920* (London: Lawrence and Wishart, 1965), 115, n. 3. Simon refers to the fact that expenditure on education reduced between 1861 and 1865. That is, as a result of the results programme.

131 Quoted in Coolahan, *The Origins of the Payment by Results Policy in Education*, 27.

at schools and of the low level of proficiency found within the schools. There was only one way of improving the situation:

> … which is to institute a searching examination by competent authority of every child in every school to which grants are to be paid, with the view of ascertaining whether these indispensable elements of knowledge are thoroughly acquired and to make the prospects and position of the teacher dependent to a considerable extent on the results of this examination.[132]

The scene was set by the adoption by the government of only one recommended resolution – Payment by Results, which was introduced in 1862. Under this scheme the onus was placed on teachers to encourage regular attendance and to advance the progress of their pupils as higher fees were paid for more senior classes.[133] However, the situation was not entirely rosy: the curriculum became very focused on the examination at year's end and was narrowed down to the detriment of subjects which were omitted and which may have benefitted pupils enormously. A great deal of pressure existed within the teaching force and also within the pupil body. The role of inspector altered from being an adviser to that of the dreaded examiner.[134] Another decade would elapse before something similar was introduced in Irish schools. In 1899 Payment by Results came to an end in Britain, having gone through modifications during the 1890s.

It is timely now to progress our investigation into developments in Ireland regarding the adoption of the results scheme, and also to intimate both the positive and negative aspects of such a regime.

132 John S. Maclure, *Educational Documents: England and Wales (1816–1947)* (London: Chapman and Hall, 1968), 73.

133 Susan M. Parkes, *A Guide to Sources for the History of Irish Education, 1780–1922* (Dublin: Four Courts Press, 2010), 49.

134 *Report of the Commissioners appointed to inquire into the state of popular education in England.* H.C. 1861 (2794), xxi, pt I, I; H.C. 1861 (2794-11-IV), xxi, pts ii–iv; H. C. 1861 (2794-VI), pt vi, 1; *Appendix to the fortieth report of the Commissioners of National Education in Ireland for the Year 1873* (C965), H.C. 1874, xix, 114–127.

CHAPTER 2

# The Adoption of Payment by Results in Irish National Primary Education

'I have never let my schooling interfere with my education.'

– Mark Twain

## Preamble and Background

In general terms, social improvement usually involves material advancement, but also it means having an effective system of education which improves the standard of literacy, amongst other aspects. Nineteenth-century Ireland was bedevilled by religious and political problems, all in many ways counterbalancing any perceived progress attained in terms of society. Yet, state intervention in financial aid for education provision was forthcoming in Ireland long before it became available in either England or Scotland.[1] It was the 1830s before state subvention in education occurred in England and Scotland, but even before the Act of Union of 1800, Ireland had had a developing tradition of state subvention in its provision. This, of course, was not always direct intervention. It is important to note that direct state intervention became associated with the national school system of 1831 in Ireland four decades ahead of a similar state-supported system in England or Scotland.[2]

1 Scotland had joined the Union through the Anglo-Scottish agreement in 1707.

2 The most noteworthy treatment of this in Akenson, *The Irish Education Experiment*, Ch. 1, 1–58.

By the end of the eighteenth century, the Irish Parliament (Grattan's), though by no means free from the clutches of the English government, had aided primary, intermediate and university levels of schooling.[3] This aid was not as philanthropic as it may seem at first glance, as many historians from a traditional perspective have claimed that the purpose of such aid was to further the English language and English culture and to promote the spread of Protestantism in Ireland. Chief among these historians is Timothy Corcoran, and one of his principal mouthpieces was *State Policy in Irish Education 1536–1816*, published in 1916.

Some of the schools prior to 1831 were, in fact, both avowedly anglicizing and proselytizing, and they were essentially established to shore up wavering loyalty within the ranks of the Old English in Ireland. Ultimately, these Protestant schools failed, but they were funded by the Crown, but in too many instances the monies allotted to them were re-directed elsewhere by the local Protestant bishop who had responsibility for the institutions in the first place. These schools were the brainchild of Henry the Eight's Tudor legislation in 1537. A similar fate befell the Diocesan schools. Neither type of school ever garnered any appreciable support from Catholic Ireland.

Later attempts by the state to spur into place a coherent network of schools had limited success. In the seventeenth century the Royal Schools of James I, but they had a very precarious existence and never had more than two hundred students. In 1733, the Incorporated Society in Dublin for Promoting English Protestant Schools in Ireland was given a charter. These charter schools were concerned with the education of the poor, and were free of charge. They were avowedly proselytizing and anglicizing, and they had some success, with some Catholics attending. None of these institutions catered adequately for the majority population, and they were supported to varying degrees by government policy.

The backdrop to education provision in Ireland in the eighteenth century was the advent of the Penal Laws, a regime that outlawed Catholic education. However, in 1782 and 1793 the most virulent of these laws were repealed, thus allowing Catholics to openly teach in school and attend school. About this time a whole host of Protestant Society schools emerged

3 See Akenson, *The Irish Education Experiment*, 20.

in Ireland. These sprang from the effects of the evangelical movement in England, which led to the formation of education societies. These societies migrated across the Irish Sea and opened schools throughout Ireland. They included The Association for Discountenancing Vice (1792); The London Hibernian Society (1806); Sunday School Society (1809); Society for promoting the Education of the Poor in Ireland, better known as The Kildare Place Society (1811); and Baptist Society for promoting the Gospel in Ireland (1814). The schools established by these societies were voluntary, supported by private subscription, but also in receipt of government grants, and from an educational fund called the Lord Lieutenant's Fund.

The most successful of the societies was the Kildare Place Society, which began life from a religiously neutral stance but was later accused of proselytism. By 1831 Kildare Place had fallen out of favour with the government, and its grant of £30,000 for that year was simply transferred to the National Board of Education, a body put in charge of the new national school system. The national school system encountered much opposition from both Catholic and Protestants alike, though in many ways it was a successful enterprise, expanding impressively during the first four decades of its existence.[4]

## Early Efforts at Payment by Results and Working Conditions

It is possible to detect some murmurings of payment by results in some proposals concerning the remuneration of teachers many years before its establishment in 1871. An early advocate of payment by results was Richard Lovell Edgeworth, whose book *Practical Education* was published in 1798. There is an indication in the book that Edgeworth toyed with the notion of some of the basic precepts of Utilitarianism. He espoused the pleasure/pain principle, and he emphasized the role of education had on the betterment of humanity:

4 Akenson, *The Irish Education Experiment*, 157–224.

> … all the pleasures of practical education tend to one distinct object; to render our pupils good and wise, that they may enjoy the greatest possible share of happiness at present and in the future.[5]

With the authority given to him by the publication of his book in 1798, Edgeworth took the issue of education to the Irish House of Commons in 1799. On 8 February 1799, soon after his arrival in the House, the Irish Commons asked that the 1791 Commissioners' report be presented and that a committee be appointed to enquire into the state of education of the poorer classes and to suggest means for its improvement. R. L. Edgeworth, was, according to his daughter, Maria, the chief influencer on that committee:

> By his exertions, a select committee was appointed, and they adopted the resolutions drawn up by him.[6]

And:

> Mr. Edgeworth reported from the Committee appointed to enquire into the state of the education of the lower Order of the People and the Means of improving the same, the Resolutions which the Committee had directed him to report to the House, which he read in his Place, and afterwards delivered in at the Table, where the same were read …[7]

Edgeworth's address to the House contained six resolutions, number four being of concern to us:

5 M. and R. L. Edgeworth, *Practical Education*, vol. 2 (London: Johnson, 1798), 729. See also T. Lyons, *The Education Work of Richard Lovell Edgeworth, 1744–1817* (Lampeter: Mellen Press, 2003), 13–31.

6 R. L. and M. Edgeworth, *Memoirs of Richard Lovell Edgeworth*, vol. 2 (Shannon: Irish University Press, 1969), 245.

7 Edward F. Burton, 'Richard Lovell Edgeworth's Education Bill of 1799: A Missing Chapter in the History of Irish Education', *The Irish Journal of Education* 13, no. 1 (1979), 24–33.

> *Resolved,* that it is the Opinion of this Committee, that the Payment of such Masters should consist partly of a fixed salary and partly of Rewards proportioned to their Exertions and Success.[8]

In his speech to the Commons, Edgeworth urged a system of education for 'working people' seeing this as the highest importance to the peace and prosperity of the country.[9] He stated:

> I do not wish for the people any other education, but what might afford them a knowledge of their duty, what would make them virtuous and loyal, useful to themselves and to the State.[10]

He was very keen on gaining a legislative underpinning for education in Ireland because of the 'defective state of education of the lower order of people in this kingdom,' the setting up of one or more schools in every parish.

The Fourth Resolution contained the germ of payment by results, but the Edgeworth Bill never got a second reading in the House, though it was ordered; the House was counted out, and references to the Bill disappeared from the Journals.

Edgeworth consoled himself that he had made an attempt:

> The honour of having proposed a plan of National Education would be his – all the obloquy of rejecting it would fall on Ministers.[11]

One of the reasons why the Bill failed was probably the preoccupation the House had with the upcoming Union with Great Britain.[12] On the other hand, there is an alternative viewpoint emanating from the Chancellor of the Exchequer, which was published in the *Dublin Evening Post:*

8 Ireland. *Journals of the House of Commons of the Kingdom of Ireland from the 22nd Day of January 1799, inclusive, to the First Day of June, 1799, inclusive*, vol. XVIII.

9 1798, the year prior to his speech, witnessed a rising in parts of Ireland, with a threat of a French invasion.

10 Newspaper Report contained in *Memoirs of RLE,* 246–248.

11 *Dublin Evening Post,* 2 April 1799.

12 This is Akenson's view. Akenson, *The Irish Education Experiment*, 75.

> … that the present distracted state of the country was such, that the public money was scarcely equal to the public exigencies, and that in every point of view it would be politic to defer the execution of such a plan till times of more tranquillity, when Government should have more leisure and more power to complete a scheme of National Education.[13]

Perhaps, Akenson is correct, and perhaps, the Chancellor of the Exchequer is correct; there is a great likelihood that both are partially correct. By any standards, it was an inopportune moment in history to spring on the Irish Parliament a motion for social reform, especially one involving financial investment. It was a period of rebellion and union, surely, a scenario of contradictory proportions. Would Catholic Ireland send their children to a school that was one of a National System? The repeal of the Penal Laws had just happened, and the mistrust caused by those laws would not evaporate overnight.[14]

Other examples of payment by results policies can be detected in some of the Protestant society schools of the period: *London Hibernian Society,* being one such example.[15] The Kildare Place Society provided the most successful of all the society schools operating in Ireland. Among its principles was:

- To maintain a system of annual inspections of all schools in connection with the Society.
- To encourage by gratuities, but not by salaries, such masters and mistresses as should appear deserving.[16]

It is very clear that payment by results was encouraged by the KPS in its schools, and it is also noteworthy that an inspectorial system was an essential part of such a system. It was the teacher who was being assessed, and not the pupils. The first inspection of schools of its type in

13 *Dublin Evening Post*, 2 April 1799.

14 See Edward F. Burton, 'Richard Lovell Edgeworth's Education Bill of 1799', 30.

15 *Report from the Select Committee on Foundation Schools and Education in Ireland*, H.C. 1837–1838, vii, (701), 345–437.

16 *Report from the Select Committee on Foundation Schools and Education in Ireland*, 355.

Ireland, England or Scotland was that of John Veevers for the Society in 1818.[17] Veevers stated that it was the 'hope of reward' that encouraged the teachers to do their very best.

As well as reporting on the scholastic endeavours of each school visited by an inspector from the KPS, the report also included reference to the neatness and cleanliness, and order of the schools in question, and wherever they were found wanting the grant was withheld.[18]

Gratuities for teachers ranged from £2 to £10 per annum. The total amount of gratuities in 1818 was £277, but in 1825 it had reached £4,009.[19]

The Commissioners' Reports of the mid-1820s endorsed the system of payment operated by the KPS. This means that the KPS was granted official recognition for such a system that offered extra payment to teachers based on the inspectors' reports. This was happening four decades before it began in England and five decades before it was introduced by the Commissioners to Ireland.

When the national system of education was introduced in 1831 Stanley's letter outlined the renumeration details for teachers; there would be a joint source of renumeration – the state and the local community. The permanent part of the teacher's salary should be provided locally, and on the fulfilment of various conditions the government would provide funds to teachers as a bonus to their permanent salaries.[20]

The Commissioners' Report of 1835 was more specific:

> We consider that the teacher of each primary school should have a salary of £25 a year and that the Commissioners should be authorised to award annually to each a further sum not exceeding £5, provided they should see cause for doing so in the inspector's report of his general conduct and the character of the school committed to him.[21]

17 H. Kingsmill-More, *An Unwritten Chapter in the History of Education* (London: Macmillan, 1904), 327.

18 Kingsmill-More, 328.

19 *First Report of the Commissioners of Irish Education Inquiry*, H.C. 1825, xii (400), 49.

20 See *Royal Commission of Inquiry into Primary Education (Ireland)*, vol. 1, pt 1: *Report of the Commissioners*, 22–26, H. C. 1870, xxviii, pt i.

21 Quoted in Coolahan, *The Origins of the Payment by Results Policy in Education*, 48.

In the 1830s teacher supply became an issue for the Commissioners of National Education. In an address to the Earl of Mulgrave, on his arrival as Lord Lieutenant in 1835, the Commissioners requested him to ensure that they would be provided:

> with adequate means by the State, not only for training schoolmasters, but also for inducting competent persons to become candidates for teacherships through a fair prospect of remuneration and advancement.[22]

As mid-century approached, there was some satisfaction felt by the Commissioners as 4,321 national schools were operating, and 2,589 teachers had been trained in Merrion Street, and later in Marlborough Street.

However, a different picture emerges when one moves away from the training aspect of teaching and concentrates on teachers' salaries and standards of living. Initially, in 1831, Stanley had envisaged a dual aspect to teachers' income; state funding and local funding. In practice, the latter contributions were minimal or non-existent. The funding from the Treasury increased from £30,000 in 1831 to £120,000 in 1849, but this amount was used for a variety of expenditures; to build a headquarters and staff it, appoint inspectors, publish school books, run a training college and conduct model schools and pay the teachers. In 1841 there was an attempt by the Commissioners to classify teachers according to ability for salary purposes, ranging from £20 a year for a first class male teacher to £10 a year for a third class female teacher.[23] In 1845 the situation became more complicated when each classification was broken up into two or three divisions, along with the introduction of probationary teachers and assistant teachers.[24]

22 See Isaac Butt, *Irish National Education: The Liberty of Teaching Vindicated* (Dublin, 1865), 85. Republished as *The Liberty of Teaching Vindicated; Reflections and Proposals on the Subject of Irish National Education with an Introductory Letter to the Right Honourable Wm. E. Gladstone, M. P.* (London: Forgotten Books, 2018), or General Books, 2012.

23 *Seventh Report of the Commissioners of National Education for the Year 1840* [353], H.C. 1842, XXIII, 162–163.

24 *Seventeenth Report of the Commissioners of National Education for the Year 1850,* [1405], H.C. 1851, XXIV, Appendix B, Table VII, 40.

The majority of teachers never got beyond class 3, and in 1849 the average salary paid by the National Board did not exceed £14.10.0 per annum. This was in fact below the rate which a parcel porter was earning, and equal to two-thirds the pay of the ordinary policeman. Coupled with that, salaries were paid half-yearly until 1849, and thereafter quarterly.[25] In such circumstances privations must have been the order of the day. The following table illustrates percentage levels of pupils reaching the stages of the Reading Courses:

Table 1. Percentages of Pupils in National Schools in Different Class Levels, 1866

| | Book I | Book II | Seq. to Book II | Book III | Book IV and above |
|---|---|---|---|---|---|
| Year 1866 | 45.39 | 29.8 | 1.93 | 15.67 | 7.13 |

*Source:* Powis Commission Report, H.C. 1870 xxviii, Pt III, p. 290.

That this is not speculation is clear from the following diary entry of William J. Thompson, a teacher in Ballinderry, who penned the following note on 19 November 1859:

> I have some very kind friends here. Mr. Creaney, who has no less than five children at school ... lent me on coming to Mr. Ligget's (his lodgings) a corner press, a table, a cup and saucer, dishes etc. and gave me some turf. This made me a great deal more comfortable ... I paid Mrs. Ligget two weeks' lodgings, 2 shillings, and she charged me nothing for washing, up till the present, and in return I would not receive any school money for two children till Monday 18th inst. I was very ill off for milk and cream since I came here, but at last I have got milk at a half-penny per pint. I take a pint every second day, and the cream does for tea, the skim milk for porridge. I got some very bad meal from Mr. Creaney. I have to let the porridge boil for three quarters of an hour, and for bread it does not do well at all ... I am sitting in the school by myself and it is getting very cold.[26]

The situation was considerably worse in parts of the south and west of the country. After one of his rounds there, an inspector reported:

25 See J. Magee, 'The Master', *An Múinteoir Náisiúnta* 27, no. 2 (1983), 19, 17–23.
26 Quoted in Magee, 'The Master', 19.

> I beg to assure the Commissioners from actual personal inspection of the interior and exterior of several of the houses and cabins in which the teachers reside, that in portions of Kerry and Cork, they are utterly deficient in the decencies, apart from the comforts, of human habitations .... On no class in the community has the awful period since 1845 fallen more heavily than on the national teachers .... Numbers of the best teachers have obtained situations in England, many have emigrated to America, and want of means alone prevents hundreds of others from doing likewise.[27]

The plight of the teacher in Ireland in the nineteenth century was more of foreboding than having any claims on romantic myths of the respectable and influential 'master' of rural Ireland. And, if the living circumstances were very bad, the working conditions of the teacher in the nineteenth century were no better. Schools operated without desks, a few had tables, squatting on the floor was not uncommon, blackboards were a commodity, the majority of schools had no clocks, and as a watch was too expensive a luxury for teachers, opening and closing and lesson length were all guesswork.[28]

Throughout the early decades of the national system of education, the Commissioners were very conscious of getting value for money, and this often meant the introduction of incentive schemes. In 1855 a plan was adopted whereby teachers could augment their income by teaching extra subjects. This was confined to teachers who possessed certificates of competency, and the subjects included, Vocal Music, Drawing, Navigation, or the Mathematical and Physical Sciences. The criteria for payment were based on a payment by results procedure – 'according to the number under instruction and the success of the teachers' efforts'.[29]

Not all school inspectors were sympathetic towards the teachers and the squalor in which they lived and worked. One particular school inspector claimed that 'there is no teacher so poor that he could not produce the lime

27 Report of James Kavanagh, Head Inspector in the *Seventeenth Report of the Commissioners of National Education for the Year 1850* [1405], H.C. 1851, XXIV, 146–147.

28 Report of James Kavanagh, 146–147.

29 Rules and Regulations of the Commissioners of National Education (Dublin: Thom, 1863), 21.

and labour to colour its walls at each vacation, and with the aid of the pupils, by the expense of a brush or broom, preserve decency and cleanliness'.

Many teachers must have resented their working conditions, not to mention the rules and regulations that went with the job, rules that curtailed their personal freedoms. Teachers were summarily dismissed if the inspectors found them to be in breach of any of the regulations. This included attending Repeal meetings, or being a member of an agrarian society.[30]

The persistent difficulties teachers had with those in charge bedevilled any semblance of 'normal' comfortable living. It was not until the 1860s that representatives began to emerge from the teaching fraternity to represent their grievances in the political and ecclesiastical arenas.

In the period after the Famine, 1850–1875, the Catholic hierarchy felt that this was an occasion of spiritual renewal and regeneration. They expected the teacher in the local school to act as coadjutor of the parish priest in what Emmet Larkin calls the 'devotional revolution'.[31]

In 1858 a *Good Service Salaries* bonus strategy was introduced to motivate teachers to be more efficient. The grant in question was in addition to the basic salary and was awarded to a limited number of teachers in each inspector's district.

As we have seen, educational provision in Ireland prior to 1860 or thereabouts, included a number of features which prefigured the introduction of a formal system of payment by results. Edgeworth's Education Bill of 1799, intimated an inclination towards some form of payment by results. Some of the Protestant society schools included a version of payment by results in the payment of their teachers, and this feature was acknowledged by the Commissioners in 1825. The National Board fixed remuneration scales based on examination performance along with inspectors' reports. By 1860 a tradition of examining teachers, both through written tests and by their teaching prowess in the classroom. Pupil progress was determined by the quality of the teaching.

30 E. Ó hÉideáin, *National School Inspection in Ireland: The Beginnings* (Dublin, 1967), 101–108.

31 E. Larkin, 'The Devotional Revolution in Ireland 1850–1875', *American Historical Review* 77 (1972), 625–652.

Though the education scene in Ireland was fully conversant with some form of payment by results, it was not until 1872 that the scheme became fully operative.

## The 1860s and Education in Ireland

In the days before the Powis Commission Report of 1870 Archbishop Murray's successor Paul Cullen was the major force in the Irish Catholic Church from the 1850s to the 1870s, and he led the Irish bishops in a campaign for denominational system of education from primary to university level. He and his fellow-bishops rejected the idea of mixed education put forward by E. G. Stanley and Thomas Wyse in the 1830s. Mixed education was not acceptable at any level. During the 1860s some modifications were made to teacher training, to the textbooks used in the national schools – the changes to the textbooks caused much denominational rancour, leading the Powis Commission to suggest that from now on the Commissioners should no longer prepare the school books.

Cullen and the Bishops required that all levels of education in Ireland be denominational; that the Model Schools be abolished, or, at least some might become denominational training colleges.[32]

Thus, denominational issues were as alive in the 1860s as much as at any time prior to that. In concert with what was happening in Ireland, the Revised Code (Payment by Results) was introduced in England in 1862, and the following document should not come as a surprise:

> I am directed by His Excellency to inform you that Her Majesty's Government are desirous of drawing the attention of the Commissioners to the important principle upon which the remuneration of the teachers of schools supported by the State has with such marked success been recently regulated in England and Scotland; I refer to the principle of State payments apportioned to the ascertained results of

32 E. F. Norman, *Catholic Church and Ireland in the Age of Rebellion, 1859–1873* (New York: Cornell University Press, 1965), 217. Published online by Cambridge University Press, 2009.

> education. The Government do not urge the Commissioners the general adoption of the principle as an immediate change in the Irish System. They propose its early introduction in certain cases where it might properly be tried at once, as in that of the Model Schools, to be followed by its gradual development, not necessarily in the precise form which it has assumed in England but with such modifications and adaptations of the Commissioners, profiting by English experience, with their own knowledge of the wants and circumstances of Ireland, may recommend.[33]

From the contents of Fortescue's letter, we see a very clear expression on the government's part a desire to introduce payment by results to primary education in Ireland.

In response to this letter, the National Board (Commissioners) met twice, on 26 June and 30 June respectively to consider the contents of Fortescue's proposal. They wrote on 30 June:

> ... without binding themselves to the adoption of any particular details, they beg to express their general approbation of those proposals and their readiness to co-operate with the Government in carrying them into practical effect.[34]

With such wholesome approval of the scheme, one would expect an immediate practical implementation of Payment by Results in Ireland, but there was some political upheaval in the British Government. The Russell Government were defeated in a vote on 18 June and the Cabinet resigned on 26 June. A new chief secretary for Ireland was appointed, and the Resident Commissioner contacted him seeking guidance on what action should be taken regarding the Fortescue proposals.[35] However, there was no early response.

The endorsement by the Board of the proposed policy changes with regard to the Model Schools was seen by the Protestant Press as giving in to Catholic demands and the pairing of this with payment by results drew the same inference. The *Daily Mail* made the following comment:

33 Chief Secretary Fortescue's Long Letter of 19 June 1866, to the Commissioners of National Education (Mayo Papers, Ms., 11217, National Library of Ireland).

34 *Minutes of the Commissioners of National Education*, Ms., 5549, 30 June 1866, 486. This response was written by the Board's secretary on behalf of the Commissioners.

35 *Minutes of the Commissioners of National Education*, Ms., 5550, 17 July 1866, 16.

> It would have given the Ultramontanes the command of a considerable outlay of money. The spirit and purpose of the whole project was Ultramontane, and had the Ministry remained in power throughout the year, these and many other 'modifications', not only in the department of education, but in other public institutions would have been accomplished by the same subterranean process.[36]

The Presbyterian Church also spoke out against the Fortescue proposals alleging their Ultramontane bias. Their statement opposed the introduction of payment by results and praised the existing system:

> To change this system would be to put the untrained and unclassed teacher, who has declined the necessary study on a level with the individual of highest quality and class.[37]

The *Freeman's Journal* opposed the classification system and supported the Fortescue proposals when it said, 'the proper and reasonable test of the value of a teacher, as fulfilling the end of his appointment, as doing the work for which he is paid, is the proficiency of his pupils in the ordinary branches of knowledge, and the general condition of his mind .... We are, therefore, for the application of 'results' as the principle for payment ....[38]

Patrick Keenan, who was heavily involved[39] with the introduction of Payment by Results in 1872, considering the issue of the remuneration of nun teachers, had the following comment to make in 1874, by which time he was Resident Commissioner:

> I suppose this generation of M.P.s knows nothing of the anxiety of those who had to steer the National System, to hit upon some plan by which the nuns, without forcing them with examinations and classification could be placed on terms of equality with the lay teachers. Payment by Results was our plan.[40]

36 *Daily Mail* (7 August 1866).
37 Printed in *Freeman's Journal*, 9 May 1867.
38 *Freeman's Journal*, 24 May 1867.
39 In fact, it was his own plan that he introduced onto the Irish education system.
40 *Monsell Papers*, Ms., 8319, National Library of Ireland: Keenan to Monsell, 15 March 1874.

Keenan had requested the former Resident Commissioner to support the policy of payment by results.

As ever, denominational disputes abounded in Irish education, and the period immediately prior to the introduction of payment by results was no exception. The policy became part of the denominational disputes.

In a speech to Parliament on 5 August 1867, Lord Naas (the new Chief Secretary for Ireland) referred to the Presbyterian objection to the Model Schools proposal, declaring government opposition to the plan. He announced that he intended setting up a Royal Commission (known as the Powis Commission) to enquire into the whole system of primary education in Ireland. One of the signposts for the Commission he used during his speech was a reference to payment by results:

> He believed it would be of the greatest advantage to the national system of education in Ireland if some system of payment by results could be introduced. Great objection to it was made because it was thought it might have the effect of diminishing the remuneration of many teachers who were already inadequately paid, and therefore it should be considered whether payment by results should not be supplementary to the salaries at present given.[41]

Before the Commission sat, it was known to its members that both the current Chief Secretary as well as the former were in favour of some form of payment by results. The setting up of the Royal Commission was delayed, and during this delay, 'the education question is the question of the day'.[42]

Teachers were generally unhappy with the existing classification system and their rates of pay, and in 1866 and 1867 presented memorials to the Commissioners seeking redress.[43] Although the teacher continued to be held in high esteem by the local community, the world of officialdom had a different view. The Commissioners considered teachers to be on the lowest rung of the ladder and laid down detailed sets of rules and regulations that ordered the teacher's life, work and behaviour. According to the 'Twelve Practical Rules for the Teachers of National Schools', teachers were

41 *The Times*, 6 August 1867.

42 *Freeman's Journal*, 12 August 1867.

43 *Minutes of the Commissioners*, Ms., 5550, 16, 392.

not allowed participate at elections, other than to vote; they were barred from attending fairs, markets and political meetings.[44] In short, teachers were barred from mixing with the people, and these rules remained largely unchanged throughout the nineteenth century.

There was, however, general agreement that teachers were poorly paid, but on the other side of the coin, contemporary concern manifested itself in a requirement that the public got value for money. Contemporary remarks by school inspectors of the period bear testimony to the impoverished state in which some teachers lived. One report said:

> Removed above labourers and artisans in their tastes, sympathies and general culture, though somewhat superior to the former, they are yet inferior to the latter in their means and modes of living …. The average income for their schools is £28. 3. 2d.[45]

Another inspector wrote that the:

> … majority of teachers are very poor, and find it hard to keep up a respectable exterior …. The wonder is not that teachers are not more respectably dressed, but that they are able to appear at their work with anything like becoming decency at all.[46]

It was in this context that Irish National Teachers Association (later Organisation) was formed in 1868. By that time the national school system had been operating for four decades. It had expanded to 6,586 recognized national schools, with 918,344 pupils taught by 13,611 recognized teachers. The parliamentary expenditure for national education had increased from over £30,000 in 1833 to £360.195 in 1868–1869. This heavily increasing bill played on the minds of those who held the purse strings, namely the Treasury and the government. Consequently, the government

44 Appendix XVII to the *Thirteenth Report of the Commissioners of National Education, Ireland*, 1846, H.C. 1847 (832), XVII, 187.

45 See Mary McNeill, *Vere Foster: An Irish Benefactor* (Newton Abbot: David and Charles, 1971), 150. See also, M. Moroney, *National Teachers' Salaries and Pensions 1831–2000: A Historical Chronology and Review of the Role of the INTO* (Dublin: Institute of Public Administration, 2007), 20–26.

46 McNeill, *Vere Foster*, 153.

was continually seeking economies and greater possibilities of efficiency in the public service generally.[47]

Further to that, there had been changes in education policy in the countries of Great Britain, namely, England, Wales and Scotland. Payment by results looked like an attractive proposition. In order to reduce public spending on education the question was 'would payment by results' achieve the desired ends?

The Fenian rising of 1867 seemed to some people that the education system in place was not achieving the desired ends of providing law-abiding citizens. It is interesting to recall that Failed Edgeworth Bill of 1799 was also upended by the 1798 rising. This Bill was an attempt, among other things, to introduce payment by results to Irish schools. It was felt by those in charge than education reform was now as urgent as ever. There were concerns about the low levels of literacy and numeracy in the schools, and this often led to crime and delinquency. *The Daily Express* bemoaned the low literacy rates:

> Surely it is time to inquire into the working of a system of National Education which has been for a whole generation in operation and yet has failed to teach three million of our countrymen even how to read and write. Ignorance is something more than the negative of knowledge. That it is the fruitful parent of crime the judicial statistics of the empire abundantly prove.[48]

## The Powis Commission

The Royal Commission did not begin work until January 1868, and its report was delayed. In May 1870, there were complaints from some MPs regarding the delay. It made a total of 129 recommendations, some of which needed immediate attention, while others could be dealt with over the succeeding years. The Powis Report was one of the most important documents in nineteenth-century education in Ireland. One of

47 See Moroney, *National Teachers' Salaries and Pensions*, 26–29.

48 *The Daily Express*, 18 August 1866.

the conclusions reached by the Report was the inadequacy of teachers' renumeration. There was only one dissentient, a Dr Wilson, Presbyterian Minister.[49]

Earl Powis was chairman of the commission, hence the alternative nomenclature the 'Powis' Commission. The commission sat for two years and carried out an exhaustive inquiry into Irish primary education. In 1870, it produced nine large volumes of a Report. The evidence given to the commission was divided along denominational lines. Cardinal Cullen made a long contribution, some written and some orally (three days). His opinion on the education of the poor indicated a rigid class-based view of education provision. He was reminiscent of Mr Lowe who had introduced payment by results in England in 1862:

> Too high an education will make the poor oftentimes discontented, and will unsuit[sic] them for following the plough, or for using the spade, or for hammering iron or building walls. The poor ought to be educated with a view to the place they hold in society, in which it will be impossible for them to cultivate the higher branches of literature and science.[50]

He took this view even further when he remarked:

> I am persuaded that there always has been and always will be to the end of the world a great distinction between rich and poor, and I think that the rich ought to get one sort of education and the poor ought to get another sort. Each class ought to be educated for the sphere of life in which they have to move.[51]

It could be claimed that his level of Christianity was bound by his own personal life style; twenty years in the Vatican, surrounded by the emblems of medieval aestheticism, and now living in a palace. The Powis Commission asked him if he favoured payment by results and his reply was a qualified one; exceptions should be made for poorer parts of the

49 *Minutes of the Royal Commission of Inquiry*, vol. 1 (Dublin: National Archives, 1 June 1869).

50 *Royal Commission of Inquiry into Primary Education*, vol. 3, Minutes of Evidence (C6–III) 1870, XXVIII, pt 3, par. 27150.

51 *Royal Commission of Inquiry into Primary Education*, vol. 3, Minutes of Evidence (C6–III) 1870, XXVIII, par. 27151.

country because it is difficult to maintain sufficient numbers in school to obtain good results.[52] There seems to be an obsession in Cullen's mind with regard to class-based divisions of society; there certainly no evidence of upward social mobility in his thinking.

The final report of the Commission was in 1870: it expressed grave concerns over the limited progress being the pupils in the national schools were making, 'and we reason to think that in Church Education schools, non-National Convent Schools, and Christian Brothers' Schools, the result is not very different'.[53]

In the considered opinion of the Commission:

> That means should be found to secure a better return for the outlay and labour of the National System, and we recommend that each teacher, besides a fixed class-salary, should receive an addition according to the number of children whom the Inspector, after individual examination, can pass as having made satisfactory progress during the year.[54]

The Commission was firmly in favour of endorsing the idea that the best way to counteract and improve the low levels of literacy and numeracy which was evident among Irish pupils was by the 'results' approach. Coupled with that, Payment by Results was also viewed as a mechanism by which it would provide value for money, or, as it were 'a return for the outlay'.

This is nothing short of a perfect example of situations in which the 'hidden' aspects of school life cannot be tested, namely, social development, attitudinal difficulties or improvements, relationships with other pupils or with the teacher. And, how would the inspector assess the difference in pupil development between the start of the school year and the end of the year. This business-like approach to assessment was very much based on the factory production model. The question of teacher employment 'ought to

52 *Royal Commission ...*, vol. 3, XXVIII, par. 26616.

53 *Report of the Commissioners of Inquiry*, H.C., 1870, XXVIII, pt 1, 293.

54 *Report of the Commissioners of Inquiry*, H.C., 1870, XXVIII, pt 1, 293. In the English System, the entire teachers' salary was based on payment by results – there was no fixed salary, unlike that which pertained in Ireland.

be viewed according to the laws of political economy'.[55] The principles of the marketplace were to be applied to the classroom. Recognizing the ideological tradition of his policies, Lowe formally called as witness the doctrines of Adam Smith on competition in education, which doctrines, as Lowe would have it, 'were true without any limitations of time or place, and can never by any change of circumstances become obsolete or inapplicable'.[56]

This was typical of nineteenth-century positivistic theory in which value is placed on sensory perceptions and other experiences such as introspection, intuition, metaphysics are meaningless. Reason and logic determine *a posteriori* facts, and in the early nineteenth century huge advances in the natural sciences encouraged philosophers to apply scientific methods to their ideas. The nineteenth century adopted a state authority notion that unless a concept cannot be 'fixed in returns' it loses its strength or, even its importance entirely. What would Auguste Comte say about the nineteenth-century concept of payment by results? Isaiah Berlin puts positivism, utilitarianism and rationalism in the same basket, as if they belong to one family. Perhaps, they do.[57]

If the 129 individual recommendations published by the Powis Commission were taken on board and implemented, a whole new structure and fundamental re-organization would ensue in the existing primary school system. In summary form, the following are the recommendations that refer specifically to payment by results:

- Aid from the Board will be obtained upon an examination in secular subjects by the Inspector
  1. ----in *Reading, Writing and Arithmetic*; each pupil who gets a pass will earn a fixed sum per head for the school, provided he/she has the minimum attendance fulfilled.

55 Robert Lowe, *The Revised Code of Regulations of the Privy Council on Education* (London: Ridgeway, 1862), 74.

56 Robert Lowe, *Middle Class Education: Endowment of Free Trade* (London: n.p., 1868), 7.

57 Isaiah Berlin, *The Power of Ideas,* with an editorial contribution from Henry Hardy (London: Pimlico, 2001), 69, 208 and 223.

2. Any child who has passed in two of these subjects will qualify for examination in extra subjects approved by the Board (Grammar, Geography, Agriculture), and earn a payment for each pass.

- The progressed of each child from year to year must be considered, and without such progress, *aid from the Board will not be forthcoming*
- It is desirable that the *State should cease to pay* for the instruction of children over a certain age
    1. No scholar above *twelve years of age* should be able to earn by examination any payment for the school unless in Book IV or V.
    2. In schools where there is an Infant Department, children may earn a fixed sum for *average attendance*, provided the Inspector is satisfied with the General Management and Instruction of the school. Such children must not be under four or over six years of age.[58]

The Commission left all the detail regarding the workings of payment by results in the hands of the Commissioners of the National Board who would work on it along the lines of the above principles.

It seems that the Powis Commission members and the Commissioners for National Education worked hand in glove when the recommendations were published. As Akenson puts it, 'the commissioners of national education seem to have swallowed this educational medicine without hesitation.'[59] There was no official debate by them on the question of payment by results. However, there was a discussion on how to effect its implementation.

Patrick Keenan, one of the Chief Inspectors of national schools, was requested by the Powis Commission to submit a plan for Payment by

58 *Report of the Commissioners of Inquiry*, H.C. 1870, XXVIII, pt 1, 524–525. The highlights are the author's. The Powis Commission were against summary dismissal of teachers by the managerial body of a particular school and they also stated that in any school receiving state aid there ought to be a formal contract of employment between managers and teachers incorporating a clause of a three-month period. *Report of the Commissioners of Inquiry*, H.C. 1870, XXVIII, pt 1, 311.

59 Akenson, *The Irish Education Experiment*, 317.

Results for schools in Ireland.[60] His submission came on 28 April 1868 with minute details for a payment by results scheme:

> He advocated that the introduction of such a scheme would result in an increase in the attendance of scholars and ensure more effective teaching by teachers; that money should be provided from the local rates for the payment of teachers; and that on retirement they should receive a pension.[61]

In a similar vein Vere Foster conducted a survey of teachers' associations on a number of specific questions. He forwarded the results to the Commissioners in April 1869. His report highlighted the 'pittance' given to teachers was so miserably inadequate that the best teachers were resigning for other posts or emigrating and that it would require an increase of at least 100 per cent to them on a par with their English counterparts. His recommendations also echoed that of Keenan's regarding pensions for teachers.

The Powis Commission adopted the payment by results scheme proposed by Keenan as a new method of paying teachers. Henceforth, teachers had two sources of income; a fixed salary, based on classification level, plus an additional payment by results element. Up to this point, there were seven different classification levels for teachers, but following Powis this was reduced to three.

The new payment by results scheme got a good welcome from the Commissioners of National Education, the inspectors and from the Catholic Hierarchy. Bishop Moriarty of Kerry sent a written submission in which he stated that he felt it was correct to pay teachers by results but that a basic classification salary ought not to be abolished.

The Powis recommendations meant a diminution of the power of the National Board and a strengthening of the denominational trend in the education system, and a good deal of the Report was in line with Catholic demands.[62] The Press quickly acknowledged the Report and expressed their individualist views in accordance with their dispositions. *The Daily Express* observed that:

60 Patrick Keenan's Memorandum in Parliamentary Papers, H.C., 1870, XXVIII, pt 3, 89–105.

61 See Moroney, *National Teachers' Salaries and Pensions*, 27.

62 Coolahan, *The Origins of the Payment by Results Policy in Education*, 80.

> ... it amounts to little more than a manifesto of the Ultramontane element in their body, modified and restrained to a certain extent by the opinions of the less resolute of their fellow-Commissioners.[63]

*The Freeman's Journal* was very supportive:

> The Report is, on the whole, to be regarded as a very decided step in the right direction, and as such will be received with satisfaction in Ireland.[64]

The same paper inserted a caveat expressing concern for schools in thinly populated areas which might be adversely affected by payment by results.

Two of the main defects to which the Powis Commission drew attention in Irish national education were the poor attendance of pupils at school and the low levels of pupil attainment. Payment by results was looked to as the method whereby amelioration of these defects might be brought about.

Improvements in attendance rates did take place over the period, indicated by Table 2:

Table 2. The Number of Pupils who made at least one attendance and the percentage of those who attended 100 days or more for each decennial period 1861–1901

| Year | Pupils who made at least one attendance | Percentage of those pupils who made 100 attendances or more |
|---|---|---|
| 1861 | 638,282 | 38.9 |
| 1871 | 862,141 | 39.3 |
| 1881 | 1,020,082 | 48.9 |
| 1891 | 988,766 | 56.7 |
| 1901 | 916,869 | 59.7 |

Compiled from Table 160 Census of Ireland, 1901, H.C. 1902, Pt II, H.C. 1902, cxxix, p. 615.

63 *The Daily Express*, 4 June 1870.
64 *The Freeman's Journal*, 6 June 1870.

The Christian Brothers, through one of their number, Br. Grace, favoured payment by results, as it would assess the quality of teaching.[65] Likewise, the Presentation Brothers agreed with the 'results' scheme.[66]

Some objections were raised, such as that of the Presbyterian Minister, Mr Berkeley in Lurgan. He held that such an examination could not test the worth of the instruction given. He felt that such a system would inhibit genuine education and he added:

> I would rather have thirty children educated under a high class teacher than three hundred merely crammed to answer certain questions.[67]

He held that a similar view was on the minds of Presbyterians in general, claiming that it would 'deteriorate the character of the education of the country'. Many were against the cramming aspect, a view which turned out to be prophetic in the long run.

Some Anglicans also opposed the 'results' model, as Protestant schools were generally smaller, thus not earning the equivalent of Catholic schools.[68]

However, senior officers within the inner circle of the National Board of Education (the Commissioners) favoured the 'results' model – Alexander McDonnell, Resident Commissioner; Patrick Keenan, Chief Inspector; and Dr Newell, Secretary of the Board. All the inspectors called to give evidence before the Commission favoured a system in which teachers' salaries would be partly paid on results fees.[69]

Only four teachers, one from each province, were called to give evidence before the Commission, and they opposed the introduction of the 'results' scheme. The Report of the Commission made the following dismissive remark:

> We have out this list (of witnesses for and against) the School teachers, whose objections however are only to the English system, and who had not considered the

65 *Royal Commission* ..., vol. 3, pars 9713–14.
66 *Royal Commission* ..., vol. 3, pars 17351–52.
67 *Royal Commission* ..., vol. 3, pars 11611, 11693.
68 *Royal Commission* ..., vol. 3, par. 21570.
69 *Report of the Commissioners*, 1870, xxviii, pt 1, 294.

subject in its modified form. When put to one of them in this way, he admitted that it might be beneficial.[70]

At a meeting on 14 January 1871 the commissioners resolved to submit proposals to the Treasury, in the estimates for 1872–1873, for a 50 per cent increase in the remuneration of teachers based on payment by results. The Treasury rejected the proposals, as it would have increased the cost of primary education in Ireland by an extra 25 per cent. It did, however, adopt Keenan's proposal on the introduction of Payment by Results, but it rejected his proposals that money should be raised from local rates, and that teachers on retirement should get a pension.[71]

The concept of a results programme appealed to the government, as expenditure on education was increasing and it was deemed to be uneconomical and inefficient, while concurrently, the results obtained from the existing system did not legitimize the growing expenditure.

The implementation of the 129 recommendations of the Powis Commission met with a sluggish response. Gladstone intended introducing legislation based on the Report, anti-Catholic feeling in England obstructed this.[72] Within the realms of participating partners, significant controversy arose. The Poor Law Guardians, the Board of National Education (which had accepted Payment by Results as early as 1866), the Catholic Church, the Presbyterian Church, the Teachers, the British Government and the Treasury all found issues with the Report. The kernel of their concerns was the manner in which education Ireland would be financed and administered locally. During the 1870s there were two occasions when the controversy boiled over: 1872/73 and 1874/75.

The Commissioners of National Education favoured a 50 per cent increase in teachers' salaries, and they duly requested the Treasury to agree to a grant of £100,000 for this purpose, and that it should be based on the principles of payment by results.[73] The Irish National Teachers' Association agreed that teachers' incomes should be increased, but payment by result was not the answer. A Teachers' deputation went to London and met

70 *Report of the Commissioners*, 1870, xxviii, pt 1, 294.
71 Moroney, *National Teachers' Salaries and Pensions*, 29.
72 Norman, *The Catholic Church and Ireland in the Age of Rebellion*, 440.
73 Minutes of the Commissioners, Ms. 5552, National Library of Ireland.

Gladstone, and they made it clear to him that factors peculiar to Ireland might be prejudicial against teachers and education. They alluded to the thinness of the population, the requirement by the labouring poor in Ireland of their children's availability for seasonal work and they also spoke of their insecurity of tenure.[74] The deputation were left with the impression that a modified version of payment by results would be put in place. Security of tenure was a big issue for teachers in the latter half of the nineteenth century, especially with the introduction of payment by results. Many teachers lived in dread of aggravating the school manager for fear of dismissal. Pádraig Ó Conchubhair highlights the:

> … lowly status of the National teacher and his insecurity of tenure …. At any moment he could be dismissed without appeal by the manager whose power was absolute and often he was held in contempt by his contemporaries who felt he could have done better than the less educated who earned more.[75]

Furthermore, teachers did not have the right of appeal until late in the century. According to D. H. Akenson, 'until the last quarter of the nineteenth century they remained unrepresented, unappreciated cogs in the system'.[76]

At the outset of payment by results there were 9,868 teachers working under the National Board, and of these, 3,461, or about 35 per cent, were trained.[77] The table below indicates the classification status of the teachers in employment in the year 1871.

The Irish National Teachers' Organisation actively campaigned for security of tenure and in 1870 the Powis Commission recommended the provision of three months' notice of dismissal. It is hardly surprising that many managers protested against this notice. However, in 1873 the National Board fulfilled this approbation in the form of written contracts for teachers acknowledging that teachers could not be dismissed except for serious misconduct.

74 *The Times*, 1 February 1871.

75 P. Ó Conchubhair, 'The Early National Teachers', *Oideas* 18 (1977), 15.

76 Akenson, *The Irish Education Experiment*, 154.

77 *Report of the Commissioners for 1871*, 293.

These written contracts, while they did offer some protection to teachers, they had, at the end of the day, little significance in reality. The Maynooth Resolution of 1894 stated that a three month notice of dismissal could not be served on a teacher by the manager until the bishop had been informed and his permission obtained to take such action.

Nevertheless, teachers continued to be dismissed from their posts, often on a summary basis, unprotected by the Maynooth Resolution.

Following a debate about Patrick Keenan's version of payment by results, it was adopted, with some alterations. They did not include Keenan's scheme, such as teachers' pensions and employment agreements. Historians and educationalists differ as to the merits of payment by results. It did increase the 'successful' teacher's income significantly, and the levels of attendance improved. Akenson refers to the advantages of payment by results as the *Three Major Blessings* to Ireland. The system was to be a powerful stimulus to the industry of teachers. It secured more equal attention to the several classes of their schools and also led to the adoption of better methods of teaching and more considerate treatment of children. Many would disagree with the 'better methods of teaching'. Under the Results' system education was seen as a product rather than as a process, and the teacher's rapport with pupils was not a consideration. The relationship between teachers and the inspectorate deteriorated during the thirty-year lifespan of the Results' Programme.

The government were only partially in favour of the Keenan scheme, and would only offer to pay third-class teachers 'as a temporary measure'. The estimates for this part were calculated at £18,573. The first recipients of a payment by results dividend in 1871, but in a very limited way. This occurrence is an indication of the Treasury's increasing control of education.[78] The Treasury argued that, in Ireland, the entire cost of education was borne by the government, and they were especially conscious of this in the wake of the Foster Education Act (1870) in England which copper fastened a role for local contributions.

78 Akenson, *The Irish Education Experiment*, 318.

Robert Lowe, who introduced payment by results in England in 1862, was now Chancellor of the Exchequer, and as such he would be keen to reduce education's dependency on public monies.

Meanwhile, in Ireland at a Presbyterian General Assembly in June 1871 a resolution was passed:

> That inasmuch as the system known as 'Payment by Results' does not set forth the true idea of education, but tends to deteriorate and degrade it, while it is utterly inapplicable to the present circumstances of Ireland, especially when not accompanied by compulsory attendance, and, inasmuch as its effect would be to deprive such of the services of good teachers, the assembly are of the opinion that the system should not be introduced into Ireland.[79]

Was this the first salvo to be fired, even before the system was fully introduced and fully operational?

The rancorous climate continued when, on 12 March 1872, the Treasury refused to sanction the Commissioners' estimates for the academic year 1872/1873. Initially, this caused shock, but it led to a very serious and acrimonious of fisticuffs between the Treasury and the Commissioners. In a milder tone, the Commissioners expressed 'unfeigned disappointment' at the treasury's refusal to sanction their estimate for payment by results. Following a lot of toing and froing with verbal shots being fired across the bows, the Commissioners delivered, what John Coolahan calls, an 'implied ultimatum':

> If the Lords of Her Majesty's Treasury persevere in refusing to sanction the Supplemental Estimate, the Board cannot but anticipate a very grave check to the Spread of Education in Ireland. The Commissioners, therefore, very earnestly and very strongly beg Lord Hartington[80]to urge a reconsideration of the decision of the Lords of Her Majesty's Treasury, with a view of obtaining the sanction of Their Lordships to the Supplemental Estimate.[81]

79 *The Daily Express*, 9 June 1871.

80 Lord Hartington succeeded Fortescue as Chief Secretary for Ireland. As the Duke of Devonshire, he was aristocratic, rich, and a Whig, but he was driven by *noblese oblige* to take public office.

81 Letter in Minutes of Commissioners, Ms. 5553, Nat. Lib. Of Ire, 171–175.

The Chief Secretary, Lord Hartington became involved when he penned a letter to the Commissioners on 1 July 1872. The letter indicated some progress on the matter of payment by results payment:

> I have to inform you, that the subject has engaged the most careful consideration of Her Majesty's Government. They have observed, with great regret, the small amount of Local Contributions to the cost of National Education in Ireland .... Her Majesty's Government hesitated to sanction a large addition to the amount provided by the State without requiring some increased contribution from local sources.[82]

This resulted in a step forward, as the National Board drew up a Form of Agreement, approved by Hartington, but with the proviso that, before any payment on results was made, School Managers had to exhibit the official form of agreement properly signed by themselves and their teachers.[83]

However, the Catholic managers found fault with this arrangement as it could mean an interference with their rights as school managers. Cardinal Cullen agreed with the managers, recommending them not to sign until it shall have been maturely examined, 'and its object and tendency fully explored'. The teachers were up in arms as they were not being paid under the terms of payment by results, the clergy were refusing to sign, while the government were holding firm on not distributing the agreed fees when the conditions of the agreement were not being met at a local managerial level.

Vere Foster, INTA President, put forward a memorial of agreement at the annual congress in December 1872. This did not work, as the memorial was defeated and Congress was abandoned in disorder. The teachers did not agree with the Payment by Results aspect being tied to the managers.

The Bishops met in January 1873 and decided to approach Lord Chancellor O'Hagan about getting the wording of the form of agreement changed.[84]

This idea was successful, and it was approved by Lord Hartington in February 1873.[85] A minority of managers still continued their opposition for

82 See Minutes of Commissioners, Ms. 5553, Nat. Lib. Ire., 308–311.

83 See Minutes of Commissioners, Ms. 5553, 27 August 1872. Nat. Lib. Ire., 368.

84 Norman, *The Catholic Church and Ireland in the Age of Rebellion*, 444.

85 Minutes of the Commissioners, Ms. 5554, Nat. Lib. Ire., 76–92.

a time, teachers were satisfied with outcome, as they got their results fees, and they also had contracts of employment. Having gone through many ups and downs payment by results was fully operational in the autumn of 1873, but what of the future?

As it turned out, Lord Hartington's agreement of 1872 was for a three-year period only, and therefore, temporary. Concerns were expressed about the issue when it came up for re-consideration in 1875. This was at a time when the results programme in England underwent notable modifications with the introduction of class subjects which did not necessitate individual examination but could be judged by inspectors on the basis of the proficiency of whole classes.[86] Other modifications followed, and by 1885 'dismantlement' was under way.

It was in this political atmosphere that payment by results in Ireland was ushered in. During the 1870s the national teachers opted for salary increases rather than the results programme. Meetings were held, M.P.s in London were lobbied, and in 1874 they organized a wide-ranging campaign for salary increases. *The Freeman's Journal* commented on the teachers plight:

> With an average income of under £1 a week, no pension, and no residence, the life of an Irish National School Teacher is one of the most sordid penury; While when he is past his work, the open gates of the workhouse are his goal.[87]

The Executive of the INTA sent a memorandum to the Commissioners of the National Board in which they clearly articulated that any increase that may be given should be in addition to the class salaries.[88]

Again, *The Freeman's Journal* reiterated its defence of the teachers and their plight, by opposing any modification that would deprive the teachers of their rightful claim to an income increase under the terms of the payment by results scheme. In its panegyric it had the following to say:

86 Cited in John Coolahan and Patrick O' Donovan, *A History of Ireland's School Inspectorate, 1831–2008* (Dublin: Four Courts Press, 2009), 53. See also, Balfour, *Educational Systems of Great Britain and Ireland* (Oxford: Clarendon Press, 1903), 38.

87 *The Freeman's Journal*, 9 January 1875.

88 *The Irish Teachers' Journal* VII, no. 39 (26 September 1874), 473.

But to tamper with the principle of payment by results – to check the spread and development of a system that, still only in its infancy here in Ireland, has wrought incalculable good, and given a vast impetus to the teaching energy of our country – would be a serious disaster, and retard the advancement of our educational progress.[89]

The Commissioners of National Education favoured the retention of the existing system of payment by results, but requested a doubling of the annual grant of £120,000 to £240,000 for the year 1875/6. The Central Executive of the INTA opposed this increase and sent a deputation to the Chief Secretary, Sir Michael Hicks-Beach in January 1875 urging him not to give an increase. The Hicks-Beach response came in March of that year that payment by results in Ireland had some defects and that an increase in class salaries should be borne in mind.[90]

Behind the scenes the government had only one real concern, and that was to ensure that education in Ireland would not cost any more than it should, and local aid should be forthcoming. With increased local aid came increased local control, and the Catholic Church was concerned about that, in case it meant the introduction of local boards of management. They were aware of the precedent which was set following the Education Act of 1870 in England which introduced local boards of management.

Hicks-Beach was on the government side in declaring that there should be a corresponding payment from local sources.[91]

Now, the government were willing to continue with the grant of £120,000, but with a change; only half would go to payment by result and the other half would go towards increasing class-based salaries. And, the government would contribute another £60,000 to the results programme provided it was matched by a local contribution from the Boards of the Poor Law Guardians. Now the Poor Law Guardians were dragged into the fray, and their contribution was a voluntary one. The government passed The National School Teachers'(Ireland) Act

89 *The Irish Teachers' Journal*, 5 June 1875.

90 Reported in *The Irish Teachers' Journal* VIII, no. 11, 155–159.

91 *The Daily Express*, 2 August 1875.

for the purpose of permitting the Poor Law Guardians to levy a rate on themselves to help finance education. This became known as the 'Permissive Act'.

Because of this measure, cynicism set in among the teachers. They were hampered by this unfavourable legislation. The increased spending on education was dependent upon a voluntary body; if the Boards of the Poor Law Guardians did not become 'contributory' then the teacher was paid only a third of the awards which was earned by the pupils' results in the examination; only 65 of the 163 Boards became contributory in 1875.[92] The teachers had canvassed the Poor Law Guardians to become contributory Unions, at the risk of ecclesiastical censure.[93]

During a period local distress in many districts in 1879–1880, because of the poor weather and famine conditions, the government decided to match whatever local communities could raise from non-contributory unions. That, coupled with the Local Taxation (Customs and Excise) Act of 1890 resulted in an increase of £78,000 per annum to the teachers.[94]

There were too many chinks in the armour of the payment by results system of teacher remuneration. During its three decades of existence its popularity increasingly waned; strained relations between teachers and the national Board could not overcome, and very often the Treasury became the main player in Irish primary education. Teachers, themselves, realized that teaching was becoming a dull routine and the inspector an adversary to be outwitted on the day of his decision.[95]

92 *The Irish Teachers' Journal* VIII, (27 November 1875), 599.
93 *The Irish Teachers' Journal*, 576.
94 See Balfour, *Educational Systems of Great Britain and Ireland*, 101.
95 T. J. O'Connell, *One Hundred Years of Progress; the Story of the INTO 1868–1968* (Dublin, 1968), 149–150.

## Patrick Keenan's Role in the Introduction of Payment by Results to Irish Schools

Patrick Keenan was a much-respected officer within the education fraternity in Ireland. At the age of 33, he was appointed Chief of Inspection of the Statistical Department in 1859. During his time as Chief Inspector, he worked very closely with the Resident Commissioner, Alexander McDonnell. Upon McDonnell's retirement in 1871, Keenan was appointed to the role of Resident Commissioner, and he held that position until his death in 1894.[96]

Keenan favoured the introduction of the 'results' scheme to primary schools in Ireland, and he outlined many reasons for this. Firstly, he pointed out that 45.5 per cent of the pupils did not get beyond Book One, and only 7.1 per cent of pupils were in Book Four or higher. However, he claimed that teachers were paid their salaries indifferently regardless of which book they were on.

The Payment by Results set forth by Keenan was to consist of three elements; Inspectors' Results Fees; Managers' Quarterly Results' Fees and Classification of salaries of principal teachers. Keenan's submission involved some variations from that which pertained in England. He opted for 90 rather than 100 days attendance per year so that pupils could qualify for the examination. And. Unlike the English system which provided payment on the results to both junior and senior pupils alike, Keenan employed a sliding scale favouring the senior pupils. His rationale behind this thinking was to encourage schools to ensure that a greater number of pupils would remain on board for the senior grades.

Keenan's Managers' Quarterly Result Fees was an answer to the prevailing haphazard attendance patterns in some areas of the country where satisfactory attendance was maintained for one-quarter of the year only. He was opposed to giving any capitation grant on mere attendance but to encourage teachers to have some 'interest in instructing them or

96 R. B. McDowell, *The Irish Administration 1801–1914* (London: Routledge and Kegan Paul, 1964), 248.

favouring their appearance at all in their schools', he suggested a quarterly examination to be carried out by the manager as a result of which the teacher would receive a fee of one shilling for each successful pupil.

Regarding Keenan's third element of his proposals, classification salaries for principal teachers – he was convinced that by the 'fruits of his teaching' the teacher's worth and capacity would be fairly enough tested if his pupils sat for the payment by results examination.[97]

He, therefore, opted for a reduced classification salary but as the following comment indicates he wished it to be viewed more as a results' award:

> To recompense the teacher for his care of the irregular attendants, the idle and the stupid, as also with a view to conferring upon him an official individuality ... I would attach a small personal classification salary to the principal of each school. This salary, I hold, will partake of the character of a results' fee, for work of a collective nature, for the general moral training of the pupils, and the tone of the school.[98]

The costings for Keenan's plan may seem excessively high, this was countered-balanced by the abolition of other forms of teacher remuneration.

Under cross-examination Keenan effective defended his scheme. The answer he gave to one particular question reveals how committed he was to payment by results. He was asked, 'Do you propose your scheme as a remedy for the defects of the National System?' His reply was:

> I propose my scheme as a remedy for certain defects to which I refer in the opening paragraphs of my memorandum; but independently of these defects I have been so much impressed with the importance of the question of paying by results, that were there no defects at all in the operation of the system I should suggest that plan of payment.[99]

It would seem that Patrick Keenan was the Robert Lowe of Ireland, and he probably ranks as the person who was most influential in spreading

97 The Memorandum and Keenan's Questioning on it are found in *Royal Commission of Inquiry 1870,* XXVIII, pt 3, 94.

98 The Memorandum and Keenan's Questioning on it are found in *Royal Commission of Inquiry* 1870, XXVIII, pt 3, 94.

99 The Memorandum and Keenan's Questioning on it are found in *Royal Commission of Inquiry 1870,* XXVIII, pt 3, 100.

payment by results in Ireland. Almost a decade of payment by results in Ireland had elapsed when we find Keenan as enthusiastic as ever about the scheme in had introduced in 1872. At the *Social Study Congress* of 1881 he declared:

> The function of educationalists is to discover methods of instruction; the function of Governments is to discover tests of efficiency. In respect of the latter function, the great discovery of modern times is the system of payment for ascertained results.[100]

There is a lot of Lowe in Keenan's thoughts, but what is overlooked is the type of efficiency applied and how it effects the methodologies already in place. It may have serious repercussions for school practice. Keenan, alluded to Adam Smith with his comments on teacher remuneration:

> The Irish master is principally paid by the public ... but the application of the system of payment by results is the safeguard even more telling than that contemplated by Adam Smith, against any possible neglect of business.[101]

Keenan continued to favour payment by results, even at a time when it was under serious criticism in England. This attitude to the 'results' programme was palpable during when he gave evidence to Cross Commission in 1886–1888.

At an earlier date, and shortly after presenting his evidence to the Powis Commission in 1869, Keenan was appointed by Earl Granville, Secretary of State for the Colonies, as a Special Commissioner to investigate the state of education in all its branches in Trinidad. He undertook a painstaking investigation into education provision in Trinidad, a colony with a multicultural population and different religious affiliations. He unearthed many educational ills and problem issues, but he relied heavily on a system of payment by results as a remedy for these problems.[102]

He proposed his tripartite scheme for the payment of teachers at primary level. He employed 100 days attendance as his qualification base and

100 *The Freeman's Journal*, 6 October 1881.
101 *The Freeman's Journal*, 6 October 1881.
102 See his *Report on the State of Education in the Island of Trinidad*, H.C. 1870 (450), L.655, 1–150.

suggested a sliding scale of payment, weighted in favour of the senior classes. He also introduced payment by results to second-level education. In 1870, the Legislative Council of Trinidad gave credence to the Keenan plans by encouraging the newly formed Board of Education to implement Keenan's scheme. With Trinidad under his belt, Keenan's next objective was Malta.

As the main author of the scheme to introduce payment by results to second-level education in Ireland, and following the passing of the Intermediate Education Act 1878, he set out for Malta. As special commissioner, and upon his arrival in Malta on 4 October 1878, he recommended payment by results, not only for primary and second-level, but as well:

> Each Professor to receive .... From the Education Department, a results fee of £2 for every student who, in the Arts Faculty or in the Professional Faculties, passes his examination with honours.[103]

Thus, it is fair to extrapolate that Sir Patrick Keenan had a high level of commitment towards the policy of payment by results, and, coupled with that, he was a most efficacious champion of the system.

## Concluding Remarks

The teachers' lot was not a happy one in the nineteenth century. The working conditions of the teacher had many shortcomings. The children had few comforts, either at home or in school. These circumstances offered the greatest curtailment to any effective form of teaching or learning, no matter what type of curriculum was in vogue. Yet, the main question within any dialogue regarding education's provision was 'who should pay for it?' Should it be voluntary provision or should it be provided fully by the state? These were, no doubt, important questions, but the greater consideration was the circumstances under which both teacher and

103 Keenan, *Report upon the Educational System of Malta*, H. C. 1880 (C2685), XLIX, 255, 100.

pupil undertook their daily routine. Those in charge of Education, the Commissioners, were hell-bent on getting value for money. And, though there had been intimations of some form of accountability in Irish primary schools, during and prior to the 1860s, it was the Powis Report of 1870 that answered the Commissioners' prayers. Powis, in one of its many recommendations made explicit the advantages of introducing a Payment by Results system.

At this juncture, the Results system became the standard bearer in improving the low levels of literacy and numeracy. However, the most important aspects of school life; interrelationships, social development, willingness to help others, recognizing difference, and accepting it, and so forth, were ignored under the results regime.

Did utilitarianism play an ideological role in educational policy in nineteenth-century Ireland?

For the last thirty years of the century policy went through a remarkable period of change in how education provision was interpreted. The Doctrine of Utility played a central role in defining education in terms of cost, and as a result the economic dimension of supply and demand, expenditure and returns was drawn upon.

The policy of the market place, payment by results, crept up on the Irish Commissioners of education. There was little or no debate among the Commissioner enclave as to the merits or otherwise of Patrick Keenan's results model. Could they have had a dialogue regarding such a model as to how it was faring in England or Scotland? It seems that they wished for a quick, simplistic solution to the teachers' disgruntlement regarding their plight as employees. One of the principal reasons why teachers were concerned about their situation was the absence of pension rights. They needed to avoid the workhouse, having toiled at the coal face for so many years. Security of tenure was becoming a big concern for teachers, and following the founding of the INTA in 1868, the teachers finally had secured an avenue through which they could express their demands and desires. Security of tenure was not a *fait accompli* in the nineteenth century, but in its later decades, its realization was gaining some momentum.

Did Irish education deserve to have the Treasury make dictatorial decisions regarding policy and administration?

There was much confusion, many errors and many modifications associated with Payment by Results and its implementation in Ireland. The system was doomed to failure from the beginning, and the Irish authorities should have been aware of what was happening to the results model in Britain in the mid-1870s. A great deal of disenchantment could have been avoided if awareness were more pronounced. When a teacher is paid to teach certain subjects, at the expense of other subjects, he or she will focus on the obvious choices. Talented and creative teachers became embroiled and hamstrung in a schooling net, while their imaginative and poetic energies dissipated.

Education becomes the victim when an external agency places a particular monetary price (not value) on teaching and learning. Then, *docendo discimus* is cast out the window. And, despite the fact that in Britain, the results scheme was perceived to be outmoded, but there was hint at this stage in the early 1880s that retreat might begin in Ireland.

During the time we are dealing with a publication called *Amalgamation of Unions, and Pauper and National Education in Ireland* by John Taylor, which was published in 1857, and it offers, among many things, a definition of a 'good' teacher:

> The teacher must love his profession, as few men ever yet attained a degree of excellency in any calling who did not love it, and place all their hopes in life on it. The great secret of teaching is to be skilful and trained to the business; to have so fully and distinctly in his mind the whole course of instruction, not only as regards the matters to be taught, but also as to all the best modes of teaching, that he may be able readily and decidedly to vary his method according to the peculiarities of each individual mind which may come under his care.[104]

Taylor also castigates the 'dull 'routine' of the 'old mechanical method'. This will not do in Ireland, he says, where 'the object of education ought to be to make immediately available, for the highest and best purposes, every particle of talent that exists in the country'. To achieve this, the teacher must be flexible and be able to adapt his teaching to every degree of intellectual capacity, 'and every kind of acquired habit'.

104 John Taylor, *Amalgamation of Unions, and Pauper and National Education in Ireland* (Dublin: John Falconer, 1857), 192–193. (Reprinted by Bibliolife, n.d.).

The results system expected a narrow focus: the teacher must zoom in on only what will be examined. The inspector must focus only on what has been rehearsed. Incidentally, inspectors could examine, what were called, sub-heads, but a pass here did not mean a merit for payment. Only the mechanical aspects of reading were measured by the examination. The comprehension of the passage read did not count as it was placed in the sub-head section.

Many of the qualitative aspects of teaching were ignored. For example, a good interesting introduction to a lesson was overlooked as it did not count. This was at a time when European countries were exploring child-centred education, while the Irish system was clinging to a wearied mechanistic scheme divorced from the realities of life.

In any case, the results programme was introduced in Ireland as a method of computing teacher salaries in 1871. Unlike Britain, it meant that a teacher's salary henceforth would be a composite one – a set basic income plus an amount based on the number of passes each pupil received from an inspector's examination each year. This also included a minimum annual attendance by the pupil – if this fell short, the pupil did not qualify for the examination.

The introduction of Payment by Results into both the primary and second-level sectors in Ireland proved to be a strong indication of the convergence of educational thinking in Great Britain and Ireland. 'The parliamentary resistance to the growing costs of an expanding education system and the counter demand that the quality of the system be raised produced the compromise enunciated by the Newcastle Commission when it sought "sound and cheap elementary education."'[105]

There was also an interesting caveat proposal in the Powis recommendations – that overt recognition be given to separate denominational schools, the final nail in the anti-Stanley lobby and his principle of multi-denominational education (mixed). This policy indicated that the old regime was over and a new one was about to begin.[106]

105 See S. Ó Buachalla, *Education Policy in Twentieth Century Ireland* (Dublin: Wolfhound Press, 1988), 25.

106 Akenson, *Irish Education Experiment,* 315.

F. S. L. Lyons, in his book, *Ireland since the Famine*, goes out of his way to make a bold and exaggerated claim that without the results system, resulting in improved literacy levels during the last decades of the nineteenth century, the foundations of a modern Irish state could not have been laid.[107] The Powis Commission, in its espousal of complete denominationalism, promoted an increase in the number of small rural schools, and thus contributed to the creation of one of the system's ongoing problems. Small rural schools also meant the creation of dire problems for the success of Payment by Results. In order for teachers to be successful in preparing their pupils for the annual inspectors' examination of their pupils it was necessary that a reasonable level of pupil/teacher ration existed in all schools. Success in one and two-teacher schools was hampered significantly, as there could be eight different levels of pupil in one classroom, with each child in each level required to be examined by the inspector. Urban schools, as a result, fared much better because teachers very often had only one level to prepare for the annual examination. Despite the population drop of a million in the period from 1870 to 1900, the number of national schools increased by over 2,000 to a total of 8,692.[108]

Both teachers and pupils laboured under the results scheme, 'an elaborate mosaic of sixpences and shillings ... making half a million children in each year the drudges of the teachers, the teachers the drudges of the inspectors, and the inspectors of the office.'[109]

In short, the results programme restricted the work of the teacher. Unhealthy cramming dominated the classroom. The Treasury gained control of the education system in Ireland and education was seen as a product that had a monetary conceptualization: it was a tangible entity that could be measured and packaged to suit government needs.

The following chapter will deal with the operational aspects of the system, the 'nuts and bolts' as it were. The central role of the inspectors is duly identified and analysed. The social conditions of the participants,

107 F. S. L. Lyons, *Ireland since the Famine* (Fontana, 1976), 88–89.

108 *Report of F. H. Dale H. M. I., on Primary Education in Ireland* (CD 1891), 984, H.C. 1904, xx. See Ó Buachalla, *Education Policy in Twentieth Century Ireland*, 25–26.

109 Quoted in O'Doherty, T. and O'Donoghue, T. *Radical Reform in Irish Schools, 1900–1922: The 'New Education' Turn* (Switzerland: Palgrave Macmillan, 2021), 18.

namely, the pupils, had an immeasurable debilitating affect on a scheme such as payments by results. This was one of the biggest problems associated with the success or otherwise of the scheme. The chapter is also illuminated with appropriate statistical Tables, which, in turn, are examined and analysed.

Table 3. Classification Status of National School Teachers in 1871

| Class | Principals | | Assistants | | Junior Assistants | Work Mistresses & Industrial Teachers |
|---|---|---|---|---|---|---|
| | Males | Females | Males | Females | | |
| $1^1$ | 122 | 72 | 5 | 2 | | |
| $1^2$ | 125 | 96 | 3 | 10 | | |
| $1^3$ | 270 | 146 | 18 | 21 | | |
| $2^1$ | 678 | 389 | 34 | 99 | | |
| $2^2$ | 700 | 443 | 65 | 154 | | |
| $3^1$ | 1,505 | 656 | 207 | 713 | | |
| $3^2$ | 518 | 288 | 132 | 379 | | |
| Probationers | 305 | 163 | 238 | 476 | 396 | |
| | *4,223* | *2,253* | *702* | *1,854* | *396* | *440* |
| *Total* | *6,476* | | *2,556* | | | |

*Source: Report of the Commissioners of National Education*, 1871, p. 293.

CHAPTER 3

# The Nuts and Bolts of the Results Programme in the Primary School System in Ireland: 'Fix Everything in Returns'

'You can never be overdressed or overeducated.'

– Oscar Wilde

## Introduction

Mid-Victorian bureaucracy introduced new powers for central government. Before the industrial age, it had been sufficient for individuals or voluntary bodies to provide services such as law and order, the relief of the poor and education. Now, with urbanization and industrialization, and demographic growth, these older methods became outmoded. New institutions and bureaucracies emerged, which would be under the control of central government. As a result, civil service departments emerged, among them the Education Department. Policy changes in Ireland were an off-shoot of policy in Britain, and this was very apparent regarding the provision of Payment by Results, first at primary level, and later at post-primary level in Ireland.

Payment by Results, or, the Results System was compulsory when it was introduced to the National School System in Ireland in 1871. Quite a significant number of primary school pupils were considerably older than those in primary education in the twentieth, and especially, the twenty-first century. The absence of adequate second-level schooling had a major bearing on this phenomenon. As well as that, those who remained in school until they were, perhaps, 14, 15, 16 or 17 years of age had in mind a white-collar occupation. If the teacher in the primary school had the wherewithal to teach pupils to a more advanced level, than primary, then it was of mutual benefit. Payment by Results was to have a major effect on the lives of those directly involved in formal education, including pupils, teachers and inspectors. Payment by Results had a significant influence on an improved school attendance.

Traditionally, many of those pupils who did attend did so for relatively short periods, and for significant numbers attending school was a seasonal affair, child labour being commonplace.[1] Before any school attendance issues were seriously addressed one measure was introduced to tackle the problem of indifference to schooling. This consisted of a new scheme, which involved paying the teacher extra fees based on the results attained by the pupils, which made its debut in Ireland in 1871[2] and it ushered in a new attitude to school efficiency and teacher accountability. Indirectly, it improved attendance to some extent though a satisfactory level of attendance was, in the eyes of various vested interest groups, deemed to be unworkable in a rural society.[3]

The 1901 Census of Ireland assessed the number of children aged 5 and under 16 years of age who were not in attendance at school the Census school week, at decennial periods and the following pattern emerged:

Table 4. Percentage over 5 and under 16 not at school

| Year | 1851 | 1861 | 1871 | 1881 | 1891 | 1901 |
|---|---|---|---|---|---|---|
| Percentage over 5 and under 16 not at school | 75 | 70 | 58 | 53 | 46 | 40 |

Compiled from Census of Ireland 1901, Pt II, p. 89.

1 Norman Atkinson, *Irish Education: A History of Educational Institutions* (Dublin: Allen Figgis, 1969), 101.

2 Akenson, *The Irish Education Experiment*, 316–319.

3 Akenson, *The Irish Education Experiment*, 316–319.

There is a continuing drop from the 1851 figure in subsequent years but it still indicates that very large numbers of children of school-going age were absent from school.

The Powis Commission report of 1870 came to the conclusion that there was no need for compulsory school attendance in rural areas; instead it emphasized the requirement for the State to provide schools in urban centres for children not at work. It was this mentality which was to bedevil Irish education for several decades to come.

A Results system had already been in place in England since 1862 (as we have seen) and the Powis Commission had looked to this rather crude and simplistic model for the poor standards of attainment and attendance which it detected among Irish school children.[4] The sound and cheap mentality had worked in Britain, now it was Ireland's turn. Teachers welcomed the system initially, but their enthusiasm waned and the results system never attained any degree of appreciable success with regard to advances in school attendance. As a result, the issue of legislation[5] began to emerge gradually and as the debate gathered pace the whole question of compulsion became embroiled in controversy.[6]

Throughout the 1870s and 1880s events in Britain were watched with interest in Ireland.[7] In the British context attendance at school proved to be much more satisfactory than was the case in Ireland. As a consequence, the Irish administration wished to emulate the standards set in England and Wales.

The matter reached the House of Commons and in 1877 Mr Shaughnessy, MP for Limerick, spoke at length on the question of

4 Atkinson, 101.

5 Compulsory education had been introduced in England and Wales in 1880. In 1883 it was unanimously resolved in the House of Commons 'that it is expedient to introduce into Ireland the principles of compulsory education with such modifications as the social and religious conditions require'. See Áine Hyland and Kenneth Milne, eds, *Irish Educational Documents*, vol. 1 (Dublin: Church of Ireland College of Education, 1987), 136.

6 Ó Buachalla, *Education Policy in Twentieth Century Ireland*, 26.

7 Edel Donohue, *Compulsory School Legislation in Ireland (Republic of Ireland and Northern Ireland), 1892–1994* (Unpublished Master of Education Thesis, Education Department, University College, Dublin, 1994), 8.

elementary education in Ireland. Cautioning against an unpopular Act of Parliament, he favoured the introduction of indirect compulsion that would bring pressure to bear on parents and employers to reduce the prevalence of child labour.[8] The O'Connor Don, MP for Roscommon, could not agree with any form of compulsion, indirect or otherwise. Mr Butt, too, could not support any proposal to introduce any form of compulsion regarding school attendance. The Chief Secretary intervened by claiming that 'it will be found in Ireland, as it had been in England that however much they disliked compulsion they would be unable to secure attendance without it'. The debate ebbed and flowed both within and without the Commons. In 1883, and again in 1885 the issue of compulsory school attendance for Ireland came to a head when Mr Campbell-Bannerman the Chief Secretary brought forward a Bill for Education in Ireland. That year, however, saw the resignation of Gladstone and his administration, and as a result the Bill was delayed. It was not until 1892 that the Bill finally became law under the title Irish Education Act (1892).

For the first time attending school was made compulsory and fees in primary schools were abolished. Children from now on were compelled to attend school between the ages of six and fourteen, though pupils were allowed to have part-time work between the ages of eleven and fourteen. It was expected that School Attendance Committees would enforce the Act, similar to the practice pertaining in Britain. It achieved some successes in improving attendance in the towns and cities, but not so in rural areas where it did not apply until the establishment of County Councils in 1898. The Act made little difference in country districts as by 1908 ten county councils had failed to apply it. Attendance still remained precarious and seasonal. And, by now, Payment by Results had been abandoned. The following table offers some indication of the haphazard attendance rates in Irish primary schools during the final decade of the nineteenth century:

8 Edel Donohue, 9. See, Tony Lyons, 'Compulsory School Attendance Legislation in Ireland, 1892–2000', in Deirdre Raftery and Karin Fischer, eds, *Educating Ireland: Schooling and Social Change, 1700–2000* (Dublin: Irish Academic Press, 2014).

Table 5. Yearly Percentages of Average Daily Attendance to Average Number on Rolls, 1891–1898

| Year | 1891 | 1982 | 1893 | 1894 | 1895 | 1896 | 1897 | 1898 |
|---|---|---|---|---|---|---|---|---|
| Percentage | 61.4 | 60.7 | 63.3 | 63.1 | 62.9 | 65.6 | 63.9 | 64.2 |

Adapted from *Sixty-fifth Report of the Commissioners, for 1898* (C.9446) H.C. 1899, XXIV, p. 9.

The system of Payment by Results had been designed to operate in a particular economic and social milieu in the last decades of the nineteenth century. Consequently, it did not operate in isolation. Educational endeavours are always prone to the vicissitudes of political, social and economic influences. The success of any curricular alteration depends on the calibre of the teachers, the attitude of the inspectors, the school building, the equipment within the school building, the reading material in use in the school, the finances available locally and nationally to support curricular alterations and the realization of planned outcomes.

In studying the history of any aspect of the history of education, no matter how minute or all-encompassing, one has to concede that the wider circumstances are extremely relevant factors. These individuals, and apparently, separate issues overlap, and are intertwined with the social fabric of any society.

The results' programme dominated all school activity during its existence, and not only that, it left a residue which continued well beyond the decades of its operation, in which an examination culture dominated the education system in Ireland.

Any changes brought about during its term of existence, affected teachers and their families. From the outset, there were issues with its implementation. The Commissioners of National Education relied on the good will of the Treasury to fulfil their obligations by paying, in full, the necessary funding to satisfy teachers' needs according to the agreements arranged under the results' scheme. Different levels were established within the new results' programme for 1871 and subsequent years, and appropriate fees were allotted to each level within the programme. As it happened, the Treasury broke the agreement by sanctioning only the part relating to third class and probationary principal teachers. However, inspectors were instructed to examine all schools and all levels, though payment of fees was restricted for the year 1871. As the instruction to the inspectors came late in the year, on 24 October 1871, results had to be in on time for the next financial year.[9]

It is indicative of the philosophy behind the Payment by Results programme that the financial year should determine when results should be collected, a year which had little or no relationship with the school year. Here, we have an example of the financial world defining what takes place, and when, within the education system.

The teacher got paid only on the results of inspection which determined how effective the he or she was as an instructor. However, the teacher was liable for deductions in results fees if other aspects of his work were deemed to be defective:

> If the moral tone, the discipline, the order and cleanliness of pupils and school-room, or the supply of books and apparatus, be unsatisfactory, a deduction, ranging from five to ten percent of the total amount of results' fees accruing to the teacher, will be made.[10]

The teacher was not acknowledged when these matters were looked after, no matter how well, but if these issues were deemed to be flawed, the teacher could be penalized by the inspector for any perceived defects.

The programme for the year 1871 catered for five classes.[11] Reading, Spelling, Writing and Arithmetic were included for all classes. Grammar and Geography became part of the curriculum from Third Class upwards, while Needlework should be available from Second class upwards, though fees were not available for Needlework. The total aggregate amount of fees per pupil went from six shillings in first class to eleven shillings in fifth class. Reading and Arithmetic were deemed to be the most lucrative for the teacher. There was no programme under payment by results for infants in

9 Circular to Inspectors, 24 October 1871, in Circulars to Inspectors, 1861–1873, Ms. 2C, 59, 7, National Archives, Dublin. The financial year ended on 5 April and began on the 6 April each year. It was also known as the tax year. It dates back to 1752 when Britain switched to the Gregorian calendar.

10 Circular to Inspectors, 24 October 1871.

11 Circular to Inspectors, 24 October 1871, 4, 5, 6.

1871, but, instead of individual examination, a collective inspection could be undertaken on the 4- to 7-year-olds, at a rate of five shillings per pupil.

Though, no payment was available for Needlework, deductions were made if a girl failed in Needlework.

There were criticisms of the 1871 programme, and a good deal of dissatisfaction emerged at such an early stage in its implementation. Teachers had the view that there was too great a gap in the standards outlined for each class division. For example, teachers felt that an extra division be introduced between First and Second Class, as expectations were deemed to be too high.[12] There was also an objection to the reduced fees for the Senior Classes.[13] Another bone of contention was the fact that the inspector could ask comprehension questions on the passage being read, even though there was no fee payment for the pupils' understanding of what they had read. Teachers wished that this practice be withdrawn. They also wanted Needlework to be included in the fee scheme.

At a conference held in July 1872, in which the Resident Commissioner, the Chiefs of Inspection and the Head Inspectors, a review was undertaken on the payment by results system. A report was duly issued on 30 July.[14]

This resulted in a new programme which was more thorough and comprehensive than the previous one and it differed in some respects from the original. The teachers' objections and suggestions were by and large adhered to, and this programme remained in place for many years. The nuts and bolts of the new format now included eight divisions, and six classes instead of five. There was also a more realistic expectation concerning each of the divisions. However, with the modifications came a reduction in the fees paid. In the Infant grade, the fee was reduced from five to three shillings. There was a distinction made between infants under 6 years of age and those over 6, but under 7 years.

Under the modified scheme, arithmetic was the most lucrative for a teacher, and fees were introduced for Needlework from third class upwards. Many of the penal clauses had been removed in the 1872 version

12 Editorial of *Irish Teachers' Journal* v, no. 50 (1 January 1872), 260.

13 Editorial of *Irish Teachers' Journal*, 1 January 1872, 301.

14 Minutes of the Commissioners, Ms., 5553 (Nat. Lib. Ire), 342.

of payment by results, but the Commissioners retained the right to exert sanctions in a general sense, if the school were found to be unsatisfactory:

> If the moral tone, the discipline, the order and cleanliness of pupils and schoolroom, the supply of requisites, or the state of the school accounts be unsatisfactory, a special representation of the facts will be made by the inspector in his report, and the Board will deal with the case as may be necessary.[15]

Though there was provision in the inspector's report for highlighting shortcomings of a general nature in a school, there was no provision made for rewarding a teacher who may have been exemplary in such matters. Many years later, in 1896, a Head Inspector, bemoaned, in a retrospective manner, the absence of such a provision:

> One of the defects of the results' system, as carried out, is that it makes no provision for directly rewarding a teacher whose school, by its good organization, order, discipline and cleanliness, merits such reward.[16]

This inspector continued in a similar vein and towards the end of his reflections, he expressed some satisfaction when this policy was deemed to be a failure, and duly withdrawn.

## 'Heads' and 'Sub-heads'

One seemingly innocuous aspect of the programme for payment by results was the distinction drawn between 'heads' and 'sub-heads'. This became controversial and contentious, and from the viewpoint of education, it offers an insight into the minds of those who were in charge of the results' scheme. The 'heads' were the portion of the programme upon which the pupil passed or failed the inspector's examination. The 'sub-heads' could

15 Programme in Minutes of the Commissioners, Ms., 5553, 330.
16 *Report of the Commissioners of National Education for 1895*, H.C., 1896. Appendix to the Report, 111.

also be examined, but did not have any bearing on the results of the examination. The 1872 version of the programme put it succinctly:

> The portions printed in italics are intended to be the tests for a 'pass' in each subject. The Inspector will, however, examine in the other portions of each subject set down, both at the results and at the Secondary inspections. The italics will not appear on the form of Programme issued to the Schools, neither will the fees for each subject. A table of the latter will be communicated to the Teacher through the Manager.[17]

The authorities were very concerned with concepts such as 'reading with ease', but, to be 'fairly acquainted' with the subject matter, to 'write from dictation' a passage read from the Reader, and so on. Most educationalists would consider what falls under the 'sub-head' label as being worthy of very sound educational principles. It is difficult to locate any aspect of the payment by results programme that inspires the imagination. Perhaps, if we examine very briefly, a comment by an education historian, David Wardle, from England, who designates the philosophy of payment by results to the doldrums. Referring to the results programme in England, Wardle makes the following observation:

> But the system had its limitations. It tended to produce teachers who were competent, but uninspired and undisposed towards originality and experiment, This characteristic was noted at the time .... Much of the instruction they exhibit is satisfactory; but it is marked by a constant tendency to fall into a groove.[18]

Not placing due emphasis on the 'sub-heads', which stretches the imagination of the pupil and allows him or her to expand their vocabulary, and extend what the writer said by bringing the material into their own consciousness and internalizing it, seems to lack any sound educational philosophy. This form of deprivation emerged very strongly during the payment by results era when teachers had a tendency, not through their own fault, to favour rule-of-thumb, unadventurous methodologies, in a confined field in which what counted were measurable results. This was

17 Minutes of the Commissioners, Ms., 5553, 328.

18 David Wardle, *English Popular Education, 1780–1975* (Cambridge University Press, 1977), 106–107.

no less than a return to the monitorial system, in which experiments in broadening the curriculum were cut short.

The teacher–inspector relationship took a hit during the results' era. At the outset, the assumption was that teaching could not be entrusted to the teachers, and they had to be minutely supervised by inspectors. This led to over-inspection, and even suspicion, and an imposition of uniformity across all the national schools in Ireland. Local circumstances did not matter; the environment did not matter; all that mattered was the material covered by italics. And, above all, the emphasis on the results' scheme during the last three decades of the nineteenth century was one of pecuniary; finding the cheapest possible method of transmitting the barest rudiments of instruction (not education) to the children of the poor. The mechanical passing on of inert facts to passive recipients was the order of the day in the results' schools, while Robert Lowe gave the classic enunciation of the argument that the poor should receive a limited education, quite different from that of the rich, and fitting them for their humble station in life:

> The lower classes ought to be educated to discharge the duties cast upon them. They should also be educated that they may appreciate and defer to a higher cultivation when they meet it, and the higher classes ought to be educated in a very different manner in order that they may exhibit to the lower classes, that higher education to which, if it were shown to them they would bow down and defer.[19]

This class-based excursion by Lowe, and the tenets which it expresses were quite acceptable among certain circles, along with the belief in the evil of child nature. Ever since the days of Rousseau, Froebel and Pestalozzi the understanding child nature was undergoing a transformation.

There seems to have been a confusion between information-giving and genuine education (*educare*). Concentration upon the three Rs was obtained at the expense of narrowing the primary school curriculum so that an individual teacher (and there are many) could delve into whatever heartfelt subject area he or she might have in mind – in such situations a teacher can offer a beacon of light to the pupils, but with payment by

19 Robert Lowe, from a pamphlet he wrote in 1867. Quoted by Wardle, *English Popular Education 1780–1975*, 25.

results the teacher's hands were tied, and the unlimited amount of 'sub-heads' he or she could draw upon never darkened the school-room door. The child-centred approach to teaching and learning was not quite ripe yet, but in certain European countries it was fomenting in the 1890s. This approach viewed childhood as basically good and only corrupted by society – this was a direct contradiction of the older belief. This thinking saw children at the centre of teaching and learning, the child's interests were paramount, and should form the basis for what is being taught. This had no place during the payment by results era, the child's interests being irrelevant. Payment by results was concerned with teacher domination of the pupil, pressing the child along a pre-determined route.

The examination by the inspector was devoted to testing what was not very important, and excluding the more important aspects of development. Thus for Reading, the meaning of the subject matter read is not essential, and neither is the meaning of the words necessary for passing the Spelling test. As far as Arithmetic is concerned, mental arithmetic is excluded as essential for passing in the various grades. Surprisingly, in the Sixth Class Reading Programme we find that the pupil should 'answer intelligently on the subject-matter of the lessons' which was included in the 'head' section. This was the only occasion when this occurred.

The division of the examination into 'heads' and 'sub-heads', with the former determining passes, would appear to have harmful long-term effects. The sections which might call for exercise of the reasoning powers, creativeness or imagination were all too often excluded from the monetary award process. This approach also tended to foster drill, rote and mechanical performance on what became known as the 'head' part of the programme. The compulsory results programme about which there was so much debate and controversy at its inception settled down in a well-run and rutted path.

There were many facets of the results' programme which undermined it. A pupil got a pass in Reading based on a parrot-like reading of a passage. Understanding the content did not count. As a result, rote learning became an important attribute of school life. This was especially true of poetry, where repetition of the poem in a sing-song manner without awareness or understanding gained a pass.

In the late 1870s teachers objected to the tendency to reduce overall results payments by a percentage if the answering in the sub-heads was deemed unsatisfactory. They held that it was a basic violation of the system of results payments.[20] Their objection must have worked as the system of 'heads' determining passes and fees was continued, and the 'sub-heads' had no say in the payment of fees. The establishment of payment by results in 1872 for all primary schools recommended by Powis, was expected to remedy the poor state of the situation then existing. The Table below sets out the percentages of examinees who passed and were promoted in the different classes during the first five years in which the results' scheme was in full operation:

Table 6. Percentage of Examinees who were Passed and Promoted in the Results Examination, 1872–1876

| | 1872 | 1873 | 1874 | 1875 | 1876 |
|---|---|---|---|---|---|
| Advanced from Infants | 48.3 | 39.2 | 40.1 | 40.0 | 40.1 |
| " " 1st Class | 78.8 | 80.4 | 57.1 | 61.8 | 62.9 |
| " " 2nd Class | 85.6 | 84.7 | 65.6 | 69.2 | 68.1 |
| " " 3rd Class | 92.6 | 90.4 | 61.0 | 63.4 | 62.3 |
| " " 4th Class | 96.6 | 94.2 | 67.2 | 51.7 | 48.7 |
| " " 5th Class | 97.3 | 96.1 | 79.0 | 48.9 | 46.1 |
| | | | | *59.4 | *56.6 |
| " " 6th Class | 87.9 | 96.4 | 72.7 | 51.2 | 51.0 |

*Source:* Annual Reports of the Commissioners 1872–1876.
*Note introduction of second stage of fifth class.

The small percentage in the Infants section relate to the fact that even though they might pass the examination, they were not necessarily promoted to First Class until they were 7 years of age.

In 1874 the percentage of success in each of the obligatory subjects was as follows:

20 Editorial in *The Teachers' Journal*, 9 November 1878.

Table 7. Percentage Success Rates in Different Subjects of the Compulsory Programme in 1874

| | |
|---|---|
| Reading 86.8 | Grammar 55.3 |
| Spelling 75.4 | Geography 54.4 |
| Writing 86.7 | Agriculture 41.1 |
| Arithmetic 69.0 | Needlework 91.8 |

*Source: Report of the Commissioners* for 1874.

Throughout its history, the results' programme was rarely without attracting objections and/or controversy. The teachers were usually at the head of the posse, but that is understandable as they were at the coal face. In 1873, a Mr W. McMillan, an inspector, opposed the concept of individual examinations in the primary school. He stated:

> The division into sub-heads, which do not affect the marks, though in some cases covering the most important part of the course, has done much harm.[21]

Throughout the period of the existence of payment by results, the Commissioners always felt that it was in their best interests to maintain a good working relationship with the teachers. They even went so far as to advise the inspectors not to adopt a severe standard.[22]

The Commissioners were, almost always, open to recommendations from others, such as the teachers and inspectors. Payment by results adopted a fluid and open stance, as 1873 witnessed significant changes in the scheme, and this was for a third successive year.[23]

Some relatively minor changes, but important, nonetheless, took place from time to time. For example, Grammar gained recognition for fees at Third Class Level, while Agriculture was put on the course for boys from fourth Class upwards, which probably balanced the Needlework course available to girls. Significant increases in the fees also occurred, and other

21 *Report of the Commissioners of National Education for 1895*, 208.

22 Abstract and Index of Circulars to Inspectors and Others, 1840–1891.

23 See the *Thirty-Ninth Report of the Commissioners of National Educational in Ireland, for 1872.* (C.805), H.C. 1873, xxv, 25.

subjects were added to the list, including Vocal Music and Drawing. A new scheme for Classics and French was introduced in 1874 – these were to be taught outside school hours, for extra payment. The Classics lessons were ten shillings, while the French lessons were five shillings.[24] Changes like these helped relations between commissioners and teachers. The teachers saw the changes 'as a great gain and a great improvement'.[25]

From 1874 onwards, there were no appreciable changes made: the following were the subjects on the compulsory programme – Reading, Spelling, Writing, Arithmetic in all classes. Grammar and Geography from Third Class upwards. Needlework for girls from Second Class, and Agriculture for boys from Fourth Class Upwards. Bookkeeping was added as a compulsory subject for Fifth and Sixth classes in 1877, and it was confined to boys from 1879. The minimum attendance levels in order to qualify for the examination was raised from ninety days to one hundred in 1877. Slight modifications occurred in the years 1882/1883, 1884/1885, 1885/1886, 1887/1888, and 1891/1892. However, the fundamentals remained intact.

In 1884, a few points that are noteworthy in developments in payment by results. In a footnote to the Programme for that year we find:

> If there are Irish-speaking pupils in a school, the teacher, if acquainted with the Irish language, should, whenever practicable, employ the vernacular as an aid to the elucidation and acquisition of the English language.[26]

In Irish-speaking areas, teachers must have had unusual problems, not readily alive in English-speaking districts.

The Programme for 1888 included a Froebelian Kindergarten Programme. Be that as it may, the Programme was set out in a very dry unattractive fashion, very much in keeping with the results scheme. It had lists of objects to be used, but it is doubtful if Froebel would be enthralled with the absence of a Froebelian spirit.

24 *Fortieth Report of the Commissioners …, for 1873*, Appendix, (C.965), H.C. 1874, xix, 118.

25 *Irish Teachers Journal*, vii, no. 13 (4 April 1874), 158.

26 *Fiftieth Report of the Commissioners of National Education, for the year 1883* (C.4053), H.C. 1884, xxv, 213.

An interesting development took place in 1889 with the announcement that Sixth Class girls were not keeping a-pace with a required standard in literary and scientific instruction expected of girls. To adjust this imbalance, the Commissioners issued a memorandum stating:

> ... the Commissioners have resolved that every girl who passes the Fifth Class shall devote the remainder of her school life mainly to Industrial Instruction.[27]

Under the new system, Industrial Instruction for girls was to account for nine shillings, while the literary would be reduced to five shillings and six pence. The Industrial part of the programme dealt with practical and utilitarian aspects of domestic life.[28] This new course was not very successful, as by 1898 it was undertaken by about one-third of national schools. The *Report* for that year carried the comment:

> In view of the comparative want of appreciation displayed by managers and teachers in regard to this scheme, we have left its adoption optional in every case.[29]

It would appear that the Commissioners were disappointed with this innovative attempt to cater for girls' 'industrial' instruction.

By way of summation, it would appear that innovation was not at the heart of the payment by results scheme. Early on we witnessed some level of flexibility, but this quickly solidified, and following 1875, very little change took place. The basic subjects were well established early on – English to include Spelling, Writing, Grammar, and Arithmetic, and these formed the core of the curriculum. Subjects like Geography, Needlework and Agriculture were also enjoined.

The programmes were designed in a very specific, unattractive manner with little or no allowance made for individuality, either from the teacher or from individual pupils. In this regime, the teacher was merely a functionary cog whose concentration dwelled upon what gave him or her a livelihood – the examination of the pupils by the inspector. There was no

27 *Fifty-Fifth Report of the Commissioners, for the Year 1888* (C.5738), H.C. 1889, 21–22.
28 *Fifty-Fifth Report of the Commissioners*, 133.
29 *Sixty-Fifth Report of the Commissioners, for the Year 1898,* (C.9446), H.C. 1899, xxiv, 412.

room for deviation from the prescribed curriculum, a curriculum which was focused and narrowed to suit the expectations of those in charge.

The curriculum made no allowances for local divergence; there was no allotted space for local history or environmental studies; and the exemption for the use of Irish in Irish-speaking districts can hardly be designated a distinguished or generous concept. Teachers became adept at preparing for the examination day – their teaching became a process of routine, habit, and well-worked practices to prepare for the inspector's visit. The school year was dominated with preparation for the annual steeplechase course, and occasionally, the obstacle to surmount was akin to Becher's Brook!

The payment by results regime was satisfied once it had located the lowest common denominator, and there was no point in probing any further. A difference in methodology or presentation or language use or the use of visuals could add value to concepts by bolstering or by enhancing a concept through renewal was never availed of.

Arguably, the division of the examination programme into 'heads' and 'sub-heads' had long-lasting effects. The money reward process frequently excluded the 'sub-heads' aspects of creativity, imagination, and development of the reasoning powers, and the child was merely on the side of the stage – all the pupil was expected to do was to repeat the prompts that were recited by the teacher during a prescribed course of studies. Again, there was no deviation from the set model. The compulsory results' regime eventually settled into a well-worn and narrowly trampled path.

## Extra Subjects

Prior to 1871 when payment by results was first introduced officially to the national school system, there were other instances of teachers being paid for certain subjects. As early as 1855, provision was made for gratuities to be paid to some teachers on the level of attendance and success rates of pupils, but without the formal patterns that developed later. Allied to that, some teachers, though few in number, were paid by the Science and Art Department based on the results of pupils in an examination carried out by that Department. Here, we have a form of payment by results for extra subjects beyond the core areas of the primary school curriculum.[30]

The policy of acknowledging extra subjects on the national school curriculum continued into the era of the formal payment by results scheme. A regulation for the inclusion of extra subjects was issued in 1872, and it read as follows:

> A fee equal to that paid for arithmetic will be paid for any pupil who, having passed in reading, spelling, writing, and arithmetic, in the fifth or sixth class, shall exhibit satisfactory proficiency in algebra, physical science, navigation, or other approved extra branch; or for any pupil who, having similarly passed in the fourth or higher classes, shall exhibit satisfactory proficiency in any system of vocal music, or any system of drawing, provided –
>
> (a) That no fees shall be paid for more than two extra subjects to the same teacher: and –
> (b) That no fees shall be paid for any pupil for whose proficiency in the same subject, grants are made by the Department of Science and Art.[31]

Not many pupils were in a position to avail of this modest expansion.[32] An and, it would appear that the Commissioners favoured concentration on the three R's as indicated in the following statement:

> Fees were not allowed for proficiency in Geography in any class lower than Third, or in Grammar in any under Fourth, the Commissioners deeming it desirable for the present to apply the stimulus of results fees only to instruction in Reading, Spelling, Writing and Arithmetic, to children of the lower classes.[33]

As the years progressed, more scope was allowed for schools with favourable circumstances to widen the range of subjects and to provide a higher level of education to pupils who would benefit from it. This was at a time when there was still no financial support from the state for second-level education (intermediate), though the demand for such was growing.

30 Minutes of the Commissioners, Ms., 5549, 270.

31 *Thirty-Ninth Report of the Commissioners, for the Year 1872*, (C.805), H.C. 1873, xxv, 25.

32 *Thirty-Ninth Report of the Commissioners, for the Year 1872*, 25.

33 *Thirty-Ninth Report of the Commissioners, for the Year 1872*, 23.

In 1874, 'superior' subjects joined the ranks of the extra subjects, and these, Greek, Latin and French, were regarded as intermediate subjects. The new arrangements for extra subjects for 1874 were as follows:

(a) Vocal Music and Drawing
(b) Classics and French
(c) Geometry, Algebra or other approved branch of Science.

The above subjects gained fees for the teacher provided that no fees shall be paid for more than two extra subjects, besides vocal music and drawing, in the same class to the same teacher. This does not extend to classics.[34]

There was a three-year course spelled out for Classics and French and the fees allotted were ten shillings each for Classics and five shillings for French, for each successful pupil per annum.

Interestingly, Irish was not included in the extra language subjects, with Classics and French. At the Annual Congress of the INTO, in 1974, a motion to include Irish as an extra subject was passed unanimously. In the following year, 1875, at the Annual meeting of the Historical and Archaeological Association of Ireland, a resolution was passed calling for the inclusion of Irish on the results' programme. The Society for the Preservation of the Irish Language, founded in 1876, made representations to the Commissioners of Education calling for the language to be included on payment by results. On 2 July 1878, at a meeting of the Commissioners it was conceded that Irish would be included, and the following notification was sent to the SPIL:

> The Commissioners are prepared to grant results fees for proficiency in the Irish language on the same conditions as are applicable to Greek, Latin and French.[35]

From 1879, Irish appeared as a results subject, earning ten shillings, but to be taught outside of normal school hours. This coincided with the

34 Appendix to the Rules and Regulations of the Commissioners, October 1874, 64.
35 Minutes from the Office of Education to J. J. McSweeney, Secretary of the Society of the Preservation of the Irish Language, 4 July 1878, Ms., 8466 (Nat. Lib. Ire).

inclusion of Celtic on Intermediate school courses under the Intermediate Education Act, 1878.

Only twelve schools embraced Irish as an extra subject[36] by 1885, but due to increasing cultural awareness it expanded subsequently, reaching eighty-three schools in 1898.[37] In 1891 German was added to the list of languages for which results fees were paid. In order to teach extra subjects, teachers had to have certificates of competency. The standard of courses available in the national schools was of an intermediate level. For example, Virgil, Ovid, Horace, Juvenal and Levy were studied on the three-year Latin course.

Teachers complained about the difficulty within the courses, but their complaints fell on deaf ears. Year after year the programmes were issued without any alterations. It seems that the intention to have the extra subjects set at a particular level meant that they were, in fact, providing a second-level standard of education within the national school system. During the period prior to 1878, when the Intermediate Education Act details were being prepared, the Irish National Teachers' Organisation felt that an encouragement of the extra subjects in national schools 'would partly compensate for the admitted deficiencies of Irish Intermediate education, and would serve as a valuable auxiliary to a proper system when established'.[38]

Under the terms of the Intermediate Act, national school teachers were barred from earning fees, though children enrolled in national schools could compete for exhibitions and prizes.

It was feared that some national school pupils might be neglected if the teachers concentrated on teaching extra subjects for extra fees. It was also argued that some parts of the country were without intermediate schools, and the national schools, if allowed, could provide an alternative means to intermediate education. It was also maintained that there were sufficient safeguards in place to ensure that the national teacher's work was not neglectful of some pupils. It was now feared, following the passing into law of

36 Annual Report of the Gaelic League, 1897, 20.

37 Report of Comisiún na Gaeltachta, 1926, 13.

38 *Irish Teachers' Journal* xii, no. 14 (6 April 1878), 171.

the Intermediate Bill, that some advanced primary school pupils would be enticed away from the national schools.

In 1878 the Commissioners of Education thought about asking the government for an increase in the education budget. However, before they had time to act on their ruminations, the Commissioners received a letter from the Chief Secretary for Ireland calling for a reduction in their educational expenditure, and this included a request to reduce teacher numbers. He went on to elaborate:

> Parliament having granted a liberal scheme of Intermediate Education for Ireland, perhaps the Commissioners will consider that it is no longer necessary for them to make an effort to have many of the extra subjects now set out in their school programme, and not perhaps properly appertaining to the instruction given in Elementary schools for the independent poor, taught and paid for by the State.[39]

The Chief Secretary was clearly pointing out that there was a demarcation line between primary and intermediate education. The Commissioners agreed to exclude about £62,000 from their estimate, but they would leave the question of extra subjects as it was, at least for some time. The Commissioners' report, later in 1878, expressed a defensive attitude to the issue of extra subjects. They alluded to the fact that payment of fees was made for the teaching of extra subjects in Great Britain, and also in Ireland. And, they also pointed out that it affected only a small number of pupils. The Commissioners made it very clear in stating that the extra subjects could only be taken by pupils who had attained a minimum of Fifth Class standard, and in 1878 22,684 pupils presented for examination, but only 14,880 passed.[40]

The commissioners ignored the Chief Secretary's request, and the schools continued with the extra subjects as before. However, there were some complaints from some inspectors regarding the intermingling of primary and intermediate education. District Inspector Cowley, in his report for 1876 observed:

39 Minutes of the Commissioners for 1878, Ms., 5557, 432.

40 *Forty-Fifth Report of the Commissioners, for the Year 1878*, 23.

> In some schools a respectable knowledge of algebra, geometry, and mensuration is imparted to a few of the senior pupils. In one or two a smattering of Latin, Greek and French, is given to one or two of the most advanced pupils; but in these schools I generally find that the junior classes have suffered, and I think that the introduction of these subjects into a system of primary education, is only rendered expedient by the present unsatisfactory state of intermediate education in Ireland.[41]

We should bear in mind that he was writing his report two years before the Intermediate Act was enacted.

Cowley was not alone in his observations, and in 1880 Mr Mullally stated that several of the extra subjects did not come within the ambit of the primary school curriculum. And, he advanced the idea that the introduction of the Intermediate System had diminished the reasons behind the continuance of including extra subjects on the primary school programme. However, he was selective in favouring the retention of languages, geometry and algebra.[42]

A Mr Connellan also felt that intermediate school subjects should not form part of the primary school curriculum. He did not give any particular reasons for his opinion.[43]

Some tightening of the regulations did occur, possibly prompted by the inspectors' expressed views, but more likely by developments taking place under the Intermediate Education Act, 1878. From 1882 onwards it was more difficult for primary school pupils to take on board a raft of extra subjects. It was no longer possible to take such a range of subjects without special sanction. The 1882 regulation stated, 'only two extra branches can in future be taught in the same national school in addition to Singing, Drawing, Algebra and Geometry, without the special sanction of the Commissioners.'[44] Hitherto a pupil could take Singing and Drawing, any two other 'approved subjects', and Classics, French or Irish.

There was a distinction made between Ordinary National Schools and other types of National Schools. The 'other types' include Model Schools, Convent or Monastery schools, in which extra subjects could be taught for

41 *Forty-Third Report of the Commissioners for the Year 1876*, Appendix A, 81.
42 *Forty-Seventh Report of the Commissioners for the Year, 1880*, Appendix B, 36.
43 *Fiftieth Report of the Commissioners, for the Year 1883*, Appendix C, 243.
44 *Forty-Eighth Report of the Commissioners for 1881*, H.C. 1882, xxiv, Appendix, 273.

fees during school hours. But, in Ordinary National Schools, where the staff and accommodation are limited, these subjects could not be taught during school hours 'with efficiency, without imperilling the proficiency in the essential elements of the programme'. However, it must be made clear that the Commissioners *did not prohibit* the teaching of these subjects during school hours.[45]

Following these regulations there was a drop in the numbers taking the extra subjects, except for Music and Drawing. However, by 1891, the numbers taking extra subjects had increased to 35,884 with 25,865 passing the examination.[46] It, therefore, emerges that the extra subjects in the primary school curriculum continued to provide for some degree of intermediate education for some pupils.

## The Role of the Inspectors During the Payment by Results Era

Prior to the introduction of the results programme in 1871, it was customary for three annual inspections of every national school in the country. Each visit resulted in a detailed report being forwarded to the Commissioners. The same inspectors were also familiar with examining individual pupils, upon whose answering gratuities were paid for extra subjects since 1855. Therefore, a tradition of individual examining had become strong. This is, in fact, attested to in a Circular to the inspectors on the occasion of the first examination under the payment by results regime:

> It is not deemed, for the present, necessary to suggest to you to employ any particular method of examination. Indeed, from experiments which have recently been made,

45 *Sixty-Seventh Report of the Commissioners for the Year, 1900.* (Cd.285), H.C., xxiii, Appendix F, 68.

46 *Report of the Commissioners for 1891*, 39.

> it would appear that, ... the plan of examination hitherto adopted by the large body of the Inspectors, who made it a rule to note the individual answering of the pupils.[47]

This statement indicates that the Commissioners had adequate confidence in the inspectorial team to undertake their duties without any major changes in procedure.

This reflection upon the ability of the inspectors was further copperfastened by Patrick Keenan; he was asked by the Powis Commission if the existing staff of inspectors would be able to carry out his proposed plan; he replied, '.... I am of the opinion that our present staff of sixty Inspectors with six Head Inspectors would perfectly equal to the duties which it would impose.'[48] Keenan intended that there would be one annual visit by the inspector for the results aspect, and one incidental visit for other aspects of the school work. It must be borne in mind that a cadre of inspectors maintained opposition to payment by results throughout its existence.[49] However, some expressed reservations about the system, claiming in particular that it emphasized mechanical teaching methodologies at the expense of the broader development of the child. And, as the teachers' income largely depended on whether sufficient pupils passed the annual test (provided they were in attendance for a minimum number of days) it was not uncommon for the teacher to falsify entries on the roll book. According to Coolahan and O'Donovan, this practice 'abounded' during the early years of the results programme.[50] Examining the roll books for such falsification became another duty of the inspectors.

While the inspectors performed their duties under the new system of payment by results with diligence, their role as inspectors became somewhat distorted. As much of their time was devoted to investigating school rolls and examining individual pupils, very little time was devoted to the

47 *The Royal Commission of Inquiry into Primary Education (Powis Commission Report)*, 24 October 1871. Ms., 2C, 59, 7. National Archives, Dublin.

48 *Powis Commission Report*, 1870, xxviii, pt iii, 98.

49 William Jacques, *The Chief Factors Determining the Developments in Primary Education in Ireland, 1831–1947* (Unpublished Doctoral Thesis, presented to Queen's University, Belfast, 1952), 131.

50 J. Coolahan and P. O'Donovan, *A History of Ireland's School Inspectorate, 1831–2008* (Dublin: Four Courts Press, 2009), 47.

broader aspects of a school inspection. It was difficult for the inspectors to allocate time in establishing teacher methodology or variety of techniques employed by the teacher. 'The quality of teachers' work was being assessed indirectly through pupil performance on a given day on a range of tests, regardless of other circumstances.'[51] This had the unwelcome side effect of portraying the inspector as an inquisitor, rather than evaluator or adviser. Allied to the changes the new regime incurred, the clerical work of the inspectors increased enormously. At home, they were obliged to tabulate the money value of the results examination and then transfer data from marking sheets to examination rolls. Other inspectors' duties included examination of monitors and teachers for promotion, local investigations relating to applications for aid to establish National Schools, and to act as a general agent of the Commissioners. Each inspector had responsibility for about 110 schools with an aggregate attendance of approximately 10,000 pupils.[52]

The practice of paying three annual visits to each school in each inspectorial district was retained when the results scheme began. One of these visits was now to be the annual results examination, and it was the only one for the teacher to have advance notice. From 1873 a fixed date for results examinations was arranged for each school. The other visits were incidental, and 'the inspector is not to give any intimation of his intended visit'.[53] There were ingenious stratagems in use to anticipate the 'surprise' visit of the inspector.[54] Coupled with the rules and regulations was the standard of the roads and transport facilities, allied to the ever-increasing numbers of National Schools, many of which were based in townlands away from towns and villages, must have placed considerable strain upon

51 J. Coolahan and P. F. O'Donovan, *A History of Ireland's School Inspectorate, 1831–2008* (Dublin: Four Courts Press, 2009), 294–295.

52 Patrick Keenan's evidence to the Powis Commission, 1870, xxviii, pt 3, 96.

53 *Rules and Regulation*, 1874, 19.

54 Mr John Lavery of Tarbert, Co. Kerry, in an interview with John Coolahan, who began his teaching career under the results programme in 1894, gives us one example of how the inspector could be hood winked. On one occasion, he says, the visit of the mew Resident Commissioner, Dr Starkie (1899–1920) was forewarned by telegram from another teacher. This was only one version of an early warning system.

the inspectors. Inclement weather often played havoc with the inspectors' timetables, and this was a significant problem during the winter of 1879/1880, when the weather was particularly treacherous. Famine at this time was also a major concern for the smooth running of schools, especially with regard to attendance levels.

Another issue which bedevilled the national school system was the fact that inspectors were recruited without having had any experience of primary school teaching. Teachers on the ground were not happy that they being examined by individuals who were university graduates but not practising primary school teachers. At the 1873 annual congress of the Irish National Teachers' Organisation (INTO) a resolution was adopted unanimously calling for the setting aside of 50 per cent of the appointments to District Inspector for teacher-candidates to the inspectorate. This resolution, however, fell on deaf ears, and the tradition of recruiting university graduates continued for many years.

In the inspectors' examinations for entry to the inspectorial team, education had a very low status, being allotted only 200 marks out of a total of 7,000. Education shared the bottom of the list with book-keeping. We should remark at this point that if a candidate for the inspectorate offered Political Economy as a subject his texts were Smith's *Wealth of Nations* – Books I, II, III, and V, and J. S. Mill's *Principles of Political Economy* – Books I, II, III, and V.[55]

On the day of the inspector's visit to undertake the individual examination, teacher and pupils were filled with trepidation and apprehension, but was this a desirable atmosphere to behold the classroom? The examination itself was undertaken with great haste, oral tests taking place while others sat at their desks or tables with arithmetic cards upon which were the written aspects of the test. Five separate 'sums' were on the card, and getting two of the five correct was enough to pass the test. Writing exercises had to be undertaken during the inspector's presence. In the early years, however, it was enough to present writing samples undertaken during the year.[56]

55 *Programme of Examinations in Rules and Regulations*, 1874. Appendix, 47–48.

56 *Recommendations on Inspection – Minutes of the Commissioners*, Ms. 5553, 332.

On the day of the examination the inspector was meant to treat the teacher and pupils with courtesy, and he was also encouraged to use a tone and methodology which would give confidence to the pupils. Accounts of inspectorial activity do exist. One account, by a Thomas Murray, described the inspectors as 'cold, awesome, distant, inquisiting [sic], but giving no guidance'.[57]

On the other side of the coin, inspectors' reports and comments following the annual examination often appear to have been overridden by the Commissioners and Chief Inspectors. A certain amount of censorship was undertaken, based upon the following resolution:

> Passages inconsistent with instructions, to be struck out in future by the Resident Commissioner, assisted by the Secretariat and Chiefs of Inspection.[58]

Similar censorship took place in England in the 1860s which resulted in the resignation of Robert Lowe from Vice-President of the Education Privy Council.

One particular inspector's report caught the eye of the *Irish Teachers' Journal*. In its editorial, the journal refers to a letter from an inspector:

> … published in our columns some time since, revealing the ugly fact, that a circular had been sent to the Inspectors forbidding them to discuss the principle of results in their reports; and our correspondent explained that circular to mean simply that while Inspectors were not at liberty to write adversely of the system, they might praise it, and point out its advantages to their hearts' content.[59]

There were obviously some reservations among the teachers regarding acceptance at face value of every comment from an inspector.

With death of Sir Patrick Keenan in 1894 came an outpouring of views from the Inspectorate on the results system. One, Thomas Fitzpatrick, who was a teacher in the early days of payment by results and had opposed it in the mid-1870s, now pointed out in an article, that with Keenan's

57 Thomas Murray, 'Our Primary Schools and their Inspectors', *New Ireland Review* 9 March–August (1898), 229–235.

58 *Minutes of the Commissioners*, Ms. 5552, Nat. Lib. Ire., 446.

59 *Irish Teachers' Journal* 12, no. 26 (June 1878), 313.

demise, inspectors changed direction in their reports, but while he was alive any criticism of the results programme might damage one's promotional prospects.[60]

In 1896, the Inspectorate was given the opportunity to express their views of the system of Payment by Results. In requesting such a response, the Commissioners specified certain sub-headings under which each inspector was to reply. These were:

- The effects of the present system of examination on the inspection of the schools.
- The effects of the present system of examination on the teaching in the schools.
- Modifications which may be made in the present arrangements, for example, (a) the omission of certain details from the Programme; (b) the change of certain obligatory subjects into optional; (c) the introduction of class examination in certain subjects instead of the individual examination now required, or any other alterations in the requirements of the school course or mode of testing the pupils' knowledge which your experience may have suggested to you as desirable.
- The possibility of determining the conditions and awarding results fees for good organization, order, discipline, and cleanliness.

This left the door open for very frank responses. While these guidelines might indicate a basic belief in the system, it, nevertheless, opens the possibility for an honest re-appraisal of the results programme. Of course, the sub-headings presented to the inspectors could be construed as a mechanism for narrowing or confining their responses. The inspectors presented their comments along the lines suggested to them.[61]

In general terms, the inspectors' reports expressed serious dissatisfaction with the results system. All the reports were in agreement when calling for drastic changes to the system. Some were more vociferous than others.

60 Thomas Fitzpatrick, 'A Peaceful Revolution', *Westminster Review* CLVI (1901), 396–410, 404.

61 *Sixty-Second Report of the Commissioners*, 1895, (C.8142), H.C. 1896, XXVIII. 'General Reports on the State of Education, and the Working of the Results System', Appendix B, 89–340.

Some said they more or less wished for its abolition, while one inspector wrote that he had been in opposition to it for twenty-four years. Some felt the process had a harmful effect on the pupils and:

> If a pupil ... has got a bare mnemonical grasp of the isolated fact, and if by a process of verbal memorising, repeated again and again, he is made to retain some vague notion of the fact until it helps him to score a mark at the examination, all that is considered practicable is supposed to be accomplished. An examiner in dealing with such pupils will not have much opportunity of pursuing his questions into the upper reaches of intelligence. Still if he gets a reasonable number of answers while on the lower heights of the field he cannot well refuse a mark.[62]

The above comments strike many a chord at a time when child-centred education was about to make a welcome appearance. The *Revised Programme* of 1900 witnessed the end of payment by results in Irish primary schools. Tangible entities were a marketable concept at the end of the nineteenth century. Teachers' pay was based on a number of processed products, as on a conveyor belt apparatus. Technical education gained in importance, as it was more easily measured. The results system had tight control over what happened in schools. Both teacher and pupil became cogs in an industrially perceived, finance-driven system for which very few had any respect.

The agents of the system, the inspectors, in their 1896 reports made a strong case for its abolition. They understood that the teachers' pedagogic contribution was redundant and irrelevant. The division between 'heads' and 'sub-heads' was the bug-bear of the whole system. In other words, what became most valuable in the following decades in Ireland and Europe, the knowledge and understanding of what the child reads and internalizes, was simply cast aside during the era of results. It was tantamount to a Prohibition Era rather than an era associated with sound educational principles.

A handful of inspectors held out some positive interpretations of the results system. Among them was a Dr Skeffington who stated that without the pecuniary aspect of the system teachers would more than likely neglect their duties. He quoted liberally from Adam Smith and John Stuart Mill

62 'General Reports on the State of Education, and the Working of the Results System', 157. Mr J. P. Dalton.

to substantiate his point of view. In fairness to the system, some weaker pupils were attended to; subjects of a mechanical nature benefited; promotion of pupils became regularized; more pupils reached the senior classes; attendance rates improved. There was, however, much disgust with the 'sub-heads' because of their inherent educational value and they were not paid for. There were some inspectors who suggested that a separate test be implemented called 'Explanations'. Frequent remarks abounded regarding the neglect of explanation, mental arithmetic and reasoning in grammar. Geography was reduced to 'dry' facts with lists of places; poetry involved meaningless repetition without feeling or understanding. Most inspectors called for the inclusion of the 'sub-heads' in the calculation of passes for payment of fees.

Inspectors also complained about the fact that the system was applied to all schools, both town and country, and to all types of children. Cramming was another issue for complaint, and it often happened that the teacher put on a 'spurt' as the designated examination day approached.

It can be safely assumed that the inspectors were very alert and aware of both the positive and negative traits of the payment by results system. In 1896 revised instructions were issued to the inspectors, though drastic changes did not appear, apart from a vague reference to paying more attention to the 'sub-heads':

> A Pass in any subject is to be awarded for proficiency in the principal head of that subject. The Inspector is, however, required to examine on the other heads carefully, and to call particular attention in his report to any case of marked neglect. This applies in a special manner to Explanation as required in connection with Reading, and to mental exercises in Arithmetic.[63]

There was also a more defined delineation made between a No. 1 and a No. 2 pass, without extra remuneration. By the time the results system was abolished and replaced by a radically different programme in 1900 the inspectors, who had become so familiar with the old system, at least some, opposed the 1900 curriculum. Dr Starkie, the Resident Commissioner,

63 *Sixty-Second Report of the Commissioners*, H. C. 1896, Appendix O, 481.

was responsible for introducing the new curriculum in 1900 expressed great concern that his inspectors embraced such a stance of opposition:

> During the first year of the new system the incapacity and disloyalty of some of the senior officials was so injurious to its success that I was constrained to use very strong language to some of my colleagues who made complaints to me on the subject, and on several occasions to lay my complaints before the Board. I pointed out that the Chief Inspectors had been disloyal to the Board from the beginning and I disapproved of making them pass judgement on a scheme which they had tried to kill.[64]

Then, it was the turn for the teachers to complain that the inspectors were examining in the old fashion. In a speech in 1911, Dr Starkie announced that some inspectors had not freed themselves 'from the methods which had enslaved them for twenty-nine years'.[65] The Vice-Regal Commission of Inquiry was set up in 1913, and it had the following statement to make:

> … we have found that some inspectors were still conducting examinations on the style of the Results system, with the effect that their verdicts have often failed to command the confidence of the managers and teachers.[66]

The evidence suggests that some inspectors were unable or unwilling to change their mode of examining from the pattern to which they had become accustomed over the last decades of the nineteenth century.

## Problems Associated with Payment by Results

Tradition tells us that in Ireland there was an healthy respect for the teacher, especially in the days when the hedge schools were very much part of the community. During those days, teachers did not teach a

64 Quoted in Coolahan, *The Origins of the Payment by Results Policy in Education*, 150.

65 Dr Starkie, *The History of Irish Primary and Secondary Education during the Last Decade,* (NP, Pamphlet, 1911), 12.

66 *Vice-Regal Commission of Inquiry into Primary Education*, (C.7325), H.C. 1914, XXVIII, 1133.

national curriculum, and when it came to retirement age there was no system in place to provide pensions. Therefore, teachers who could not work any longer had to rely on family aid or go end up in the workhouse, as many did. In the mid-1820s it was estimated that there were a total of 11,823 schools in Ireland: 9,352 were pay schools or hedge schools, 1,979 were of Protestant Education Societies, 322 schools belonged to Catholic teaching religious orders, and Catholic Day Schools, 170 others.[67] These figures emerged from a survey carried out in 1824 in which all clergymen, both Catholic and Protestant, completed a questionnaire for each parish in the country.

Prior to 1831 the payment of teachers was haphazard and it varied enormously from place to place and from time to time. Payment often depended on what the teacher was willing or able to teach. Consequently, at retirement time the Poor Laws, under parish schemes, were invoked.[68] In contrast with the plight of the pay school teacher, those who taught for the Protestant Education Societies were remunerated on a regular basis, and they were also supplied with residences. These, of course, were in the minority.[69]

While the respect for the local teacher, at local level, continued in the post-1831 era, the prestige for the teacher did not find favour at official level, and his position in the community was below that of the professions. His recruitment came from the lower and working classes and he was not expected to have a great deal of learning. The teacher, in the eyes of officialdom, was seen as a functionary who would impart a certain level of numeracy and literacy, while at the same time remaining just ahead of the more advanced pupils. Perhaps, E. B Castle sums up this state of affairs to best advantage for us:

67 *Second Report of the Commissioners of Irish Education Inquiry*, 125–127, H.C. 1826–1827 (12), XII, Appendix no. 22, 229–1331.

68 See M. Moroney, *The Remuneration of National Teachers, 1831–1900* (Unpublished M.Litt. Thesis, submitted to Trinity College, Dublin, 2001).

69 See *First Report of the Commissioners of Irish Education Inquiry*, 1825, H.C. 1825 (400), XII, 39–40.

> This sad situation was due to the low social status of the families from which the teachers came, no matter how respectable they were; to the meagre demands of the teacher's work on his knowledge and personal culture; to the correspondingly poor quality of the instruction he received to qualify for his job; and not only to the parsimony of those who paid for his training but to the fact that it came from public funds.[70]

Castle was referring to the teachers' circumstances in Britain, and it seems that the teachers' lot was not appreciably different from that in Ireland. Following that, the trainee teacher was required to undergo a public examination in order to secure a place in one of the several Model Schools. While in the Model School, the aspirant was known as a candidate-teacher, spending six months there, again at teaching and study, after which he went out to serve with pay, for two years in a school. At the end of this, he proceeded to Marlborough Street Training Institute for his final training, a stay of about four months.[71] Thus enriched and fortified, the successful teacher set out on his life's work. This, he must do only in Ireland, as his training was not recognized by the Department of Education in England.[72]

From the middle of the nineteenth century, aspirant for the teaching profession was appointed as a paid monitor in a national school, and followed a graded syllabus of practical teaching and study.

There were two sources of income for the teacher in the nineteenth century. From 1831 until 1922 the Board of Commissioners contributed only a small gratuity towards teachers' pay, and as a result, many became dependent upon this meagre amount as the community contribution did not always manifest itself. Parents were either unwilling or unable to pay. Even with the local contribution teachers' standard of living was poor, they being unable to meet ordinary living expenses. Throughout the period under review, the Commissioners maintained a discriminatory attitude towards female remuneration. There were minor improvements in teacher

70 E. B. Castle, *The Teacher* (Oxford: Oxford University Press, 1970), 192.

71 P. J. Dowling, *A History of Irish Education* (Cork: Mercier Press, 1971), 123.

72 W. J. Walsh, *Statement of Chief Grievances of the Irish Catholics in the Matter of Education: Primary, Intermediate, and University* (Dublin: Browne and Nolan, 1890), 106.

payment from time to time. The first Board of Commissioners consisted of seven members – three from the Established Church, two Catholics and two Dissenters. The Board underwent four constitutional changes; 1838, 1848, 1851 and again in 1861 when, in response to Catholic pressure, the principle of equality among the denominations was accepted. In that year, a National Board of Education consisting of ten Catholics and ten Protestants was constituted, and this was maintained until 1922, when the entire edifice was dismantled by the Free State.

One of the perennial problems with teacher training in Ireland was the stance taken by the Catholic hierarchy. Catholic aspirants to the teaching force were reluctant to attend the stints in the Model Schools and in Marlborough Street. This resulted in a huge disproportion of untrained Catholic teachers operating within the system. This number increased as the years rolled by. The number, which stood at 4,369 in 1866, had risen to 6284 in 1874, and by 1883 had reached 7,067.[73] A tradition of opposition had built up over the years to the Model Schools and the central training institute. The tone had been set at the Synod of Thurles in 1850, but as late as 1875, and following what was called 'a devotional revolution' in post-Famine Ireland, the Maynooth Synod of Bishops, renewed their earlier ruling against the attendance of Catholics at the Dublin Training establishment and protested at the government's continued failure to endow denominational training colleges.[74] The bishops pointed to England where the idea of mixed training colleges had been abandoned as long ago as 1839, after a trial period of a few years.[75] The bishops argued that Britain had denominational training colleges,[76] but the National Board remained intransigent, more intent on selling the idea of mixed education to unwilling customers than tackling the huge backlog of untrained teachers. The precarious and unattractive nature of teaching continued, with some other niggling issues thrown into the melting pot. A less important contributary cause to the teaching force's lot was an economic one; while the trainee teacher was

73 Walsh, *Statement of Chief Grievances*, 119.

74 P. J. Corish, ed., *A History of Irish Catholicism*, vol. v: Catholic Education (Dublin: Gill and MacMillan, 1971), 43.

75 Walsh, *Statement of Chief Grievances*, 100.

76 Walsh, *Statement of Chief Grievances*, 102.

in the Marlborough Street Institute, he had to pay his substitute – few could afford to do so. That aside, the main reason for the deplorable state of teaching within the national school system was the pressure exerted by the Catholic hierarchy in discouraging would-be candidates from attending the Training College and the Model Schools.

Suffice to state at this point that by century's end denominational colleges were granted with the concession from the Commissioners that unmixed policies might be the way of the future. All of these colleges were under private management: St. Patrick's, Drumcondra, Our Lady of Mercy, Baggott St., Dublin, the Church of Ireland College in Kildare Place and Mary Immaculate College, Limerick. From now on the normal length of training would be two years, but in the case of already serving teachers, when the period stipulated would be one year.[77]

With the advent of the new colleges, between 1883 and 1898, one would expect the shortfall in teacher numbers with qualifications to be vastly reduced or even obliterated. However, such was not the case: a glance at the statistics showing the demand for new teachers indicates that despite the best efforts the deficiency was still far in excess of the numbers trained. In 1888, the number of female vacancies was 264, but the number trained was only 99, leaving a gap of 165, to be made up by using monitors and pupil-teachers, all provisionally certificated.[78] By 1899, the vacancies for female teachers had risen to an average of 290 annually, while the supply of teachers had risen to 150 per annum, improving the situation marginally.[79]

Though officialdom did not invest the teaching body with any great degree of approbation, the same officialdom expected high personal qualities in the teacher; officialdom also placed restrictions on his civic life and made a multiplicity of demands on him. Certain personal and professional qualities were deemed essential in a teacher; they should be of Christian sentiment, of calm temper and discretion, and that they should be imbued with a spirit of peace, of obedience to the law, and of loyalty

77 Akenson, *The Irish Education Experiment*, 356–357.

78 *Sixty-Ninth Report of the Commissioners of National Education* for 1902, Table 42. Demand for new teachers and means of supplying them, 31.

79 *Sixty-Sixth Report of the Commissioners of National Education for 1899*, Appendix 1, *Report on Training Colleges*, 172.

to their Sovereign.[80] Teachers were not allowed mix with the people: they were not allowed to attend fairs or markets, and meetings of a political nature. Taking part in elections was forbidden, other than to vote; neither could they own or reside in a public house. Coupled with all the above prohibitions was the range of their school duties. School ventilation, white-washing the school building, keeping registers, report books and class rolls accurately were some of the key duties that teachers should attend to. One of the key facets of a teacher's duty was to ensure that there was 'a time and a place for everything, and everything in its proper time and place'.[81] This was one of the catch-all phrases of the nineteenth century, and it applied to the results era as much as it did at any other time. Teachers were also expected to promote 'cleanliness, neatness and decency' and to undertake personal inspections of their pupils on a daily basis with regard to hygiene. All this had to be carried out while dealing with inspectors' visits, trouble-some managers and unwilling pupils. As teaching became more complex and more onerous, it was inevitable that the teaching fraternity needed some support.

Much of the complexity stemmed from the manner in which teachers were classified. The seven categories were assigned as follows:

- First Class, First Division [1–1]
- First Class, Second Division [1–2]
- First Class, Third Division [1–3]
- Second Class, First Division [2–1]
- Second Class, Second Division [2–2]
- Third Class, First Division [3–1]
- Third Class, Second Division [3–2][82]

80 *Rules and Regulations of the National Board* (Dublin: Thom, 1874), 20. Also, see Powis Commissions, XII.

81 *Rules and Regulations*, 20.

82 A teacher designated [1–1] was often described as 'a first of first' and likewise with all the categories, such as [2–2] being described as 'second od second'.

The salaries awarded to male teachers from 1848 onwards ranged from £30 to £14 per annum, and for female teachers from £24 to £12. Probationary teachers and needlework mistresses were on lower rates of pay.[83]

In 1867, Robert M. Chamney Henly and Vere Foster agreed to publish a monthly journal, the *Irish Teachers' Journal*. Its launch in 1867 proved to be the catalyst for the setting up of the *Irish National Teachers' Association* (INTA) in 1868. The first edition of the journal in 1868 featured a long letter from Vere Foster in which he drew attention to the long list of grievances experienced by teachers in the national system of education. Amongst these were hardships being experienced by teachers; he called for an increase in salaries to help alleviate this issue; he also called for pensions for teachers in line with others operating as civil servants. And, in order to promote their cause, Foster urged teachers to form Teachers' Associations. This resulted in a teachers' united front when agitating for better conditions.[84]

The INTA went from strength to strength, forming a strong centralized organization, with a clear framework as to how the Local Teachers' Associations might work to best advantage. Coinciding with the formation of the INTA in 1868 was the government proposal to undertake a national investigation into primary education. A Royal Commission (Powis Commission) was established and it reported in nine detailed volumes in 1870. Teachers viewed this as an opportunity to remedy the problems of remuneration and conditions of service. It became incumbent upon local teachers' associations to prepare petitions and memorials for submission to the Commission.

At a meeting on 20 June 1868, the Dublin Central Teachers' Association decided to hold a conference in Dublin on 15 August to consult members regarding petitions or memorials that might be put to the Commission. Apart from the issues of salaries and conditions of service, this conference felt it their right to speak out about the impending introduction of payment by results to Irish schools, similar to that which had pertained in Great Britain for ten years. A second conference was held on the 29 and 30 of December in the same year. Vere Foster was appointed President

83 See Moroney, *National Teachers' Salaries and Pensions*, 16.
84 See Moroney, *National Teachers' Salaries and Pensions*, 24–27.

of the INTA and a constitution was adopted. Soon afterwards, the word 'Association' was dropped from the INTA and replaced with 'Organisation'. The INTO had its work cut out for the future. Since 1848 national teachers were paid according to a merit hierarchy of three classes with sub-divisions in each class. The classification depended on the teacher's performance in written examinations and on the inspector's report of the teacher's ability in the classroom. Some had been trained in the Central Training Institution at Marlborough, Dublin, while other were trained in the District Model Schools. However, for religious reasons, the Catholic hierarchy had opposed both of these institutions, resulting in fewer teachers being trained in either of them. They had to fall back on the older system of monitorial apprenticeship training with an experienced teacher and passing monitors' examinations.[85]

At the outset of payment by results there were 9,868 teachers working under the National Board, and of these, 3,461 were trained. That is about 35 per cent.[86] Therefore, it can be deduced that the calibre of the teaching force at the inception of payment by results, as 6,427 teachers were ranked as third class or lower. The average income for classified male principal teachers in 1871 was £42. 0. 4 and of classified female principals £34. 10. 3. Assistant teachers were granted £22. 0. 4. for males and £19. 1.1. for females.[87] For several years prior to this the low incomes for teachers was the cause of much unrest and disquiet. When, eventually, in 1872 the Treasury opened its purse strings and granted an extra £100,000 for national teachers, the method adopted for its disbursement was the payment by results system.

Soon after the establishment of the national system in 1831 most of the schools run by monks and nuns applied to come under the aegis of the National Board. Initially, six Christian Brothers' schools joined but they withdrew in 1836 due to the difficulties they had with the Board's inspectors. There were other issues regarding the connection to the Board which were of concern to the Brothers from the beginning: the Rules relating to religious instruction, that is, the separate nature of religion from the other

85 See Coolahan, *The Origins of the Payment by Results Policy in Education*, 154.

86 *Report of the Commissioners for 1871*, 293.

87 *Report of the Commissioners for 1871*, 293.

school work throughout the school day; the Board's control of the school textbooks; and the public's right to visit schools under the National Board. Upon their leaving the national system of education several attempts were made to re-introduce them, but to no avail. It was not until 1925 that the Christian Brothers re-joined the fold of the national system of education.

From 1839 teachers' pay changed from being a capitation grant to an annual salary determined by the classification into which each teacher was placed. Religious teaching communities were given the option of retaining the old system of capitation grants or the new classification system. The majority opted for the capitation grant system, resulting in two types of national schools being created for religious-run schools – 'Capitation Schools' and 'Classification Schools'.[88]

Teachers complained that the payment by results rewards favoured Convent and Model Schools, as opposed to rural schools and schools in back-streets of cities. *The Teachers' Journal* objected to this trend by stating:

> But we maintain that it was not for these schools the grant was principally intended, since their conductors put forward no plea of poverty; it was to relieve the dire necessities of the ordinary teachers.[89]

It was the experience of many teachers that the grant for results payments was not going to do very much for the ordinary national teacher. 'It is well known, and now fully acknowledged that the teachers who stood most in need of the grant have gained but a mere *bagatelle* by it.'[90]

Following on from these reports the Executive Committee of the INTO launched a campaign to ensure that future grants would be paid by fixed salary rather than by results. The INTO claimed that Convent Schools and Model Schools were located in places where attendance rates were high. These schools also had superior facilities and better equipment. The Executive pointed to the dire straits many ordinary teachers found themselves in, and in 1872 and 1873 that 852 teachers had left the profession.[91]

88 See Moroney, *National Teachers' Salaries and Pensions*, 13–17.
89 *The Teachers' Journal* VI, no. 4 (13 May 1873), 51.
90 *The Teachers' Journal* VI, no. 4 (15 February 1873), 183.
91 *The Teachers' Journal* VI, no. 4, (13 July 1874), 284.

The upshot was the partial success of the campaign, with £60,000 of the grant now being allocated to classification salaries. In the provisions of the National School Teachers (Ireland) Act, 1875, Poor Law Unions were permitted to tax themselves in order to raise results fees to a maximum of £60,000 extra in results fees. However, this Act proved a failure in the long term and some teachers suffered a reduction in their results if they lived in non-contributary unions.[92] John Ferguson, President of the INTO, pointed out huge discrepancies in the incomes of teachers in Ireland when compared with those in England and Scotland.[93] Such was the state of play in the middle of the results era. A pension scheme was introduced on 1 January 1880 under the National School Teachers (Ireland) Act (42 and 43 Victoria), 1879.

The parliamentary grant for national education increased significantly over the period, and the Table below gives an idea of the expansion which took place in each decade from 1870 to 1900:

Table 8. Educational Provision in Association with the Board of National Education, 1870–1900

| Year | Parliamentary Grant | Number of Schools |
|---|---|---|
| 1870 | £394,209 | 6,806 |
| 1880 | £722,366 | 7,590 |
| 1890 | £734,467 | 8,298 |
| 1900 | £1,145,721 | 8,684 |

Compiled from D. H. Akenson, *Irish Education Experiment,* 321, 325, 346.

Increases in classification salaries can be illustrated by those for principal teachers in the first division of each class. For males in 1872 these stood at £52, £30, £24. By 1880 these were raised to £70, £44, and £35. For female principals the corresponding figures were 1872 – £42, £24, and £20 and the reached £58, £34.5, and £27.5 in 1880.[94] While improvements in

92 *Forty-Seventh Report of the Commissioners*, Appendix, 516.

93 See John Ferguson, 'A Few Observations on the Present Position of Irish National Teachers', *Journal of the Statistical and Social Inquiry Society* 8 (1882), 359–363.

94 *Forty-Seventh Report of the Commissioners*, for 1880, Appendix O, 518.

remuneration did take place during the results era, teachers' incomes still remained quite low. Uncertainty, though, was replaced by a definite character in teachers' incomes.

Another issue that concerned teachers was the haphazard nature of teacher training. In 1866 there were 4,369 untrained teachers in the system. A few years later the Powis Commission took up the mantle of untrained teachers. It recommended state support for denominational training. However, nothing was done, even though the numbers of untrained personnel continued to increase. By 1883 the number of untrained teachers had reached 7,067, or 66 per cent of all the certified teachers in the National School System.[95] One major outcome from Catholic opposition to the Model Schools and the Central Training Institution was that only about 27 per cent of Catholic teachers received any training.[96]

Very often, the matter of teachers' remuneration or teachers' training depended on what type of person held key political roles in the Irish administration. In 1883 George Trevelyan, Liberal and Chief Secretary for Ireland, concerned himself with the matter of teacher training and issued a statement on the subject, it 'must no longer be considered as one of speculation or expediency, but as one of absolute urgency'.[97] As far as he was concerned the matter of so many untrained teachers in the schools the work being done must be 'infinitely less fruitful' than it ought to be. He promised that Parliament would vote for a huge increase in the grant for education in Ireland.[98] Parliament accepted his proposals and state support for voluntary or denominational training colleges, fulfilling certain conditions, was accepted. This resulted in great expansion during the last decades of the nineteenth century, in which training colleges were established, the training course was extended to two years duration, or one year in the case of a certified teacher.[99]

95 *Fortieth Report of the Commissioners*, for 1883 (C4053), 1884, XXV, 471–477, 473.

96 See Coolahan, *The Origins of the Payment by Results Policy in Education*, 160.

97 See *Fortieth Report of the Commissioners*, for 1883 (C4053), 1884, XXV, 471–477, 475.

98 *Fortieth Report*, 475.

99 Graham Balfour, *Educational Systems of Britain and Ireland* (HardPress Publishing, Reprint, 2012), 102.

The course content in the new training colleges emphasized pragmatic and practical approaches to teaching in the classroom. Now, teachers emerging from these institutions were expected to have a knowledge of the content of school subjects, but also be familiar with classroom management, including a variety of methodologies. The student teachers were grounded in organizational methods rather than in educational theoretical principles. There was also a great deal of stress placed on an apprenticeship approach in which the young trainee teacher would model his or her lessons on another's demonstrated lessons.[100]

The two chief texts used in the colleges were Robinson's *Manual of Method and Organization* but, of much greater use and importance was Joyce's *Handbook of School Management.*[101] Joyce's text was based very closely on Patrick Keenan's lectures from the 1850s in which he delivered to school organizers, of which Joyce was one. Joyce emphasized the practical as opposed to the theoretical:

> While carefully avoiding all mere theory, I have endeavoured to render the instruction contained in it plain, useful and practical.[102]

Joyce's book went through several editions, and in the 1887 publication two extra chapters were added under the headings 'Kindergarten' and 'The Human Mind in Relation to Education'. The content of the book included furniture apparatus, school organization, methodologies of teaching, simultaneous instruction and class teaching, reminders for monitors, classification, notes of lessons, manner of answering, and apart from a general statement that pupils should be told everything but, should also be led to find out for themselves. A large section of the book was devoted to the different subjects a teacher might teach in a typical

100 Prevailing trends in England at the time were not dissimilar to what was happening in Ireland. See R. J. W. Selleck, *The New Education* (London: Pitman, 1968), 45 and 58.

101 R. Robinson, *Manual of Method and Organization* (Château – 92200 Neuilly sur Seine, Ulan Press, 2012) and P. W. Joyce, *Handbook of School Management and Methods of Teaching* (McGlashan and Gill, 1863). Reprinted by Andesite Press, New York and London, 2017).

102 This statement was in the Preface to the 1863 edition. P. W.

national school. This included hints and guidelines on how to approach each topic. Great detail was evident in this section of the book. One hundred and fifty pages were devoted to this section, while nine pages were devoted to the new chapter on 'Kindergarten'.

The emphasis on the subject content of the primary school programme continued, and it may have been as a result of the paucity of intermediate schools available. The emphasis on curricular content was very much in keeping with the idea that inspired the payment by results scheme.

While teachers who were being trained by the system increased to 47.8 per cent in 1899,[103] this still meant that over half the national teachers were still untrained when we reach the end of the results era. Possibly allied to this issue was the ongoing practice by teachers, once they graduated from the colleges and took up teaching posts, of teaching in a mechanical manner towards the results examination. Very few engaged in sound pedagogical approaches to methodology and planning. The favoured route was the shortcut towards results. The Head Inspector, Mr Strong, reporting in 1897 indicated that some teachers were unable or unwilling to stand back from the role drill of the results routine. In his statement, he is very condemnatory of what was happening in the schools:

> But in all other schools – and these are an over whelming majority – the personal influence of the Inspector has under the present system fallen to a very low ebb indeed. The teachers have got into a groove, into a certain stereotyped round of work, with the single object in view of having as many passes as possible at the next Results examination. The adoption of a new routine in school organisation or the introduction of new methods would lead to a dislocation of the ordinary mechanical round[sic] and involve alterations in the manner of imparting instruction. To make changes would require additional thought and labour, and cause such a loss of time as would tell against the success of their pupils at the next examination. The teacher has sunk to the level of a mere mechanical drudge.[104]

However, it is pretty certain that all teachers did not succumb to the standard of 'a mere mechanical drudge'. Of course, teachers did replace, what might be termed sound educational practices, with methodologies

103 *Sixty-Sixth Report of the Commissioners*, for 1899, 220.

104 Cited by Coolahan, *The Origins of the Payment by Results Policy in Education*, 165.

that were 'inspired' by the pecuniary advance which in turn was preceded by a rigid emphasis on certain narrow methodologies. These methodologies had the general effect of lowering the tone of schools, and of depriving pupils from experiences which, might otherwise be of enormous value to them. This situation also deprived those teachers who were passionate about their work, and who were constricted to instructing as many individual pupils as possible to ensure payment for the teacher on the basis of the results. This was a classic case of the end justifying the means.

## Other Issues

A multiplicity of issues caused a great strain on the lives and work of teachers during the results era. Rural schools felt the brunt of misfortune as much or more than urban schools. For example, Mr O'Donnell was appointed principal of Glenrue NS in 1871. This teacher was classified as Class II status on qualifying. Not long after his appointment, he fell ill, and resigned in 1882. Out of necessity, he worked in the school up to the day he died. He lost his life four days after he had resigned, leaving his family in very poor circumstances. The school manager, Fr. John Kelly, wrote seeking assistance from the National Board of Education for the teacher's family, but the Commissioners responded by saying that they 'had no funds at their disposal to make any grant to the family of the deceased teacher in consideration of the retiring gratuity to which the teacher might have been entitled had he lived'.[105] In other words, if the teacher did not have the required number of years served the gratuity was miniscule or non-existent. In keeping with the ideology of payment by results, it was truly a time when only the fittest survived. William O'Donnell was only 33 years old when he died. His wife and three children were left in severe want. At the time, widows and orphans did not

105 N. Ó Duinnín, ed., *Scoil Mhuire Anseo!: Glenrue N.S.* (Glenrue: Pub. By Scoil Mhuire 75 Committee, 2010).

have much recourse to pensions to help them in their hour of need. Alas, Mr O'Donnell's teaching career was too short to warrant a grant.

*The Irish Teachers' Journal* was wary of the results scheme quite early on:

> The cardinal point for consideration, ... is that the Results Scheme is now an accomplished fact, and has assumed a character of permanency; and, therefore, all that can be done is to watch its operation carefully, and endeavour to turn it to best account.[106]

A very serious issue, and of great concern to teachers, was the problem of pupil attendance. Resolutions were passed by the INTO regarding the provision of enforcing pupils to attend school.

At this juncture, it should be noted that there was no School Attendance legislation in Ireland. As a consequence, children attended when not required at home to undertake some work. There were about 300,000 small farmers and cottiers whose holdings were only fifteen acres or less, the labour of whose children was a very valuable asset to such families.[107] Some rural districts were worse off than others. A teacher from Swinford, Co. Mayo wrote of the annual migration to England from the district leaving the care of cattle or pigs, sowing and tilling to the women and older children. Another teacher complained that his school was nearly empty in Spring, Summer and early Autumn.[108]

Attending school was a seasonal affair, and not only that, but based on the type of weather pertaining in any particular location at a particular time. The vagaries of the weather had enormous influence on school attendance. In 1872, the first year of full payment by results, the weather was particularly inclement. In the Autumn of that year it rained continuously for fifty days, resulting in closed schools, and as one teacher explained, 'a tremendous fall of aquatic fluid flooding the road and school premises, to such an extent as to preclude the ingress of pupils.'[109] Poor transport facilities also impeded school attendance.

106 *Irish Teachers' Journal* V, no. 66 (1872), 467. Note that the Results System had recently begun in all schools.

107 See Keenan's Memorandum to the Powis Commission, 93.

108 *Irish Teachers' Journal* VIII, no. 10 (1875), 43.

109 Cited by Jacques, *Factors Determining Developments in Primary Education* (Thesis), 134.

Local events such as fairs, race meetings also hampered regular school attendance. And, as fate would have, these events took place about the time of the Inspector's visit to the local school to carry out the 'dreaded' examination. Perhaps, many factors were outside teachers' control, but it must also be pointed out that the atmosphere in schools had become so dull and routinized that pupils' enthusiasm for attending waned significantly during the period in question.

The freedom of 'good' teachers was curtailed by the results programme, the *Teachers' Journal* remarking:

> The INTO claimed that a system which remunerates a teacher based on the 'exertions' of the teacher will fail if it is not accompanied by an enforcement of school attendance.[110] It was not until 1892 that Compulsory School Attendance Legislation was introduced in Ireland.[111]

For the first time attending school was made compulsory and fees in primary schools were abolished. Children from now on were compelled to attend school between the ages of six and fourteen, though pupils were allowed to have part-time work between the ages of eleven and fourteen. It was expected that School Attendance Committees would enforce the Act, similar to the practice pertaining in Britain. It achieved some successes in improving attendance in the towns and cities, but not so in rural areas where it did not apply until the establishment of County Councils in 1898.[112] The Act made little difference in country districts as by 1908

110 *Irish Teachers' Journal* V, no. 50 (1872), 280.

111 See Lyons, Tony, 'Compulsory School Attendance Legislation in Ireland, 1892–2000', in Thomas G. Grenham and Patricia Kieran, eds, *New Educational Horizons in Contemporary Ireland: Trends and Challenges* (Oxford: Peter Lang, 2012).

112 Susan Parkes, *A Guide to Sources for the History of Irish Education, 1780–1922* (Dublin: Four Courts Press, 2010), 50. See also N. Atkinson, *Irish Education: A History of Educational Institutions* (Dublin: Allen Figgis, 1969), 103. For a very comprehensive discussion on the enforcement of the Act see Frank Shalloo, *Compulsory Schooling as an Irish Education Issue: An Empirical Investigation* (Unpublished Master of Education Thesis, University of Dublin, School of Education, 1977), Chap. 3.

ten county councils had failed to apply it. Attendance still remained precarious and seasonal.

During the results era teachers pointed out the large numbers of irregular attenders along with those children who, nowadays would be classified as special needs, had had no provision for them within the payment by results arrangements, and in normal circumstances would require extra attention from the teacher. It should be recognized that Keenan in his submission to the Powis Commission included a clause to encourage teachers to cater for such pupils. In 1872 only about 30 per cent of pupils were examined under the results programme. The others did not attend, for one reason or another, for the required minimum number of days. *The Teachers' Journal* felt that this was a 'delusion of fancy' that such pupils did not get a great deal of attention from the teachers.[113]

*The Teachers' Journal* made some very apt comments on the results scheme on more than one occasion. From 1873, we get the following remarks:

> The child from the back-streets of Dublin or Belfast is to be subjected to the same course of treatment as the child in the remotest and least frequented part of Dingle or Mayo .... It is the essence of any scheme of results that the same course of instruction is to be carried out, and the same test applied, in every school and under every circumstance.[114]

Within the results programme there was no allowance made for cultivating local interest in one's immediate environment, and neither did the scheme make any tangible allowance for the very weak child. The system proceeded on the assumption that all pupils, regardless of ability or other circumstances, in application, or in attendance levels could progress harmoniously together, and that the same system suited all types of children.

One commentator, who delivered a paper outlining the shortcomings of the results scheme, challenged the basic approach of a payment by results scheme as applied to the teachers' work. Thomas Fitzpatrick, speaking in 1875, remarked that a piece-work criterion could be applied to the work

113 *The Irish Teachers' Journal* XII, no. 24 (1872), 290.

114 *Irish Teachers' Journal* V, no. 50 (1873), 301.

of a bricklayer, but to extend that analogy to teaching was fundamentally wrong. The nature of a teacher's work did not lend itself to a crude form of measurement, in circumstances which very often depended upon contingencies beyond the teacher's control. He stated:

> By all means pay teachers on the results of their labours if you can do them the simple justice of taking cognizance in your estimate of all the work done. (original underlining)

Clearly, from his point of view the system of payment by results failed to do that.[115]Similar comments were issued by other teachers who felt that the title 'payment by results' was captivating and appealing to the general public but was, in essence, misleading. Suggestions were made for a replacement title, such as 'payment by Fortuitous Circumstances into which Good or Bad Teaching plays only a minor part'.[116]

A typical teachers' day in the late nineteenth century under the watchful eye of the National Board's Commissioners, and their Inspectors, had many vicissitudes to contend with; some could be planned for, but it is the one's that could not be planned for that cause the greatest strife; then there are the easily determined responsibilities such as rolls, reports and other records; if monitors are in the school, attending to them may take place when the pupils have gone hope, or in the morning before they get to school; there is also the instruction in extra branches for those who do have an intermediate school to attend, but remain with national school teacher until they know enough to pass the civil service examination; the teacher must also light the fire in the morning and tend to it throughout the day; the teacher was expected to offer a set of clean rooms for any would-be visitor; there was often a lack of suitable textbooks, not to mention copies, pencils, pens, and so on – this was a cause of annoyance; and the teacher had to supply his own ink, chalk and duster for use in the school.[117]

115 Text of Address printed in *Irish Teachers' Journal* VIII, no. 9 (1875), 128–130.

116 Quoted by Coolahan, *The Origins of the Payment by Results Policy in Education*, 171.

117 This detail comes from an interview J. Coolahan had with Mr Jack Lavery, who was a teacher at the time of the results era. Coolahan, *The Origins of the Payment by Results Policy in Education*, 171–172.

School buildings were poorly serviced; toilet facilities suffered from the absence of running water, and if there was a very serious breakdown, it was usually the school principal who came to the rescue, in the absence of a caretaker. In 1898, two visiting Scottish teachers were more than shocked at what they encountered in the schools they inspected in Ireland. They observed:

> The schools, insufficient in accommodation and equipment for the existing demand, are miserably inadequate to what the demand ought to be. They are systematically denied the simplest of educational requisites. Applications for books – and these half a century out of date – slates, etc., are only half granted, and that after an interval calculated to call Patience herself down from the monument. Many of the teachers supply out of their pittances the scanty maps and pictures with which they make a futile attempt to conceal the dilapidations of the buildings, which are ill ventilated, badly lighted, and often in an almost ruinous condition.[118]

To add to the woes of school life as described above, corporal punishment was acceptable as a means of discipline, and in the smaller schools, which had come to predominate the educational scene in Ireland, dealing with children of wide-ranging abilities and ages, meant that classroom management was a significant problem. Unruly pupils were often dealt with in a summary fashion.

Pupils came to school bringing with them many problems, and not always challenges to the teacher's authority. A report from 1898 comments:

> School begins at 10 am and continues, with an interval of half an hour, till 3pm. During these five hours the luckless children, many of whom have had but the veriest[sic] apology for a breakfast, followed by a walk of two, three, or even four hours, have to sustain their mental activity on crusts of bread or a few cold potatoes .... Whatever may be the causes, inattentive, and utterly devoid of the eager desire to learn which rejoices the heart of a Scottish teacher. To those accustomed to the quick responsiveness of Scottish scholars, the tongue-tied stolidity of these quick-witted Irish children is simply amazing.[119]

118 Edith F. Hogg and A. D. Innes, 'Irish Elementary Education', *The Contemporary Review* 73 (1898), 564–581, 574.

119 Hogg and Innes, 'Irish Elementary Education', 474.

By this time, payment by results had been abolished in Scotland, and is it possible that the atmosphere created by the payment by results scheme (still operating in Ireland) had something to do with the perceived lack of interest or desire to learn among the scholars in this Irish scenario?

Added to the already existing plethora of miseries which bedevilled the Irish teacher's lot, he was still further disappointed with the delay in receiving the results of the Inspector's examination. Delays could be up six months in duration, and the *Irish Teachers' Journal* found much wanting in these delays:

> It is then essential that after the annual field-day, the teacher should at once commence his preparations for the next; and to do this, he should know exactly the casualties of the engagement just concluded, how many pupils have emerged from the struggle entirely untouched, with a row of crosses entirely un-profaned by what is termed in the language of competing marksmen, a 'duck's egg', how many have received wounds in the contest, though still in the main victorious; but above all it is essential that he should know those who have been left entirely *hors-de-combat* by failing even to achieve a 'pass'.[120]

Delays in the return of the examination roll was a further concern and hindrance to the teacher under the Payment by Results System.

## Concluding Remarks

It was important for the Victorian mind to be able to 'fix everything in returns'. Payment by Results was tailor-made for this concept. One of the more pernicious aspects of Payment by Results was the practice of dividing knowledge into 'Heads' and 'Sub-heads'. This proved to be detrimental for both pupil and teacher; it precluded any sense of initiative on the teacher's part and it deprived the child from developing the imagination.

120 *Irish Teachers' Journal* VI, no. 27(1875), 326. Also, VII, no. 6, 69.5.

The role of the inspector was of paramount importance during the existence of the results regime, and as the years rolled by, teachers became very adept at outwitting the inspector. The questions he was likely to ask during his visit to the school were often worked out by the teacher in advance, which in its own way diluted whatever sound educational principles may have existed.

The programme of 1872 laid down ninety attendances per year as the minimum whereby pupils could qualify for the upcoming examination on which results were payable. Those who did not reach the minimum of ninety days were not allowed take the examination, but the inspector could examine them if he had time, but whatever the result, it did not count for payment purposes.

The teachers were generally in acceptance of the modified (slightly) programme of 1872, and this was followed by advice to the inspectors from the Commissioners that they should not 'adopt a severe standard'. This was issued in Circular to the inspectors on 11 October 1872.[121]

A regulation was introduced in 1874 which substituted the passing in Reading, Writing and Arithmetic, for passing in Reading and any one other programme subject as the condition, which applied prior to 1874, of promotion of pupils of First and Higher classes.[122] Under the old regulation it was found that pupils were advanced too quickly.

Although a series of programmes were issued continually with the label 'Revised', to be operative from certain subsequent dates, the most striking feature that emerges from a scrutiny of them is the lack of change effected in any of the basic programme components. Any changes that could be classified as such were so minute as not to warrant consideration. In fact, it can be stated that a habit of innovation was not a feature of the evolution of the compulsory programme in the period under review. The early years had a certain fluidity for review but this quickly solidified, and for the period following 1875, no changes of any significance did occur.

121 *Abstract and Index of Circulars to Inspectors and Others, 1840–1891*. Issued by the Education Office.

122 *Forty-Third Report of the Commissioners of National Education for the Year 1876* (C.1757) H.C. 1877, XXXI, 27.

Extra fees were paid to teachers for teaching extra subjects. However, in 1872 the numbers of pupils who presented for the examination in extra subjects was small.[123] Succeeding years saw an expansion in this area. In 1873 Vocal Music was included as an extra subject from Second Class upwards, while Drawing was now to be paid for from Third Class upwards. In 1874, a further expansion took place, when Greek, Latin and French were added to the list. It was now possible in the senior classes for a pupil to be taught the compulsory course with the addition of Vocal Music, Drawing, and two other extra subjects, and one of Greek, Latin or French.[124]

From 1879 Irish appeared as a subject on the extra list for which fees could be earned outside school hours. The inclusion of Irish had a very slow start, with only twelve schools availing of it as an extra subject by 1885.[125] With the expanding fervour associated with cultural nationalism, more and more schools took Irish on board.[126] In 1891 German was added to the list, but it had little success, and was abandoned in 1895. It was difficult to find teachers who had the correct certificates to teach the extra subjects.

Initially, the Commissioners had faith in the inspectors to undertake their duties as they had been doing in previous years. This was, in fact, an error as the new regime required a whole new method of inspection. The inspection personnel should have been thoroughly briefed on what was expected of them when writing reports and examining each individual pupil. There was also another issue of an ongoing nature in the nucleus of the inspectorate which from time to time came to the surface. This cadre opposed the concept of the results programme *ab initio.*

Much of the inspector's time was devoted to examining individual pupils and investigating any irregularities in the roll book. Other duties included examination of monitors and teachers for promotion. Local applications for aid to establish a new school was also part of the brief to be examined by the inspector. Each inspector was responsible for approximately 110 schools with an aggregate attendance of about 10,000 pupils.

123 *Thirty-Ninth Report of the Commissioners of National Education for the Year 1872*, (C.805), H.C. 1873, XXV, 25.

124 *Appendix to Rules and Regulations of the Commissioners*, October 1874, 64.

125 *Annual Report of the Gaelic League*, Dublin, 1897, 20.

126 *Report of Comisiún na Gaeltachta*, DuBlin, 1926, 13.

Monitoring all this had to be in three visit per school, with one of the visits devoted exclusively to examining individual pupils for the results award.

One of the issues regarding the recruitment of inspectors caused great difficulty when they were visiting schools. No inspector had any experience of teaching at primary school level, and this irked some teachers. In practice, some teachers expressed reservations about the comments made by the inspectors in their reports following a school visit.

One of the reasons for a great deal of the problems associated with school inspected stemmed from the fact that nobody enlightened the inspectors regarding the methodologies of the new approach to teaching in the national school. As Patrick Keenan had supported its introduction to the schools it surely fell to him to organize special courses for the inspectors and teachers to enable them to become familiar with what the new approach entailed.

There were many issues which militated against the success implementation of a results regime in Irish primary schools. Rural schools felt the brunt of the problems more than those in urban settings. It was often the survival of the fittest.

Poor pupil attendance was an ongoing issue for teachers. It affected their pedagogical aims and objectives, but it also affected their pocket. The vagaries of the weather often determined school attendance or not. Local events such as fairs and race meetings also played their part. Classroom atmosphere had become dull and routinized and this dampened any enthusiasm for attending school. The blame for this must be placed at the feet of the Payment by Results system. The Attendance Act of 1892 had little import in rural districts. It did not apply until 1898 when County Councils were established, and ten years later ten County Councils had failed to apply the Act. Thus, school attendance remained haphazard and precarious.

There were no provisions within the results programme for children with special needs, even though Patrick Keenan, in his response to the Powis Commission drew attention to the need for some extra intervention in that area. All children were expected to progress harmoniously regardless of ability, application or family circumstances.

School buildings did not have a favourable infrastructure to enable any success rate with any kind of curriculum. Classroom management was a significant issue in a country with an expanding number of one-teacher schools. These brought multiclass situations into the fray, and the teacher in such schools was usually in charge of eight different levels.

Chapter Four addresses the issues which brought the results era to a close. One of the chief factors was the Belmore Commission of 1898, which introduced new educational concepts, and the 1890s proved to be a decade of new and fresh ideas, not only at home, but internationally as well. The appointment of a new Chief Secretary, Augustine Birrell, heralded a new way of thinking. Ireland was on the cusp of the 'New Education Movement'. Teaching conditions were attracting attention, and following decades of inadequacies, some measures to alleviate the situation were being considered. Vere Foster had been instrumental in this. Very few regretted the demise of the results era.

CHAPTER 4

# The Ebbing and Demise of Payment by Results within the National School System

'It does not matter how slowly you go as long as you do not stop.'

– Confucius

## Introduction

By 1895 the Payment by Results scheme had gone out of favour in England and Scotland, and was abandoned in 1897. In Ireland, the INTO had never been in favour of the system, and when it was discarded in Britain, they used this to put pressure on the government to act on the glaring inequalities that existed between teachers' conditions and incomes compared with their counterparts across the water. One feature of the pressure amounted to a request to form a Vice-Regal Commission to report on the Educational System under the Commissioners of National Education in Ireland.[1] The Belmore Commission was the result, and it published its reports in 1897 and 1898. Its recommendations sounded the death knell of Payment by Results in Ireland. This was a period of radical revision of school curricula at an international level, and Ireland proved to be no exception in this regard. The Belmore Commission was instrumental in enabling Ireland to adjust the national school curriculum in such a way that child-centred and practical education

1 See Moroney, *National Teachers' Salaries and Pensions*, 52.

would become a central focus in what went on in schools during the first two decades of the new century.

Belmore concluded that Irish education was antiquated and it would benefit from major reform. The Final Report, in June 1898, spelled out the attitudes and thinking of the European-wide child-centred movement which was alive at the turn of the twentieth century.

## Belmore Commission

The following synopsis offers a flavour of what Belmore entailed:

(a) *Kindergarten*: It recommended the extension of this model of education to all schools in which infants were attending.
(b) *Educational Handwork*: Belmore felt that kindergarten methods and principles should expand to include classes I, II and III. In practice, this included paper-folding, cardboard work, brick-laying, clay-modelling. These exercises came under the umbrella title, 'hand and eye training'. Woodwork should be included for boys in the senior classes.
(c) *Drawing*: This should be a compulsory subject in all schools.
(d) *Elementary Science*: This was meant to be part of the daily work of the school. 'Object' lessons would be part of the methodology in junior classes, while experiments would form part of the syllabus in senior classes.
(e) *Agriculture*: Belmore recommended that this subject be discontinued in primary schools.
(f) *Needlework*: This should be an important subject for girls in the schools.
(g) *Cookery, Laundry Work and Domestic Science*: These subjects to be taught in girls' schools, but as far as practicable.
(h) *Singing*: For all children in national schools.

(i) *Drill and Physical Exercise*: Various types to be introduced to all classes in national schools.[2]

In their concern for practical subjects and this type of curriculum in general, the Commissioners were in line with the mainstream of thought in Europe, where the movement in favour of introducing manual training into elementary schools was gaining strength in many countries. There was no general agreement, however, as to the precise aim of such training, nor as to the relation which it should bear to the rest of the curriculum.[3]

There were six distinct categories identified[4] upon which the 'New Education' was finely balanced. Firstly, there were the 'practical educationists' who favoured a curriculum which included practical subjects – such subjects as drawing, science, woodwork, physical drill, cookery, nature study, and so on. Secondly, there were the 'social reformers' who wished to replace military drill in schools with physical education, and they also promoted the idea that schools should provide school meals, medical inspection, and child-friendly school furniture. On an ideological basis, they felt that schools should offer social change and access to schools should be provided democratically. Thirdly, there were the 'naturalists' who revisited the likes of Froebel and Pestalozzi. 'Child-centred' education was at the core of their beliefs. In this, they referred to Montessori, Steiner, Dewey and Homer Lane. Kindergarten played a major role in their views. Fourth, Herbart's systematic lesson instruction played a crucial role. Herbart's view of the curriculum was that it should embrace the humanities, the sciences and practical subjects.[5] Fifth, the 'scientific educationists' whose origins were in Germany, but spread to the United States. Darwinism led the way in their views, and Galton in Britain and Binet in France took up the mantle of the 'scientific educationists'. Sixth, we have the moral educationists. Very

2 Cited in Hyland and Milne, eds, *Irish Educational Documents*, vol. 1, 142–146.

3 See Helen Keogh, *The Starkie Era – the System of National Education in Ireland, 1899–1922* (Unpublished MA Thesis, University College, Galway, 1974).

4 R. J. W. Selleck, *New Education: The English Background, 1870–1914* (Melbourne: Pitman, 1968).

5 See O'Doherty, T. and O'Donoghue, T. *Radical Reform in Irish Schools, 1900–1922*, 6–7.

much a nineteenth-century concept in educational matters, where religion, humanism and politics were its driving forces. The core element of moral education was to protect against an emerging plurality of values in society.

And, Dr Starkie, the new Resident Commissioner, appointed at the time the results system had drawn to a close referred to it in forthright and unambiguous terms:

> The elaborate mosaic of sixpences and shillings ... which has made half a million of children in each year the drudges of the teachers, the teachers the drudges of the inspectors, and the inspectors the drudges of the Office ... and the rigidity of the procedure unavoidably resulted in that monotony and uniformity of training which has paralysed the intellects of a whole generation.[6]

The same inspectors had been at the centrality of the results regime, and many of them had found it difficult to cope, as they found it difficult to advise teachers on certain topic because they were spending most of their time 'examining'. They could no longer keep 'au courant' with advances in education, as the only free day they had in the week was Sunday.

Though the Payment by Results policy in Irish education had many shortcomings, as we have attested to, it had one important advantage. This was an advantage that did not favour the close participants, the pupils and teachers, but from the standpoint of administration, it enabled its operation to run smoothly year after year, that is, once a pattern had been developed. Those engaged in its operation at the coal face learned very quickly how to carry out rules and regulations associated with the scheme, and, as time passed by, it could be claimed that fulfilling these regulations became almost automatic. Following on from twenty years of working under the system, it must have seemed to some teachers that this was the given order in which the world operated. It must also have appeared to some if not many teachers that such a system could assume a permanence as if it were the only way by which education could be conducted.

6 Speech by Dr Starkie at Albert Model Farm, Glasnevin, Dublin. Reported in the *Daily Independent*, February 20, 1900.

## The Results Programme Endorsed

Throughout its period of existence in Ireland, Payment by Results, got, on occasions, one or two endorsements. One in particular must be mentioned. In March 1885, the Episcopal Committee on Education of the Catholic Archbishops and Bishops of Ireland sent a memorandum to the Lord Lieutenant of Ireland. Its terms were very specific and left no doubt in the mind of the Lord Lieutenant how forceful the hierarchy were, and how authoritative they felt they were regarding education in Ireland:

> …., the system established under the Board of National Education of paying teachers partly by salary and partly by results-fees, has contributed largely to the improvement of primary education in Ireland. After several years' experience of its operation the managers of schools are unanimous in stating:
>
> 1. That in regard to teachers it has acted as a powerful stimulus to their industry, has secured their more equal attention to the several classes of their schools, and has led to the adoption of better methods of teaching, as well as to a more considerate treatment of their pupils.
> 2. That in respect to pupils this system has contributed steadily to a large increase of their numbers and to greater regularity of attendance; it has also increased their application to study, by the anxiety it inspired for their own success and that of their teachers and schools; and,
> 3. That it has given managers of schools a livelier interest in the success both of teachers and of pupils, and to lead them to look more closely into the everyday working of their schools.

The Bishops would, therefore, view with extreme regret any change in the existing system of the remuneration of teachers. In furtherance of those views, and in anticipation of the new Treasury grants which are expected for National Schools, we beg to express to your Excellency our opinion, and at the same time to declare our earnest wish, that in the interest of primary education in Ireland those grants should be made by raising the scale of results fees.[7]

7 Memorandum in *Parliamentary Papers* H.C. 1884–1885, LXI, 449–450, 449.

One might well ask, from where did the bishops and managers derive their understanding in order to comment on 'better methods of teaching', as well as 'more considerate treatment of their pupils'.

Most teachers would have had reservations regarding the desirability of 'anxiety' as a motivating agency for children's application to study. Perhaps, it was true that managers 'looked' more closely into the conditions of their schools. However, judging by the conditions of these schools at the dawn of the twentieth century, it may have been more effective if they did more than just 'look'. The hierarchy went directly counter to the views of the INTO in urging that any increased grants for teachers' salaries should be given by way of results' payments.

## Teaching Conditions and Vere Foster

The school buildings were almost universally deprived of adequate teaching equipment and apparatus. Many teachers operated in school buildings which lacked basic amenities and adequate shelter. While school inspectors were doing their rounds during the course of a year they were expected to note the condition of the school building, and they were quite adept at highlighting the shortcomings on view. One such account comes from a school visit quite late during the era of Payment by Results:

> Manager is requested to reprimand the Principal and Assistant Teachers on the very discreditable condition into which the school has fallen. If a material improvement be not observed at next Results Examination the Principal Teacher will be depressed in classification and the Assistant fined.[8]

At the outset of payment by results there were 9,868 teachers working under the National Board, and of these, 3,461, or about 35 per cent, were trained.[9]

8 From Report of a Results Examination of Swinford Male National School, 24 January 1895, by Mr O' Riordan, District Inspector.

9 *Report of the Commissioners for the Year* 1871, 293.

Due to the lack of training for 35 per cent of the teaching force, the above table would indicate (among other factors) why the bulk of teachers worked within the lower half of the classification scale.

There was a dearth of philanthropists or benefactors who might come to the aid of procuring an infrastructure for Irish primary education in the absence of state intervention – the exception being Vere Foster. During the late 1850s and early 1860s, he had encountered many unsatisfactory buildings, on his travels throughout much of the country, in which there was meant to be sound education under way. Some schools appalled him:

> Two per cent of the schools are still, however, wretched hovels – structures under the roof of which it is lamentable to have to gather together as many children as constitute a school, the means of ventilation are so bad, the lighting so imperfect, and the earthen floors so damp and unhealthy.[10]

Foster was very taken aback with low standards of earthen floors, so much so, that between 1859 and 1863 he was in a position to supply wooden floors to 1,400 schools.[11] The Commissioners were thankful for his timely prescience, which resulted in hordes of children attending school for a variety of reasons:

> … the schools in cold and mountainous districts were, during the winter, crowded with children, who came for shelter and warmth if not for education. The want of turf pressed so heavily on the poor that even in the winter months the fire was out on many hearths.[12]

From early in the twentieth century, the Irish National Teachers' Organization drew attention to sorry state of school buildings. At each of the congresses in 1904, 1906, 1907 and 1908, there was a very conscious move to urge the government to realize the urgent need for serious attention in replacing many existing schools, and to introduce regular cleaning, heating and sanitary procedures.[13] Based on the descriptions provided by

10 See McNeill, *Vere Foster*, 112.
11 McNeill, *Vere Foster*, 119.
12 McNeill, *Vere Foster*, 118–119.
13 See S. Ó Buachalla, *Education Policy in Twentieth-Century Ireland*, 102.

delegates and presidential addresses, one speaker could not be accused of exaggeration when he claimed in 1908 that 'the ducks in St. Stephen's Green are better housed, better cared for and better looked after than the majority of children attending our national schools'.[14] Birrell's attempt at an accelerated building programme met with little success – funding for education matters was reduced during the years of the Great War, and closer to home, the political unrest during the period 1916–1923 ensured that any major building programmes or any serious infrastructure investment would have to wait until a new regime, in the form of a Free State government, with its new Department of Education established in 1924, many some inroads into advancing a programme of infrastructural development.

Throughout the period with Augustine Birrell as Chief Secretary we witness a genuine attempt by him at undertaking some level of education reform. Possibly, his greatest achievement was the passing of the Irish Universities' Act in 1908. This Act formed the basis for what was to become National University of Ireland. He also announced an injection of funds in the post-primary sector, 'to raise the status of secondary schools which can only be done by raising the present status of the teachers in these schools'.[15]

Many were hopeful with Birrell's appointment to Ireland. His reputation preceded him, and as one Irish Nationalist politician so eloquently expressed in an address to the Foxford Association of National Teachers. John Dillon said of the Chief Secretary, in the context of the 1906 Education Bill in England, as:

> … a great friend and a valuable ally … a great friend too of education, and whatever may be the difficulties which may yet have to be overcome in the work of redressing your grievances and putting Irish primary education on a satisfactory basis, these difficulties, I am convinced, will spring from the National Board and from the Treasury and not Mr. Birrell.[16]

14 Presidential Address, *The Irish School Weekly*, 25 April 1908. See Ó Buachalla, 102.

15 *The Irish Teachers' Journal*, no. 7 (1911), 97.

16 Quoted in J. McBride, *A Study of the Contribution of Chief Secretary Augustine Birrell to Primary and Post-Primary Education in Ireland*, 37–38.

*The Irish School Weekly* editorial was also quite enthusiastic about Birrell's appointment – 'there is no more pressing question in Ireland at the present moment than that of primary education, and the time and the man have arrived'.[17]

In 1870 the Powis Commission categorized as 'Good' the state of the roofs as 67.19 per cent of schools; the condition of the walls of 68.46 per cent; the windows in 65.38 per cent of schools, and the 'character and repair of the general fabric' in 61.69 per cent of the schools. These figures mean that 33 per cent of schools were described as 'Fair' or 'Bad'. Earthen floors were found in over half of the schools; over half had no pictorial charts; 392 schools were short of enough desks; 788 schools were without maps; 36.5 per cent of schools had no out-offices or toilets.[18]

During the results era the number of national schools increased greatly. Many complaints came forth from the teachers regarding the condition of schools.[19] The 1871 census showed a population of 5,412,377 for which the Powis Commission for the year 1867 found that there were 6,520 national schools. By 1901, the population had fallen to 4,458,775, but the number of schools had increased to 8,692 and increase of more than 2,000.[20]

The majority of these schools were one and two-teacher establishments, lacking in funds for their upkeep. The burden of upkeep rested with the local community, including the teacher or teachers. To that end, the Commissioners issued a strongly worded Circular to school managers in 1903. It paints a ghastly image:

> The Commissioners of National Education wish to direct the earnest and immediate attention of Managers generally to the extremely unsatisfactory condition of many of the National School-houses in regard to repair and cleanliness, and particularly to the disgraceful state of the out-offices, which in numerous instances have been reported to be in such a state of filth as to constitute a grave menace to the health of the children attending the schools in question. Broken and dilapidated doors and

17 See McBride, *A Study of the Contribution of Chief Secretary Augustine Birrell*, 38.

18 *Report of the Royal Commission of Inquiry into Primary Education* (Powis), H.C. 1870, xxviii, pt 1, 227–232.

19 *Irish Teachers' Journal* viii, no. 9, 129.

20 *Report of Mr Dale on Primary Education in Ireland*, H. C. 1904, XX, 984.

> windows are not calculated to make the schools attractive to the children; and in too many instances this a true picture of the defects to be found in the school-houses.[21]

Some schools were managed better than the ones addressed above, but it is difficult to avoid the ongoing declamatory remarks and reports that continually draw our attention to squalor, to the dreadful conditions, the grisly and grim circumstances under which teachers and pupils worked. We have encountered some forbidding, spectral, hideous and repellent scenes.

With appointment of a new Resident Commissioner in 1899, Dr Starkie was appalled at the conditions of schools. Such conditions continued for years following his appointment, and in a comment he made, it seems that he understood, at least, how intimidating and uninspiring it was to work under such frightful conditions:

> I spend a couple of months every year in inspecting schools, and really I am ashamed of my country when I see the abominable state of filth and degradation in which our children are brought up.[22]

Patrick Keenan, who was largely responsible for introducing the scheme to Ireland, lost very little of his enthusiasm for payment by results with the passage of time. In his evidence to the Cross Commission (1886–1888) in England he outlined his views about the scheme:

> It works admirably. It stimulates the teacher enormously, and it has produced a most wonderful improvement in the proficiency of the children .... The character of the instruction of the results fee scheme has enormously improved both in range and character.[23]

Despite such affirmations and apparent consolidation for the results scheme, the following decade witnessed certain influences and tendencies

21 *Circular to Managers of National Schools* (Dublin: Office of Education, May 1903).

22 Dr Starkie, *The History of Primary and Secondary Education in Ireland* (Address delivered 3 July 1911), np.

23 *Royal Commission on Elementary Education*, 1887–1888, H.C. 1887; XXX, Keenan's Evidence, 413–430, 424/6.

which brought about a process which ultimately led to the scheme's abolition.

The Cross Commission, in its 1888 report, could not make up its mind about abolition or retention in England. It did suggest, however, that the system should be mitigated and that teachers should be protected by paying the larger part of the grant in the form of fixed salaries.[24] Some other changes were introduced in England: From 1890, the Codes were changed. In the Code of that year a fixed grant on average attendance was introduced, examination was to be by sample, and not less than one-third of the pupils were to be individually examined.[25] The year 1897 was the last year of payment by results in English elementary schools.[26] It is very likely that Ireland was influenced by events in England in the 1890s as she had been by events in England in the 1860s.

By way of summation, the results fees were paid to the teacher through the manager, the results fees on an annual basis and the salaries on a quarterly basis. Teachers often complained about the dire exigencies they suffered, including the difficulty they had getting credit from local shopkeepers, due to this form of remuneration. And, at that, payments were not always forthcoming on time, as *The Teachers' Journal* recorded:

> Hundreds of letters come to our hands in which these poor men – weary and fagged after the labors [sic] of the school, describe the repeated journeys they have to make to their manager's abode, often five, ten, or more miles distant from their own, before they succeed in getting their paltry pittance, the date of its arrival being utterly uncertain.[27]

The INTO sought monthly, rather than quarterly salary payments for teachers, but to no avail.[28] The teachers had a long wait before their salaries were paid monthly, in 1918.

24 M. Sturt, *The Education of the People*, 373.
25 Balfour, *The Educational Systems of Great Britain and Ireland*, 38.
26 Balfour, *The Educational Systems of Great Britain and Ireland*, 38.
27 *Irish Teachers' Journal* VI, no. 26 (1875), 316.
28 *Irish Teachers' Journal*, 333 and 351. See T. J. O'Connell, *100 Years of Progress: The Story of the Irish National Teachers Organisation 1868–1968* (Dublin: Irish national Teachers' Organisation, 1968), 147–154.

During the results era, the lot of the Irish primary teacher was not a happy one. Their monetary reward was haphazard and poor. Allied to that, many teachers were not suited to the classroom, and a large number of factors militated against their effective and efficient performance as pedagogues. One of the main problems was poor pupil attendance, and they got no help concerning compulsory school attendance. Poor school attendance mitigated against optimum results fees, resulting in a subsistence standard of living for the teacher. Many aspects of the social and economic environment had deleterious effects on the teacher's work.

In England, socialist thinkers were attacking the nature of education available for working-class children alluding to its class basis of its structure and content. One particular victim of this assault was Payment by Results and Brian Simon includes the following denunciation of it by a socialist, one H. W. Hobart:

> Week by week, month by month in the most barren and sterile ground #, the teacher has to hammer and drive the course of education laid down by law. The children are urged, persuaded, and coaxed into trying to become efficient for the so-called examinations.[29]

Socialist thinking was seeking reform to enable education match the requirements of working-class children. It was hoped that this reform would facilitate these children to realize their full potential within the full range of their human possibilities. Advocates of this reform felt that the existing nature of Payment by Results militated against this achievement.

## The 1890s

The 1890s decade proved to be a maelstrom of educational thought and concern. Ireland formed part of this British and European movement. Even during the period of the results programme, there were indications

29 Simon, *Education and the Labour Movement 1870–1920*, 146.

within the powers that be, such as the Commissioners of Education, that alternative choices were essential for the general benefit of a greater number of people. One such measure was the Commissioners' introduction of an Industrial Programme for Girls in 1889. Coupled with that was a number of initiatives endeavouring to introduce extra subjects such as drawing. However, in 1897 it was bemoaned: 'In Drawing, progress is apparent, but too slow for what we deem to be the requirements of the country.'[30] Nevertheless the Commissioners hesitated and did not make such subjects compulsory contenting themselves with advice such as:

> We are fully alive to the importance of these subjects as part of the course of instruction in all National Schools, and we are of opinion that teachers should not be content with their work so long as they fail to include these subjects in their ordinary curriculum.[31]

While very little or no action was taken at this particular juncture, the Commissioners gave the impression that they were aware of the need to give the curriculum a more technical or industrial dimension. Perhaps, a further comment by the Commissioners in 1897 may encapsulate succinctly what precisely they had in mind:

> … we are only groping, and may in time discover a perfect system when the pupil will be taught what is useful and interesting during his school career, and will not look back on his school days as time wasted.[32]

This statement expresses a very common-sense approach, and laudable in its realistic objectives.

During the last decade of the century, and while under the results system, some extra subjects found their way onto the curriculum. The number of schools embracing these subjects increased over the decade. The subjects included: Kindergarten; Domestic Economy for Girls; Sewing and Dressmaking; Cookery; management of Poultry; Dairy Management;

30 *Sixty-Fourth Report of the Commissioners*, for 1897, 217.

31 *Sixty-Fourth Report of the Commissioners*, 217. It was suggested that along with Drawing, Craft-work and Music should be added.

32 *Sixty-Fourth of the Commissioners for the Year 1897*, 217.

Handicraft; Weaving; Hygiene; Net-Making; Algebra; Magnetism and Electricity; Physiology; Light and Sound; Geography; Botany; French; Irish; Latin; Greek; Bee-keeping; Shorthand; Typewriting; Laundry Work; and Wool-spinning.[33] This is not an exhaustive list. The most popular subjects were Kindergarten; Vocal Music; Drawing and Algebra.

The 1890s witnessed a body of opinion, exclusive of the Commissioners and teachers, that sought changes in the school programme which would lend itself to embracing a wider corpus of subjects, and which would allow for more freedom and elasticity in teaching methodologies. There was a particular concern regarding the academic or 'bookish' nature of the curriculum under Payment by Results. In such circumstances important areas such as the child's experience or mode of expression were ignored. Dr Patrick Weston Joyce, writing in 1892 had the following comment to make:

> It is now generally admitted that the education given in our schools is too exclusively intellectual, too bookish. It is too much an education of words; too little an education of things.[34]

And, furthermore, he elaborated:

> Manual instruction should be placed among the ordinary branches in the programme of every school and all children, boys and girls, from infancy upwards, should be taught in schools to use their hands at some sort of work.[35]

In March 1896 Archbishop Walsh, a member of the National Board, convinced his fellow board members to pass a resolution requesting from the Lord Lieutenant a Commission to enquire into the subject of manual and practical instruction for primary schools.[36] On 25 January 1897, the Lord Lieutenant appointed a commission of fourteen members, ten of whom were Commissioners of National Education.[37] This Commission

33 *Sixty-Sixth Report of the Commissioners*, 222.

34 P. W. Joyce, *The Teaching of Manual Work in Schools* (Dublin: Gill, 1892), 3.

35 Joyce, *Teaching of manual Work*, 5.

36 *Vice-Regal Committee of Inquiry into Primary Education (Ireland)* 1913, Final Report, 4, (Cd 7235), H.C. 1914, xxviii.

37 We must not forget that the commissioners of national education were all amateurs.

undertook extensive inquiries into primary education, both at home and internationally. Their Final Report, popularly known from its first chairman, as the Belmore Commission, was signed on 25 June 1898.

The phrase 'manual and practical' instruction was interpreted by the Commission, as embracing all subjects other than literary subjects and arithmetic. The findings of the Commission were therefore not limited to what would, today, be strictly defined as manual and practical instruction.

The First Report was published on 26 February 1897, one month following the Commission's inauguration, and the Second Report appeared on 5 July, in the same year. Both of these reports contained transcripts of evidence from educationalists in Ireland, England and Scotland. The Third Report was submitted on 31 July 1897,[38] and included a special report on a visit to Sweden by three of the Commissioners, the Earl of Belmore, Rev. Dr Evans and Mr Struthers. The Final Report was issued on 25 June 1898. This report indicated that in all, ninety-three meeting had been held; that evidence had been taken from one hundred and eighty-six persons, and that one hundred and nineteen schools had been visited. Four assistants, Purser, Rolleston, Wyse and Hughes-Dowling travelled to Germany, France, Switzerland and Holland, seeking information on foreign practice. Prof. Fitzgerald visited the United States and inspected primary schools there, and acquired further information on Schools in America from the United States Bureau of Education.[39]

The witnesses were chosen from specific areas within the field of education. These included members of the Board's Inspectorate, Training College Staff, representatives of the Technical Education Association, the Irish National Trades' Association, as well as teachers, both in Ireland and abroad.[40]

38 Due cognizance needs to be observed of the Earl of Belmore's efficiency and expediency in ensuring the publication of all three reports in such a timely manner.

39 *Commission on Manual and Practical Instruction in Primary Schools under the Board of National Education in Ireland, Final Report*, 1.

40 See Maura O' Connor, *The Development of Infant Education in Ireland from 1881–1948* (Unpublished M.Ed., thesis submitted to Trinity College, Dublin, 1984), 106–108.

The Final Report suggested that Kindergarten and Froebelian spirit behind it ought to inspire the work of the school. Drawing, Singing, Drill and Physical Exercises should be obligatory in all schools. There was a strong recommendation that elementary science should be introduced as a subject and be made obligatory 'as soon as teachers can be trained to give it'. Needlework was to continue for girls while Cookery, Laundry and Domestic Science should be taught to girls 'as far as may be found practicable'.[41]

The Commission was opposed to the awarding of results fees for the subjects it proposed, thus pre-empting the decision to abandon the results system in 1900. The Report stated:

> While it should be open to the Inspector to examine individual pupils, we think that the grants awarded to the teacher, in these subjects, should largely depend on the general evidence of his own zeal and industry, on the efficiency of his method of teaching, and on his power to arrest and hold the attention of his class.[42]

This change was to have important repercussions for the traditional method of inspection. Later, the inspector was instructed to assess the 'tone' of the school rather than specific tests of information retained. This was another nail in the coffin for Payment by Results. In fact, the entire 'tone' of the Belmore Report smacks of nothing to do with assessing how much information a child retains. And, the word 'information' is used rather than 'knowledge', knowledge being information that is internalized by the pupil so that it becomes meaningful to him or to her. Information is what was decried by nineteenth-century writers like Coleridge, and especially Dickens.

The Commission went further in its Report:

> The new system of national education modified as we propose would give an all-round training to the faculties of the children, and would thus lay a solid foundation for any system of higher education – literary, scientific or technical – which might afterwards be found suitable to their talents and circumstances.[43]

41 *Vice-Regal Committee of Inquiry into Primary Education* (Ireland), 9–10, 45.

42 *Vice-Regal Committee of Inquiry into Primary Education (Ireland)*, 10.

43 *Vice-Regal Committee of Inquiry into Primary Education* (Ireland), 6.

This view was in advance of that hitherto prevailing which saw the school mainly as a training ground for literacy. We need to bear in mind that prospects of completing primary education were remote for many pupils, not to mention intermediate or higher education. Nevertheless, the thinking behind the Belmore Commission on primary education were in line with what was being planned at intermediate level at the time, and which aimed at breaking the dominance of the academic, literary curriculum into more diverse patterns termed the classical, scientific, mathematical and commercial.

There is very little doubt that the national schools were highly instrumental in the reduction of illiteracy in the English language in the nineteenth century. The Table below reveals the pattern of this change from the first reliable census, 1841. Accepting the figures at face value and rounding the percentages for the sake of convenience it reads:

Table 9. Literacy trends in Ireland in 1841–1901 in Percentage terms of the Population over five years

| | 1841 | 1851 | 1861 | 1871 | 1881 | 1891 | 1901 |
|---|---|---|---|---|---|---|---|
| Those who could | 28 | 33 | 41 | 49 | 59 | 71 | 79 |
| Read and Write | | | | | | | |
| Able to Read only | 19 | 20 | 20 | 17 | 16 | 11 | 7 |
| Could neither Read | | | | | | | |
| Nor Write | 53 | 47 | 39 | 33 | 25 | 18 | 14 |

*Source:* Census of Population 1901, p. 571.

(Comment: It can be seen from this Table that by the end of the century there were only 14 per cent of the population over five unable to read or write. This was quite a remarkable achievement when one considers the social conditions, the school buildings condition and the fact that so many teachers had no training. When one examines the pattern of the decline in illiteracy, one notices that from 1841 to 1871, the year of the introduction of payment by results, the decline was just 20 per cent, while the rate between the years 1871 to 1901, another thirty-year span, was 19 per cent).

It also mirrored the thinking behind the setting up of the Department of Agriculture and Technical Instruction (DATI) in 1899 and the aspirational aim for a more technical orientation in education courses.

The Report was considered by the Commissioners of National Education, and approved by them in February 1899.[44]

The Report of the Commission displays an inordinate influence from the thinking involved in the New Education Movement. The ideas of Froebel, Pestalozzi and the 'practical educationists' clearly affected the Report's recommendations. There was a move away from 'that exclusive, or almost exclusive devotion to the three Rs' which prevailed in the results system to a radically different concept of the curriculum and school life. The Report stood firmly behind the value of manual and practical instruction.

An analysis of the evidence submitted by the various witnesses to the Commission, offers a clear interpretation of the thinking of educationalists of the day on the matter of manual instruction in general, and Kindergarten practice in particular. The evidence as it related to Kindergarten may be discussed under titles such as the following: the existence, organization and examination of Kindergarten in the primary schools; the aims and objectives of the training college curriculum; the obstacles to the spread of the Kindergarten philosophy; and the advice tendered on Kindergarten teaching abroad. Of the one hundred and seventy-four female candidates who passed their examination in the training colleges in 1896, only sixty-three were awarded Certificates of Proficiency in Kindergarten.[45] The examiners noted that the students' knowledge of Kindergarten was acquired from textbooks.[46]

The Revised Programme for Training Colleges which was operative for the examinations of 1897 listed Kindergarten and a knowledge of Froebelian theory as part of the Theory of Method programme. Despite the dissatisfaction expressed by the examiners at the lack of knowledge displayed by the Queen's Scholars of practical implications of the Froebelian system, the Theory of Method for female students set out in 1896 the following two

44 *Minutes of the Commissioners of National Education*, Ms. 5573 (NLI), 8.

45 *Commission on Manual and Practical Instruction, First Report*, 12.

46 *Sixty-Third Report of the Commissioners of National Education in Ireland for 1896*, Appendix, Section III, XIII, 259.

questions pertaining to Froebelian theories for candidates in the Second Division of First and Second Class:

> 1. Describe the fourth Kindergarten gift; point out its relation to the third, and the manner of using it.
> 2. What are the universal properties of things to which the law of contracts and their connecting links refer? Explain what Froebel meant by these terms.[47]

The structure of these questions indicates that factual answers were sought after, and the answers were expected to be focused and precise. Little scope was allowed for discussion, analysis or evaluation on the part of the student.

This type of examination paper was denounced by Professor Thomas H. Teegan, Principal of Marlborough Street Training College in 1897. He was particularly concerned that Kindergarten had 'to be learned from a book …, in order to suit the purpose of the examination'.[48]

Considering all the troubles, all the divisions over religion or secularism, the national system of education in Ireland closed the century with buoyant anticipation. This tone was sounded by the Commission on Manual and Practical Instruction (known popularly as the Belmore Commission) in national schools, and other primary schools. In fact, the Commission could have been referred to as the Walsh Commission, as Archbishop Walsh was mainly responsible for its creation.[49]

The Report, in its finer detail, recommended that Kindergarten be extended to all schools, where possible, and that in infants and first class cardboard work, clay-modelling and similar exercises be introduced. Elementary Science should also form part of the daily life of national schools.

47 *Sixty-Fourth report of the Commissioners of National Education in Ireland for 1897*, Appendix, Section III, XV, 188.

48 *Commission on Manual and Practical Instruction, Fourth Volume of minutes of evidence being a supplement to the Final Report of the Commissioners* (C.8924), H.C. 1898, XLIV, 342–350.

49 See Akenson, *The Irish Education Experiment*, 372.

The Belmore Commission, in its final *Report* from 1898 gave a considered assessment of the results programme:

> The present system which consists largely in the study of books is one-sided in character and it leaves some of the most useful faculties of the mind absolutely untrained.[50]

Some key concerns were emerging at the end of the nineteenth century; there was a desire for more balanced curriculum – practical and theoretical-practical education had been largely abandoned by the system of Payment by Results, in favour of a strong emphasis on academia. True, extra subject were introduced from time to time, but the application of these was not universal. There was also a growing mission in the minds of many to have a more technical design on the school curriculum which would, in turn, aid in the industrial development of the country.[51]

The Belmore Commission, in its fastidious endeavours, was responsible for two major changes in Irish education. There was a complete revision of the school curriculum at primary level, and even more noteworthy the results programmed was abandoned.

The commission took this concern on board:

> A strong desire exists throughout this country, and it is growing stronger every day, for the introduction of a general system of Technical Education.[52]

Certain key individuals on the Commission for National Education, namely, Archbishop Walsh, Lord Chief Baron Palles and Professor Fitzgerald, had become convinced that a radical change in the national school curriculum was necessary.[53]

50 *Commission on Manual and Practical Instruction in Primary Schools, Final Report*, 10, (C.8923) H.C. 1898, XLIV.

51 See J. Comerton, 'A Plea for Reform in Irish Education', *New Ireland Review* 11 (January 1895), 706–719; G. T. P. 'Manual Training and Technical Instruction in Ireland', *New Ireland Review* XII (February 1900), 171–187; F. Gorman, 'Practical Education in National Schools', *New Ireland Review*, 350–357; E. Hogg and A. D. Innes, 'Irish Elementary Education', *Contemporary Review* 73 (April 1898), 564–581.

52 *Commission on Manual and Practical Instruction, Final Report*, 12.

53 See Akenson, *The Irish Education Experiment*, 372–373.

Meanwhile, Horace Plunkett and his co-operative movement were making strides in the fields of agriculture and technical instruction. In 1899 the Agriculture and Technical Instruction Act created a Department, with Plunkett as Vice-President, and this department took responsibility for technical instruction.

In 1894 the Irish Agricultural Organisation Society had been formed. This Society forged ahead with the improvement of conditions of the agricultural population of Ireland. It set about teaching the principles and methods of co-operation as applicable to farming and associated industries; it endeavoured to promote industrial organization for any purposes which may appear to be beneficial; and to counsel and advise those engaged in agricultural pursuits. Co-operative development was the key element of the IAOS. By 1900, there were 237 Dairy Co-operative Societies, and by 1903 the number had reached 800, with almost 200 agricultural banks, 50 home industries societies and 40 poultry societies.

Organized self-help was the cornerstone of the Society's philosophy. As the number of local co-operatives grew, the complexion of rural life assumed a confident glow reflected in recreational pursuits of the people, and in the setting up of facilities such as village libraries. The success of this Society, it could be claimed, led to the founding of other organizations, such as Young Farmers' Movement and Muintir na Tíre.

Throughout the period in question, it was hoped that a reformed primary school sector would help prepare pupils to engage in formal technical instruction later. Other organizations were adept at establishing their own network of classes. In particular, the Congested Districts Board, which was established in 1891, encouraged crafts such as lace-making, knitting, weaving, net-making, and so on. This was taking place in the congested districts along the western seaboard. It should be noted that the subjects mentioned above were also part of extra curriculum in the primary schools.[54]

A visitor to early twentieth-century Ireland, Paul Dubois, Belgian artist, was scathing in his criticism of the education system of the period. He wrote:

54 Joseph Lee, *The Modernisation of Irish Society, 1848–1918* (Dublin: Gill, 1973), 123–124.

> How shall I describe the public education of Ireland? A university system which is anti-national and practically closed to Catholics; a bad primary and worse secondary system; no single central and competent authority, but independent 'Boards' of irresponsible amateurs; an education which forms neither intellect nor character; a programme of instruction almost entirely mechanical and for examination purposes, and denuded on principle of everything that would make for nationality; and finally, a public opinion that manifests but little zeal and little competence in educational matters.[55]

While Dubois was on a visit to Ireland, the New Education Movement, as well as incorporating theorists who sought more practical work with a view to industrial pursuits, was also influenced, and perhaps, urged, by the educational ideas of the likes of Froebel and Pestalozzi. Froebel's *The School, an Essay towards Humane Education* was translated by M. Herford, and published in 1889, and M. J. Lyschinska's *The Kindergarten Principle: Its Educational Value and Chief Applications* (1893) greatly aided in spreading an awareness of Froebel's ideas. Lawrence, in her work on the Froebel movement, states that by the period 1893–1895, knowledge of Froebel and his attitudes towards education had spread widely in England.[56]

Coupled with the interest engendered in the infant school for kindergarten was a concern for manual training for older children. Pestalozzi's ideas in this regard had gained wide currency in England by this time.[57]

Another important publication was that of Otto Solomon's *The Theory of Educational Slojd*[58] in England in 1893, which gave a strong impetus to hand and eye training. Evelyn Lawrence states:

> .... The idea of hand and eye training by graded woodwork became popular in the last decade of the century, leading to the introduction of other forms of handwork

55 Paul Du Bois, *Contemporary Ireland* (Dublin: Maunsel and Co., 1908), 59.

56 Evelyn Lawrence, *Frederick Froebel and English Education* (London: London University Press, 1952), 41.

57 See F. H. Hayward, *The Educational Ideas of Froebel and Pestalozzi* (London: Ralph Holland, 1904), 27.

58 Slöjd: In Swedish elementary schools, students between the ages of nine and fifteen, have classes in Slöjd. In most schools, the course is divided into two parts: soft materials (textiles) and hard materials (Woodwork and metalwork).

> in schools for older children. It may be said that it was due to Slöjd Association of Great Britain and Ireland[59] that manual training received definite recognition in the upper standards.[60]

One of the champions of the new trends in England was Sir Joshua Fitch. He admired the new subjects because they allowed children express themselves in many and varied ways. Children's talents, from a wide spectrum, could now be developed. Fitch's comment elucidates further:

> But after all, language is not the only instrument of expression. There are many other ways in which thought can find utterance .... It may take the forms of delineation, of modelling, of design, of invention, of product of the skilled hand, the physical powers, or the finer sense .... Drawing, representation, construction and decorative work are educational processes, as real and vital as reading and writing. They touch, as nearly, the springs of all that is best in human character.[61]

Another exponent of the ideas of Frobel and Pestalozzi was Sir Michael Sadler who wrote of 'the formative and penetrating' effect of German educational ideas on the school system of England towards the end of the nineteenth century, and particularly stressed the influence of Froebel and Fichte.[62]

With Paul Dubois' comments in mind regarding the educational scene in Ireland in the early twentieth century, it is timely to place his observations against the appointment of Augustine Birrell as Chief Secretary for Ireland in early 1907, when education in Ireland was undergoing an unprecedented state of activity and regeneration. Cultural nationalism was at the forefront of a popular surge to claw back the years and revitalize the country as a bastion of Irishness and cast aside the imperial yoke. The Gaelic League, in particular, saw the imperial ethos of the school system as anathema, a total negation of national identity, with the re-organization of the system along

59 Founded in 1888.

60 Lawrence, *Froebel and English Education*, 74.

61 Sir Joshua Fitch, *Educational Aims and Methods* (Cambridge: Cambridge University Press, 1900), 147–176, in particular, 164–166.

62 Sir Michael Sadler, 'The History of Education', in J. H. Rose, ed., *Germany in the Nineteenth Century* (Manchester: Manchester University Press, 1912), 101–127, 124.

Irish lines as the very *raison d'etre* of its existence.[63] The League's aspirations encompassed much more than the inclusion of the Irish language in the school curriculum.[64] Through its mouthpiece, *An Claidheamh Solais* (The Sword of Light), the League promoted educational issues, from infancy to university level. This had a wide readership.[65] This cultural emphasis was underway while there was a war in South Africa, and while the average Irish person knew little and probably cared less about Kruger and Rhodes, it was a different story on the other side of the Irish Sea, and indeed among the Unionist population in Ireland.

The new programme would be expensive to implement: materials and equipment would have to be procured, at the expense of the Treasury; teachers would have to undergo in-service training, and many organizers would have to be employed to undertake such training. The indifference of the Treasury with regard to reform of Irish education, coupled with the concerted intransigence of the Catholic Church, did not bode well for any serious reconstruction of primary education in Ireland.

The new century also coincided with the death of Queen Victoria, and the removal of the familiar mother figure produced a sense of unease and a realization that the twentieth century was going to be very different from the nineteenth.[66]

As far as Ireland was concerned, an 'intimate' working relationship had developed between the Liberals and the Nationalists, led by John Redmond, and the Gladstonians who had a traditional commitment to Home Rule for Ireland. Therefore, there was some hope of some type of political settlement for Ireland. The Liberal leader, Henry Campbell-Bannerman, had stated in 1905:

63 Joseph McBride, *A Study of the Contribution of Chief Secretary Augustine Birrell to Primary and Post-Primary Education in Ireland, 1907–1916* (Unpublished M. Ed., Thesis, presented to the Education Depart at Maynooth College, 1997), 18–19.

64 Seán Ó Tuama, ed., *The Gaelic League Idea* (Cork: Mercier Press, 1972).

65 See S. Ó Buachalla, 'An Claidheamh Soluis', 1903–1909. 'An Piarsach mar Oideachasóir', *Feasta xxxix*, 5, 7 (1976).

66 See McBride, *A Study of the Contribution of Chief Secretary Augustine Birrell*, 6.

If I were asked for advice by an ardent Irish Nationalist I would say "Your desire is as mine is to see the effective management of Irish affairs in the hands of a representative Irish Parliament." Perhaps, C B was courting a future potential ally! However, in the election soon after an unprecedented Liberal landslide neutralized the bargaining power of the eighty-three Nationalists, their hopes of holding the balance of power unrealized.[67]

## Augustine Birrell as Chief Secretary

The Chief Secretary for Ireland was a key political office in the British administration in Ireland. Nominally subordinate to the Lord Lieutenant, and officially the 'Chief Secretary to the Lord Lieutenant' from the early nineteenth century until the end of British rule he was effectively the government minister with responsibility for governing Ireland, roughly equivalent to the role of a Secretary of State, such as the similar role of Secretary of State for Scotland. Usually it was the Chief Secretary, rather than the Lord Lieutenant, who sat in the British Cabinet. The Chief Secretary was *ex officio* President of the Local Government Board for Ireland from its creation in 1872.

James Bryce preceded Augustine Birrell as Chief Secretary, and very few regretted Bryce's departure from the post, particularly within the education sphere. He was viewed as a person who spoke a lot about getting policy enacted, but, more often than not, his words were rarely, if ever, matched by action. He seemed to be a man who was indifferent to his responsibilities. However, T. J. O'Connell sees a slightly different Bryce in his account in *100 Years of Progress: The Story of the Irish National Teachers' Organisation 1868–1968* when he outlines his interpretation of the Chief Secretary. In this account, there is a token semblance of hope for the departing Chief Secretary:

During his short period of office he displayed some interest in the question of university education and had made known his views on the solution of that problem, which

67 See McBride, *A Study of the Contribution of Chief Secretary Augustine Birrell*, 8.

> was a burning one at the time. But his coming made little impact on the fortunes of the national teachers. He was lavish of promises which he was either unwilling or unable to implement. When questioned in Parliament concerning Irish educational administration, he was content to supply the answers prepared for him by the Education Office in Dublin, whose actions and attitude he was rather too ready to explain and defend. No section of the Irish community, least of all the teachers, regretted his departure.[68]

Following his departure from Ireland, Bryce took up a post as Ambassador to the United States from 1907 to 1913. He had relatively more success in that post. Bryce was an academic and historian, and he was much travelled Viscount. Perhaps, had he been in the position of Chief Secretary for more than fifteen or sixteen months, he may have made an impression on the landscape of Irish education.

Augustine Birrell (19 January 1850 – 20 November 1933) was a British Liberal Party politician, who was Chief Secretary for Ireland from 1907 to 1916. In this post, he was praised for enabling tenant farmers to own their property, and for extending university education for Catholics. But he was criticized for failing to take action against the rebels before the Easter Rising, and resigned. A barrister by training, he was also an author, noted for humorous essays. Birrell's appointment as Chief Secretary introduced a person who contrasted overwhelmingly with his predecessor, as a reformer, and with his recent experience in England as President of the Board of Education, expectations ran very high that here was a person who would bring energy and hope to nearly all levels of education in Ireland. One of his political opponents in England went so far as to sidestep political infighting and offer some adulatory praise for his erstwhile opponent:

> I suppose the transition from the Board of Education is a promotion, and if it is, no man has it more than the Right Honourable Gentleman.[69]

Soon after his arrival in Ireland, he realized that the ghost of Bryce still lingered in the halls of administration. His predecessor's false promises,

68 O'Connell, *100 Years of Progress*, 155.
69 *Parliamentary Debates*, IV CLXIX, 22 January 1907, 72.

coupled with insincerity and deviousness, and one newspaper continued with the ghostly metaphor:

> The new Chief Secretary is haunted by the shadow of Mr. Bryce. At Question Time today, Mr. Birrell, with a tone of utter dreariness declared himself to be 'greatly embarrassed by pledges and promises given by his predecessor'.[70]

Upon his appointment to the post, Birrell expressed some sympathy with the plight of teachers, at both primary and post-primary levels. On one such occasion, while speaking at the Irish National Teachers' Organization congress 1907, he secured the immediate support of the teachers by declaring them to be 'the victims of a bad system' and assured them that their salary scales were meagre and insufficient. The following year proved him to be true to his word when he secured an increase for all primary teachers. This was the only increase in income between 1900 and 1920.[71]

Joseph McBride believes that the appointment of Augustine Birrell as Chief Secretary for Ireland was the announcement of a man who brought with him to the post a certain cautious and consultative approach to his work.[72]

The *Irish School Weekly* was very hopeful that reform in Irish education would take onboard a different hue than had been the case before Birrell's arrival:

> If any person is likely to carry out a thorough reform in Irish education and to make the lot of the teacher a happier and more desirable one all round, we honestly think it is Mr. Birrell.[73]

And, it was not for the want of effort in engaging with the relevant stakeholders that Birrell did not fully realize the full potential of his endeavours. One of the principal stakeholders was the Irish National Teachers'

70 *Irish Times*, 27 February 1907. Quoted in McBride, *A Study of the Contribution of Chief Secretary Augustine Birrell*, 48.
71 See Ó Buachalla, *Education Policy in Twentieth-Century Ireland*, 92.
72 See McBride, *A Study of the Contribution of Chief Secretary Augustine Birrell*, 9.
73 *Irish School Weekly*, 9 March 1907, 145.

Organisation (INTO), and in February 1907, he met with their delegation in the House of Commons. At this meeting, he

> ... listened with close attention, frequently interposed with a query which indicated his keen interest in the subject. He took copious notes of all the points submitted to him, and seemed to be impressed by many of them.[74]

Resulting from this meeting was an invitation to Mr Birrell to attend the annual INTO Congress the following month in Dublin. His speech was carried in the *Irish School Weekly*, and in the Irish daily press. It was reported that the Chief Secretary promised to return with 'full hands'. Two weeks following his speech in Dublin, Mr Asquith, the Chancellor of the Exchequer made his budget speech, and though there was a surplus available, none of this found its way across the Irish Sea and into the coffers of the Education fund. In fact, there was only one mention of Irish education by Asquith, and that referred to the Irish development grant, 'which was intended to serve the purpose of Irish education' but, instead was used to buy out some Irish landlords. This reference by the Chancellor was no doubt intended to discourage any Irish M.P.s who might consider the claims of Irish teachers more deserving than those of the Irish landlords, as well as to make it clear that the previous Government was responsible for it.[75]

With nothing in the coffers for Irish education, though England (£200,000) and Scotland (£500,000) benefited handsomely from the Westminster largesse, the INTO still persisted with claims for Irish teachers. In November of 1907 they submitted a claim amounting to £500,000.[76] The Commissioners replied with some unacceptable proposals. Other than that nothing happened.

It was well-known that a tight-fisted Treasury would not accede to the teachers' claim of half-million. Rumour had it that the first offer made to Mr Birrell was £50,000, that later it was raised to £75,000. It would appear that this was the Treasury's final offer. However, due to pressure from the

74 *Irish School Weekly*, 2 March 1907, 124.

75 See O'Connell, *100 Years of Progress*, 159.

76 *Irish School Weekly*, 14 December 1907, 540.

teachers and by the Chief Secretary, along with some Irish M.P.s, the Birrell Grant, as it was known, increased to £114,000. It was a far cry from the amount requested by the teachers. Coincidentally. The Irish Universities Bill was going through Parliament, and this was used an excuse for Treasury niggardliness. Allied to that, was the method of distribution – the Treasury announced that the monies to be allocated would be based on average attendance, position or grade of the teacher, and not by capitation or bonus. This was the method used to distribute the Birrell Grant.

Soon after Birrell's appointment as Chief Secretary he introduced the Irish Council Bill to Parliament. The Bill was drafted by Anthony MacDonald, under-secretary, and would be composed of 82 elected members and 24 nominated members. The Bill proposed to amalgamate eight of the forty-five boards and put them under the control of the council.[77] The Council was an administrative body without legislative powers. The boards to be amalgamated included the national board, the intermediate board and the department of agriculture and technical instruction. The Council would receive an annual grant from the Treasury and distribute the monies in line with services rendered.

William Martin Murphy, owner of the *Irish Independent*, launched a campaign against the Bill; Tim Healy, who kept a watchful eye on issues at Westminster on behalf of the Irish Catholic hierarchy, said it was the meanest measure ever submitted to Parliament; Dr Foley, the hierarchy's representative on the national board condemned the Bill.

The Catholic hierarchy objected to the Bill on the grounds that it was the long-awaited education reform bill. Cardinal Logue described the Bill as 'ludicrously disappointing ... and in some of its provisions mischievous'.[78] Logue went further in his condemnation of the Bill, warning 'the Irish party not to support the Bill and stated that "any politician who will try to secure its acceptance at the forthcoming convention will incur grave suspicion of endeavouring to deceive his countrymen in the interests of the ministry"'.[79]

77 Hyland and Milne, eds, *Irish Educational Documents*, vol. 1, 168–169.

78 See Hyland and Milne, eds, *Irish Educational Documents*, 169.

79 Quoted in Hyland and Milne, eds, *Irish Educational Documents*, 169.

Following a proposal by John Redmond at the Irish party convention in May 1907 the Bill was rejected unanimously, and later withdrawn.

The debate surrounding the Irish Council Bill of 1907 simply brings to the surface the power of the Catholic hierarchy. Education was their fiefdom, and they were adamant that no secular authority would upset that cosy relationship. This was an opportunity in 1907 to introduce educational reform, which was sorely needed, to Ireland. Alas, the opportunity was lost amidst clerical and political infighting and disagreement. This was not the first time, nor the last, that the Catholic hierarchy interfered in educational affairs because of their own self-interests and the detriment of the greater good.

## New Education Movement

The period coming into the twentieth century gave rise the emergence of many different components of thought, but all focused and united in opposition to the 'instrumentary' education as espoused by the Payment by Results system. In Ireland, the group most associated with this movement were, what Selleck defined as 'practical educationalists'.[80] Perhaps, one or two quotations from 'practical' educationists may help elucidate what they meant by 'practical'. H. T. Mark stated:

> Historically, the phrase 'the new education' has attached itself to the deliverance of pupil and teacher from the excessive bondage to books, and to learning from books, which characterised the 'old education', and a direction of their attention towards the world in which they live, as the natural arena for the exercise of the child's intelligence.[81]

Another commentator on the new direction for education was Mr Philip Magnus. He was very much a proponent of what was in an embryonic

80 R. J. W. Selleck, *The New Education* (New Jersey: Pitman Publishing, 1968), 102–151.

81 Quoted in Selleck, *The New Education*, 103.

state, but he serves to delineate more specifically the trend which the new movement wished to introduce:

> For many years I have regarded manual training as the basis of the new education, the essential principle that would modernise our methods of instruction.[82]

Of greatest concern to the new educationists were subjects such as manual training, science, nature study and physical education or training.[83] This type of thinking emerged at a time when Britain was losing its position of industrial pre-eminence to other countries like Germany and the United States. For this reason, educational considerations may have taken a back seat while the subjects now at the top of the pile were shot through with utilitarian motives. The elementary education system was not preparing young people adequately enough to engage in industrial pursuits. The existing programme, under the weight of the payment by results regime, was regarded as being too rigid and too centred on literacy and not sufficiently related to 'real life'. New subjects and new methods were needed 'in order to adapt better the instruction to the practical needs of artisan life'. As Mr Magnus put it, 'the school workshop is the emblem of the change in our methods of instruction, which corresponds to these changed conditions of existence.'[84]

At this time too, Socialists in England were attacking the nature of the education available for working-class children pointing out the class basis of its structure and content. In particular the payment by results system was attacked, and the following comment by H. W. Hobart offers a denunciation of the results scheme:

> Week by week, month by month in the most barren and sterile ground, the teacher has to hammer and drive the course of education laid down by law. The children are urged, persuaded, and coaxed into trying to become efficient for the so-called examinations.[85]

82 Quoted in Selleck, *The New Education*, 104.
83 Selleck, *The New Education*, 107.
84 Quoted in Selleck, *The New Education*, 106.
85 Simon, *Education and the Labour Movement 1870–1920*, 146.

The socialist belief held that education reform was essential to enable working-class children realize their optimum potential in the education system. To that end, the very nature and tone of payment by results militated against these children ever realizing their human possibilities. A new system was required, which would not inhibit or prevent children's development to the fullest.

The 1890s proved to be a decade of murmurings with some outpourings of anguish regarding the existing education system, and Ireland formed a part of this general maelstrom of educational thought and concern. Even in the Commissioners' Reports, one can detect an awareness of existing trends. The Commissioners had introduced an Industrial Programme for girls in 1889, and on that occasion it was remarked, 'the Commissioners have resolved that every girl who passes the fifth class shall devote the remainder of her school life mainly to Industrial Education'.[86]

In practice the programme for girls was designed to teach them domestic and craft skills. It was not as successful as the Commissioners would have wished, however, and the *Report* for 1898 registered their disappointment.

The *Report* for 1894 contained the following comment on drawing:

> We do not consider that the circumstances of our schools at present would warrant us in making Drawing a compulsory subject, as it is to a large extent in England, but we should be very glad to see it more extensively taught in the National Schools than at present, as it is that form of technical instruction which is most appropriate for elementary schools.[87]

In England, there had been a strong movement supporting Drawing as a subject in elementary schools. The Technical Instruction Commission had urged in 1884. The reasoning behind the desire for Drawing to be made available in elementary schools is manifest in the following statement. T. R. Ablett, of the London School Board said:

86 Memorandum in the *Fifty-Fifth Report of the Commissioners for 1888*, 132.

87 *Sixty-First Report of the Commissioners, for 1894*, 30.

> How to teach drawing in the elementary schools, so that the graphic language of the workshop may be known to those who need it is a matter of first importance in any steps we take to maintain England's supremacy in manufacturing.[88]

Drawing was made obligatory in most elementary schools in England in 1890. On the other side of the Irish Sea, the Irish Commissioners urged that more schools should offer Drawing and Music to their pupils.[89] Some progress was made but in 1897 it was lamented that 'in Drawing, progress is apparent, but too slow for what we deem to be the requirements of the country'.[90] Be that as it may, the Commissioners were content to hesitate in making the subjects compulsory, and were quite happy to act in accordance with the following 'watery' statement:

> We are fully alive to the importance of these subjects as part of the course of instruction in all National Schools, and we are of opinion that teachers should not be content with their work so long as they fail to include these subjects in their ordinary curriculum.[91]

While no official action was taken to formally include the two subjects on the national school curriculum, the Commissioners were aware of the need to change the hue of the curriculum by emphasizing the need for more technical and industrial subjects.

Due to official beseeches, there was an expansion in the number of schools offering optional and extra subjects over the last decade of the century. See the following table, which sets out the position with regard to extra and optional subjects as it stood after the last examination of the payment by results era in 1899.

88 Selleck, *The New Education*, 121.

89 See the *Sixty-Second Report of the Commissioners, for 1895*, 51.

90 *Sixty-Fourth Report of the Commissioners, for 1897*, 217.

91 *Sixty-Fourth Report of the Commissioners, for 1897*, 217.

Table 10. Percentage Success Rates in Different Subjects of the Compulsory Programme in 1880 and in 1899

| Subject | 1880 | 1899 | Subject | 1880 | 1899 |
|---|---|---|---|---|---|
| Reading | 91.4 | 90.7 | Grammar | 59.8 | 72.0 |
| Spelling | 80.6 | 85.2 | Geography | 58.6 | 79.0 |
| Writing | 93.8 | 94.6 | Agriculture | 46.3 | 66.2 |
| Arithmetic | 74.8 | 81.7 | Needlework | 94.4 | 93.1 |

*Source:* Reports of the Commissioners for 1881 and for 1899.

These figures represent significant progress that was made in the standards recorded in the compulsory subjects over the thirty-year period of payment by results. This probably reveals improvement in attainment levels in these subjects by the pupils though to some degree one suspects that teachers had become very adept at preparing their charges for the well-known course.

## Reflective Remarks

Interpreting the Payment by Results policy in Irish education history from the viewpoint of some generally accepted educational principles from our own day could lead to the temptation of dismissing it denigratingly in a brusque manner. To say the least, this would be very 'unhistorical'. Hindsight can have many advantages, often of great assistance to our understanding of past events and movements, but from time to time its dangers can lead us to superimpose contemporary understandings and attitudes on events of a former time. This does not entirely mean that we have to be bound steadfastly in a final assessment of a scheme by the value-criteria of the earlier era, if one is to understand and gain worthwhile insight into a policy pursued by others at a particular time in our past. In gaining insight and comprehension into the past event, one finds it necessary to identify and take cognisance of the ambitions, desires and general state in which that policy was commenced and operated. Payment by

Results was a significant state policy in education about which many economic, social and political measures revolved. It should never be viewed as an isolated concept. It existed for a considerable number of years, and its effects, whether good or evil, were felt by generations of pupils. As such it deserves more serious study that has hitherto been given to it. The operation of such a system at such a time reveals a great deal about the kind of society and value system in existence at the time. Its existence also reveals a great deal about those denizens of power with whom the system was associated. The historical study of such a topic ought to form a constituent strand in any fabric which aims at giving a measured account of the political and social life of the period.

It has been seen that utilitarian and Classical Economic Theory incorporated a framework of reference within which Payment by Results could be readily conceived. The simplicity and apparent rectitude of the formula 'Payment by Results' had an obvious appeal to the common sense of the general public, who were particularly well attuned to the axioms of self-help and value for the pound. If it were proved possible to test the work of a teacher in the same manner as that of a bricklayer, there seemed to be no earthly reason why the teacher ought not be rewarded on a similar basis. The age in question seems to have come up with such an evaluative mechanism – examinations, in many and varied forms. The teacher's renumeration could then be based on the number of 'products' that were deemed satisfactory by the examination testing mechanism.

Basic to the thought of Utilitarian theorists was the twin radical challenges to the existing system. Firstly, it favoured an extension to the provision of education and set itself against the tradition which saw in the introduction of the wide-scale provision of education, it was felt, would occur due to the increased awareness of people, with resulting danger of a toppling of the political and social order. Coupled with this was a desire for extending the curricula of schools, especially post-primary schools, to take greater cognizance of subjects of a scientific and technical nature, and to demote the hegemony associated with classical and literary studies. Secondly, Utilitarianism desired secularization of education and the dislodgment of the denominational control of education, exercised in England in the early nineteenth century mainly by the Anglican Church.

However, the 'radicalism' and 'liberalism' of Utilitarianism, while sponsoring administrative and social reforms, was nevertheless constrained within narrow limits. Its benefits were, by and large, confined to the emerging middle classes. The economic and social theory of the Utilitarians was directed, not at the undermining and overthrow of the existing English social fabric but rather, at reforming it to make it more efficient and flourishing. The traditional economic policy of *laissez-faire* involving free trade, open-market competition, utility, and non-state intervention, betokened the arrival of free-enterprise entrepreneurism on an unprecedented scale. Many welcomed this revolution of a dilution of the power of the aristocracy of Church and State, and of the land-owning classes. However, Utilitarianism was by no means a social leveller, though a greater place in society was allowed for the middle classes. In truth, the basic elements of the economic structure of society were being buttressed rather than abraded.

## Appraisal and Conclusion

Sir Patrick Keenan, who, as Resident Commissioner since the start of the results period, had championed payment by results died in November 1894. In 1896 inspectors were asked their frank opinions of the operation of payment by results and were asked to submit modifications along certain lines. Many of them were critical of aspects of the operation of payment by results and made suggestions at improving the system. It was as if change was in the air and it was not long until machinery was set in motion to bring it about as a reality.

By the middle 1890s several Commissioners of the National Board were dissatisfied with the results system and aimed at setting the process afoot whereby the curriculum might be reformed. One of the foremost protagonists for reform was Archbishop Walsh[92] who was appointed as

92 Dr Walsh, Catholic Archbishop of Dublin, was closely associated with educational and cultural affairs during his term of office as Archbishop.

a Commissioner of the Board of National Education in 1895. As early as 1886 Dr Walsh spoke out on the need for manual training and education in primary schools.[93] Other Commissioners, such as Chief Baron Palles[94] and Professor Fitzgerald,[95] were also behind the Walsh idea.

When evaluating the introduction of a Payment by Results policy to primary education in Ireland, one has to be mindful of the circumstances in which it was fostered and supported as a worthwhile means of educating and assessing those involved in the system. Super-imposing today's value system on an event which took place in the 1870s may well do a disservice to the earlier time and also to our own time. What may be regarded as altogether unsuitable for the conditions prevailing at one point in history may have a valuable function to perform at an earlier stage in the development of the school system. With regard to these concerns, C. E. Beeby's analysis of the organic stages of development of school systems is of relevance. Perhaps, his study of developing countries and their schools and curricular progress may offer useful signposts for the Irish situation in the closing decades of the nineteenth century. He put forward the hypothesis that there are stages of development in the life history of a primary education system, stages through which all systems, at least of a certain type, must pass, and which, though they may be shortened, cannot be skipped.[96]

By far the most popular Extra Subjects under the Payment by Results scheme were, Kindergarten, Vocal Music, Drawing and Algebra. Though this list gives some cause for optimism, only a fraction of schools offered such subjects. In 1899 it was estimated that there were 905,004 children in the country between the ages of five and thirteen, inclusive. Of these, 513,852 were in average daily attendance at school, and this was seven years after the Compulsory Attendance Act was passed.[97] Taking these figures

93 Patrick J. Walsh, *William J. Walsh, Archbishop of Dublin* (London: Longmans, Green, 1928), 507.

94 The Right Hon. Christopher Palles LL.D., Lord Chief Baron.

95 Professor G. F. Fitzgerald, Professor of Science and Fellow of Trinity College, Dublin.

96 C. E. Beeby, *The Quality of Education in Developing Countries* (Cambridge, MA: Harvard University Press, 1966), 51.

97 *Sixty-Sixth Report of the Commissioners of National Education for the year 1899*, 234, 5.

into account, and infants and first class excluded from extra subjects, the uptake on extra subjects is still very inadequate from the overall perspective.

Towards the end of the results lifespan, dissatisfaction began to come to the surface. This was part of a wider movement towards a more liberal, flexible, balanced curriculum which was taking hold in England. Peculiar to Ireland was the non-Irish content of the curriculum which was being increasingly objected to by groups like the Gaelic League, founded in 1893.

Sir Patrick, who championed the results programme, died in 1894. As Resident Commissioner, he had been a key supporting figure of the system. In 1896 the inspectors were asked their frank opinion of the results regime. They were also asked to submit modifications which could be applied to the programme. It was as if change was in the air.

Archbishop Walsh, of Dublin, and a member of the Commission since 1895, spoke out on the need for manual training in primary schools.[98] Other commissioners followed suit.

The upshot was the final curtain for the results system; few shed a tear for its demise. It no longer matched the needs of the spirit of the times, and, just as thirty years before it was in fashion to extol it, but it was now no longer fashionable to see merit in it. With the dawning of the new century confidence entered the fray, and the new arrangements were welcomed by all those involved.

98 Walsh, *William J. Walsh, Archbishop of Dublin*, 507.

# Conclusion

'The cure for boredom is curiosity. There is no cure for curiosity.'

– Dorothy Parker

The Powis Report of 1870 prepared the educational route for the introduction of the Results Programme to Irish primary schools, while the Belmore Report of 1898 sounded its death knell. Entirely discredited outside Ireland, it had brought about an educational curriculum which was hopelessly obsolete.[1] It had divided the Irish educational field into two camps. It had brought the national progressive growth of Irish education to an end by its iron grip. The experimenter became the 'oddity' in the classroom, a person under suspicion.

By adopting payments by results as a single policy measure and by ignoring altogether or greatly delaying other proposals made contemporaneously by the Powis Commission, the Authorities were adopting an easy way out in seeking the amelioration of defects in national education at the time. Further, the office of teacher was being unfairly put upon, and he was being used as a means to effect improvements in some matters extraneous to his work of teaching. No thought was taken for the many vagaries which might affect the attendance of the pupils and so render the remuneration less.

The sense of rigidity was fostered by the nature of the curriculum under payment by results. A common set curriculum was laid down for the examination in all schools regardless of size or location throughout the country. The system allowed for no flexibility or local orientations in the courses. Children in the back-streets of Dublin were examined in the

1 Balfour, *The Educational Systems of Great Britain and Ireland*, of later generations; Introduction.

same manner as those in the grasslands of Meath, and as those from impoverished holdings in Connemara or the Dingle Peninsula.

The obligatory curriculum remained narrow over the whole results period. By the end of the results period, the Irish curriculum in the national schools was significantly narrower in range than that in other countries, and this led to a drastic overhaul in 1900. During the period in question, the inclusion of subjects like Singing, Drawing, Manual Craft or Physical Education, would surely have made life a little brighter and more interesting. The affective and aesthetic aspect of subjects were neglected. The teaching pattern was didactic, acting on the assumption that it was the teacher's duty to fill the pupils' heads with the information and skills required to pass the examination. The pulse of inquiry, experiment, wonder and awe was withheld from pupils. The antipathy which pupils held towards their schooldays had a generational effect, and the experience had long-term cyclic reactions which affected the educational environment of future generations. Lowndes states:

> Finally children hated their school days, left them behind as soon as possible, soon forgot what they had learnt, and when they came to be parents of the next generation (and marriages took place early) in all too many cases could neither contribute culture to their own children in the home nor readily modify the attitude which they had learnt towards their teachers in their own schooldays.[2]

The study of Payments by Results as a phenomenon of its time is worthwhile and significant for its own sake. Examining it in the cultural diagnostic sense unearths an education policy adopted by society which is reflective of the values inherent within that particular society. Perhaps, aspects of its thinking need not altogether be restricted to the location and time of its most obvious expression. Expressions of its thought and practice are liable to re-emerge at different eras, especially at times of economic distress and exactitude. For example, recent decades in the United States have witnessed a drive for educational accountability in the form of contract performance programmes.

2 G. A. N. Lowndes, *The Silent Social Revolution* (Oxford: Oxford University Press, 1970), 11.

All political, social and economic evolutions have a starting-point, or, at least a spot in history which can highlight some particular event which gives rise to a particular movement, or, in this case a policy injection.

In Ireland, the policy of Payment by Results was introduced, tentatively at first, in 1871 and in the following year the policy became widespread throughout the country.

Between 1871 and 1900, Irish primary schools gained significant experience from the application of Payment by Results. Its introduction to Ireland was accompanied by denominational tensions, which had been a recurring problem for several decades prior to this. At first, some individuals felt that this new system would be good for education, but it had intense consequences on what was being taught in schools, and, also on the teaching methods employed.

The pages of the book examine the operation of Payment by Results at the coalface in which critique, investigation and appraisal are blended. Programmes of examination are studied, along with the prevailing methodologies, the schools' condition and suitability, the pupils' success rates, coupled with attendance rates, teacher renumeration and conditions of employment, the textbooks in use, and equipment available to the teacher. There were many reactions to the results policy, and these are explored. Emerging insights from official commissions' reports are taken on board on how the results policy was performing.

A major assessment and appraisal of the national school system was undertaken by the Royal Commission of Inquiry into Primary Education (1870) – known as the Powis Commission. Having examined various forms of evidence, the Commissioners came to the conclusion that the progress of the children in the national schools of Ireland was very much less than it ought to be. They were particularly disturbed by the low standards of reading, and they asserted in this regard that the results hitherto achieved were far below what was desirable. *The Report* pointed out that a minority of pupils were not achieving higher than Book Three. The reading standards felt the brunt of the results regime, as subject mechanical reading replaced understanding and where the necessity for explanation was forgotten, because there was no fee for it.

As a remedy for this standard of attainment, the Powis Commission recommended the adoption of a Payment by Results scheme which had been introduced in England under the Revised Code of 1862. The *Report* recommended 'that each teacher, besides a fixed-class salary, should receive an addition according to the number of children whom the Inspector, after individual examination, can pass as having made satisfactory progress during the year'. In a climate of teacher accountability and concerns about low standards the Commission hoped that this system would 'be an effectual inducement to more work on the part of the teachers'. It was hoped that teachers would promote younger pupils to higher Books as efficiently as possible. The inducement here was greater fees for the teacher when senior pupils were examined.

The Utilitarians wanted curricular reform for middle-class education because they felt that the existing system was outdated and, on the general grounds of utility, could not be justified. Science and technology were the subjects which the middle classes of the industrial age required. Education could be made available to the working class, and the state could support such elementary education, but the nature of that education was confined to strictly utilitarian limits, the provision of a literate workforce to serve the industrial needs of the day. In this the Utilitarians were opposed by the Socialists whose influence, however, did not prove very significant until the twentieth century.

One side effect of the utilitarian results regime was the strengthening of a denominational hold on the national school system. Its introduction in Ireland was affected by denominational interests, as all educational policy was. Catholic spokespersons desired its adoption in Ireland as it was held that convent schools would benefit from the rewards of its operation. Contemporary efforts by the Treasury in London to limit managerial authority by insisting on contracts of employment for teachers, and the call for local funding of education, as in England, was successfully countered.

Another aspect of the results scheme hinged about demographic and social interests. While the results regime based on pupil attendance would seem appropriate in England, with its large conurbations, its introduction to Ireland under similar criteria, with its widely scattered rural communities and its large number of small one and two-teacher schools would seem to have presaged some foreboding. The only saving grace the teacher had in Ireland was that there was only a partial dependence upon results fees, as opposed to full reliance in England. Without such a modification, the condition of many Irish teachers, in the absence of compulsory school attendance legislation (until 1892), would most certainly be impecunious and insolvent. The Irish National Teachers' Organisation felt that the Payment by Results system did not favour the bulk of the national teachers. To that end, the INTO fought on behalf of their teachers to have the grant extended for teacher remuneration through Payment by Results. By the time the end was nigh for the system the portion of the teachers' income from the results fees had reduced significantly. Luckily, for the Irish teacher, his/her income had been modified by the policy-makers, and thus, the worst effects of the full rigour of the results scheme had been circumvented. This, of course, was a departure from the original Revised Code in England and its stipulation that the teacher be thrown among the children with the full onus of earning a livelihood, based on the examination results of the pupils.

The child's locality did not matter under the results scheme, and to a young child the locale is of prime importance – the local familiar world becomes the whole world. The repetition of the same programme based on the same textbooks year after year tended to foster attitudes of routine and habit as pupils were trained to surmount the familiar hurdles of the annual examinations. One the more baleful aspects of the results scheme was concerned with the manner in which pupils were examined annually. Reading material, for example, was divided into 'heads' and 'sub-heads'. In practice, this meant that if a child could read with ease (heads) but not necessarily understanding what was being read, payment was secured for the teacher. On the other hand, the inspector was entitled to ask the pupil some comprehension questions on the passage being read, but this fell under the 'sub-head' label, and did not count for payment purposes. Thus, the mechanics of reading were deemed to be more important than understanding the content of what was being read. A bright pupil could learn a passage off by heart and recite it, parrot-like in a sing-song manner for the inspector, without being aware of the substance of the content, and yet, gain payment for the teacher. Very few educationists would subscribe to such methodology.

The policy of Payment by Results emerged at a time when societal attitudes allowed such a phenomenon to take root, in countries like England, Wales, Scotland, Ireland, and in such places as Trinidad and Malta. This system bore fruit in the context of an alignment between political and social dispositions that were favourable towards such an educational policy.

During the period of Payment by Results, education became tangible, a commodity that could be measured very easily and in a simplistic manner. It amounted to teacher-testing being analogous to that of a bricklayer's worth being measured by the number of bricks or blocks he or she lays in a day. In the late nineteenth century teachers were seen as processed products, whose worth could be easily computed, resulting in an increase in the value of technical education: the perception was that elements of technical education could be more easily assessed because of its tactile and palpable nature. Perhaps, the use of this crude instrument was the cardinal error of the results regime. What could not be easily measured was omitted from the test, the lowest common denominator being the most important criterion. Vital elements, associated with the classroom were ignored; life enriching interrelationships which often exit between pupil and teacher were overlooked; instead of addressing these issues, the results scheme merely fastened on certain criteria which would indicate basic levels of instruction or training, and thereby, embalming and rigidifying existing poor techniques. Quality of classroom relationships was ignored in favour of quantity. The employment of a results policy merely sanctioned a functional interpretation of the teacher's work in the classroom. The teacher was seen more as an instructor than an educator. Perhaps, in order to counter-balance the argument we should invoke the sentiments of a teacher in Ireland in the twentieth century, when she describes the various incidents and events in the classroom in a typical day: the teacher is a 'guiding hand;' 'initiative, imagination, capability, self-confidence, adaptability and balanced personality' are the qualities a teacher should develop in the pupil. She also writes that classroom

> … work should be a pleasure and the fun/work idea should pervade the curriculum. The children should be taught to associate work well done with a feeling of

> satisfaction, and learn to admire what they have achieved. This feeling of personal satisfaction will encourage them to avail of further education.[3]

The constricting set of rules and regulations laid down in the schools acting as a restraint on teachers, and these constrictions, were likely in the long run to have a degenerative effect on teachers' sense of initiative and ardour. A retired chief inspector in England had the following observation to make regarding Payment by Results. Surely, it applies to Ireland as well:

> It (the results system) did all his thinking for the teacher. It told him in precise detail what he was to do each year in each 'Standard', how he was to handle each subject, and how far he was to go in it; what width of ground he was to cover, what degree of accuracy was required for a 'pass'. In other words, it provided him with his ideals, his general conceptions his more immediate aims, his schemes of work.[4]

On the plus side, as it were, the teacher became very familiar with the type of questions asked by the inspectors on their annual rounds and became very practised at planning for each visit. Cramming and rote learning became the order of the day in the teacher's planning, and memorization was fostered as a methodology in the classroom. The result was all that mattered, the process was inconsequential. Allied to the narrow methodology was the narrow curriculum which remained unchanged throughout the results period. In Ireland the full onus of earning a living was not thrown on the teacher – he/she received a basic salary. This was not the case in England. However, the results programme determined what took place in the primary schools, and because of the annual visit by the inspector, a certain degree of fear entered the classroom – an issue that had quite a lengthy legacy. The inspector became a figure not to be welcomed in Irish classrooms.

Teachers were not the only participants who felt restricted within the system, as inspectors also felt somewhat aggrieved. The *Vice-Regal*

3 Beetie Culloo, 'Years After: Ní Críoch ach Ath-fhás', in Marcus Ó hEochaidh, ed., *Modhscoil Luimnigh, 1855–1986* (Luimneach: An Bórd Bainistíochta, Modhscoil Luimnigh, 1986), 80, 82.

4 Edmond Holmes, *What is and What Might Be* (London: Constable, 1911), 104.

*Committee of Inquiry* of 1913 offers an insight into the plight of the inspector under the results scheme:

> The style of examination, owing to the numbers who had to be examined, the limited time for the work of examination, and the narrow range of subjects, inevitably tended to become mechanical. The limits of the examination were well understood and rigidly defined, and the inspector never deviated from the lines laid down, by rule or custom.[5]

The inspectors' time in the classroom, it seems, was spent as a functionary, when the time could be better spent advancing the cause of education in Irish schools. This form of assessment, year after year, caused much rancour between teacher and inspector, and the child's interests were never listened to or taken into account. One positive aspect of the Payment by Results era cannot be ignored: there was a marginal improvement in literacy levels; we have to be cautious with regard to this phenomenon, as the literacy rates had been improving during the three decades immediately prior to the introduction of the results scheme. However, all the ills of the national school system during the final third of the nineteenth century cannot be attributed to the effects of Payment by Results; the spirit of the age coincided with its introduction to the education system. Perhaps, it may have been desirable to introduce the results scheme for a set period of time when it might operate as a transitional stimulus and beneficial tightening of the national system and help establish some general standards of attainment.[6] William Butler Yeats remarked in another sphere that 'Too long a sacrifice can make a stone of the heart,' and perhaps, too long a devotion to the fixation of 'results' had the effect of deadening the heart and killing the vitality of the education process in Irish primary schools. Schools, unfortunately, became institutionalized into treadmill straitjackets. The policy-makers saw no need to revamp the programme, as they were quite content to allow the serene routine prevail. The trite elements of thought which this denoted only served to compact the cramping hold of the results regime on educational matters

5 *Vice-Regal Committee of Inquiry into Primary Education* (Ireland), 1913 (Cd.7235), H.C. 1914, XXVIII, 1088.

6 Coolahan, *The Origins of the Payment by Results Policy in Education*, 403.

as year followed year in dismal repetition. The adoption of Payment by Results in Irish primary schools between 1872 and 1900 (Model Schools began with the programme in 1871) led to many grave and detrimental effects on education. It was conceived, less as an educational endeavour, but more as a political and administrative tactic. The concept of the results programme was tied up with societal expectations which sought accountability of all aspects of public expenditure. It was part of a centralized bureaucracy monitoring and controlling the workings of the education system. In order to avoid complications, deviation form a set course was not allowed. However, such inflexibility can be dangerous when applied to a process which is strongly based on human individuality and variability as in education. In genuine education teacher-pupil reaction is crucial and unavoidable; such was not the case under the results scheme, as the main concern was the running of schools as opposed to sound educational practice being developed. And, Lowe was wrong as it required a large number of civil servants to run it, and they cost money. In short, the Payment by Results policy failed, and it can only be barely contemplated that it was either 'cheap' or 'efficient'. Though from time to education costs, from the state's viewpoint, can absorb the economy's allotted funds far beyond what had been planned for, it is still imperative to ensure that the liability criteria applied on such occasions are informed and not deleterious to spirit of sound educational principles.

However, hope was at hand, when in both England and Ireland a new approach was introduced in 1900. From now on the stress was on means and methods of education rather than a narrow assessment of the results of the instruction. The policy of 1900 emphasized the quality rather the quantity of instruction and concerned itself with the nature of the curriculum in relation to children's needs and stages of development. The fostering of pedagogic methods and techniques which were educationally valid were part of the philosophy of the Revised Programme of 1900. Education was being directed along channels to expanding seas rather than being trapped in the eddying of the results regime.

The importance of examinations and testing in Irish education gained an incalculable currency, thereby allowing examinations exert a dominant influence on Irish education, an influence which still has a major input in schools in Ireland. The results system controlled what happened in schools. The programmes were laid down for the teachers; they were religiously followed and very closely examined.

One other difference between the Irish and English results schemes was that in Ireland teachers could earn money for teaching extra subjects. Something similar was introduced in England from 1875 onwards – 'Class Subjects', such as History, Geography and Needlework.

Of crucial significance in the late nineteenth century was the chronic attendance levels of pupils – schooling was a seasonal affair. A second drawback to successful teaching and learning was the poor training of teachers. Many teachers had no training at all, and that, coupled with a poor infrastructure and a plethora of one and two-teacher schools, with multiclass levels in situ, all fed into a disreputable primary school system serving the needs of society. Such factors existed irrespective of the results system and, with or without a results policy, would place serious restrictions on what the teacher could achieve. The results scheme cannot take the blame for such conditions and defects, but the policy-makers must bear the brunt of culpability for the conditions which prevailed and we need to have reservations regarding the general political and educational policy which allowed schooling to operate to the extent that it did.

It is most likely that school procedures would have followed similar lines regardless of the existence of Payment by Results. Regardless of prevailing conditions the importance of teaching the basic curriculum with an emphasis on the three Rs would have been the norm at the time, and its place on the curriculum would be a priority. An educational utopia would hardly have replaced the results system upon its abandonment; we have witnessed how the system following 1900 was so ill-conceived and prone to so many flaws. It could be claimed, however, that the clarion call for change in the post-1900 period had to wrestle with a teaching force that had become habituated to the techniques and procedures of Payment by Results. Teachers found it difficult to adjust to the more open and experimental curriculum of the Revised Programme and this contributed to the difficulties in its fruitful implementation. Many of the features associated with the Revised Programme were deficient during the results era but, because of circumstances, an automatic improvement in the classroom of Ireland in the post-1900 era was not necessarily a *fait accompli*.

One positive aspect of the Payment by Results era cannot be ignored: there was a marginal improvement in literacy levels; we have to be cautious with regard to this phenomenon, as the literacy rates had been improving during the three decades immediately prior to the introduction of the results scheme. However, all the ills of the national school system during the final third of the nineteenth century cannot be attributed to the effects of Payment by Results; the spirit of the age coincided with its introduction to the education system. Perhaps, it may have been desirable to introduce the results scheme for a set period of time when it might operate as a transitional stimulus and beneficial tightening of the national system and help establish some general standards of attainment.[7] William Butler Yeats remarked in another sphere that 'Too long a sacrifice can make a stone of the heart,' and perhaps, too long a devotion to the fixation of 'results' had the effect of deadening the heart and killing the vitality of the education process in Irish primary schools. Schools, unfortunately, became institutionalized into treadmill straitjackets. The policy-makers saw no need to revamp the programme, as they were quite content to allow the serene routine prevail. The trite elements of thought which this denoted only served to compact the cramping hold of the results regime on educational matters as year followed year in dismal repetition. The adoption of Payment by Results in Irish primary schools between 1872 and 1900 (Model Schools began with the programme in 1871) led to many grave and detrimental effects on education. It was conceived, less as an educational endeavour, but more as a political and administrative tactic. The concept of the results programme was tied up with societal expectations which sought accountability of all aspects of public expenditure. It was part of a centralized bureaucracy monitoring and controlling the workings of the education system. In order to avoid complications, deviation from a set course was not allowed. However, such inflexibility can be dangerous when applied to a process which is strongly based on human individuality and variability as in education. In genuine education teacher-pupil reaction is

7 Coolahan, *The Origins of the Payment by Results Policy in Education*, 403.

crucial and unavoidable; such was not the case under the results scheme, as the main concern was the running of schools as opposed to sound educational practice being developed. And, Lowe was wrong as it required a large number of civil servants to run it, and they cost money. In short, the Payment by Results policy failed, and it can only be barely contemplated that it was either 'cheap' or 'efficient'. Though from time to education costs, from the state's viewpoint, can absorb the economy's allotted funds far beyond what had been planned for, it is still imperative to ensure that the liability criteria applied on such occasions are informed and not deleterious to spirit of sound educational principles.

By the time we reach the late 1890s we find many commentators seeking an alternative to the narrow system that had been in place since 1871. The Commission on Manual and Practical Instruction in Primary Schools, otherwise known as the Belmore Commission, offered some solace for the future. This Commission, under the guidance of the Earl of Belmore, was a reaction to the progressive commissioners, most notably Lord Chief Baron Palles and the very influential Archbishop Walsh of Dublin. Both of these individuals viewed the existing curriculum in the primary schools as being unsuitable, especially since it emphasized the three Rs to such a degree.

The Belmore Report was radical, indeed revolutionary, emphasizing a new type of curriculum that would include Music, Sewing, Elementary Science, Art and Physical Education. It had investigated schools, not only in Ireland, but in England, Scotland, Germany, Holland, Switzerland and Denmark. Not only did these 'new' subjects get an airing, but methodology would also embrace child-centredness, reflecting first-hand experience, all in tune with international thinking at this time. School life would become brighter and happier. The new Resident Commissioner responded very positively by designing a whole new curriculum, to be termed the Revised Programme of 1900.

This new curriculum mirrored the sentiments of the Belmore Report of 1898. This curriculum was expansive, child-orientated, and person-driven rather than book-driven, and it was far removed from what had gone immediately before it. By this time, the results regime had been abandoned.

Theoretically, the Revised Programme was in keeping with international standards, and it encapsulated the more advanced elements of

European practices at the time. In practice, it was a different story. Starkie, in his wisdom, failed to engage with any of the stakeholders at the developmental stage of the Revised Programme. In hindsight, this proved to be a major stumbling block when it came to its implementation. Neither did the Resident Commissioner offer any recognition to the work of the Belmore Commission and the useful direct contribution it made to the substance of the Revised Programme. Teachers and inspectors were never fully prepared for such a momentous change to their daily routine. Granted, some in-service courses were provided by the Commissioners, but nearly not enough. Another issue was the absence of adequate financial support – a new curriculum, with new subjects proved to be too financially onerous on communities, without support from central authority. On a classroom level, many teachers did not know how to cope with the new regime; they did not understand well enough the peregrinations of child-centredness; neither did they have much familiarity with Froebel or Pestalozzi. Teachers too, underwent changes to their pre-service training, and there were changes made in the manner in which they were paid. The inspection system underwent fundamental changes also. An education system that wishes to introduce radical changes while its teachers and inspectors are disgruntled, is ill-advised.

Regardless of the problems associated with the introduction of the Revised Programme to Irish primary schools in September 1900, some progress was made, though expectations out-paced the reality. Not long after its launch, the process of its revision began, first in 1902 and again in 1904. An English inspector of schools, Mr F. H. Dale, produced his report in 1904. Some changes were made to curriculum: manual instruction was dropped; arithmetic was revised to include more concrete work; cookery now applied to fifth and sixth classes only, and kindergarten received especial attention.

Also, in Gaeltacht and Breac-Ghaeltacht schools, a bilingual programme was introduced in 1904. This had a slow start, but as time went by, it grew in popularity, so that in 1920 it was available in 232 schools.[8]

8 Thomas Walsh, 'The Revised Programme of Instruction, 1900–1922', *Irish Educational Studies* 26, no. 2 (2007), 127–143, 138.

Other aspects of school life also improved in the post-1900 period – the curriculum was enriched by the new subjects; the new methodologies were a welcome facet to schools (where these were employed); following a protracted series of curricula in the nineteenth century, the child was now at the centre of classroom activity (where practised); one could claim that heuristic methods were now in vogue.

Towards the end of the period under review (approximately 1870–1920), we find another report being published and this Killanin Report, not unlike its earlier counterpart, the Belmore Report, laid the foundation stones for another attempt at improving the status of Irish primary education.

The Killanin Vice-Regal Committee on teachers' salaries was established in 1918. One of the results of Killanin was the introduction of a basic salary scheme for all teachers, to replace the existing system of graded salaries. The new scheme included incremental payments. This was not the only reform that Killanin wished to introduce. In order to pay for those reforms, Killanin urged that a local tax rate be applied; local education committees to be set up to look after heating and maintenance in schools; local committees to be established to look after medical and dental care of school children, and amalgamation of small schools. It was a report that addressed most of the key issues in Irish primary education. Many people lauded the initiative, but, also surprisingly some did not agree with the proposals.

To take the suggestions a bit further, the government attempted to introduce legislation in 1919 in order to give the most important aspects of the Killanin Report a firm legal foundation. The MacPherson Bill of 1919 took on the mantle of the efforts at legislation and in this it represented the most comprehensive single effort at legislation for first and second-level schools in the history of Irish education.

There was a generally favourable response to the proposals. However, one of the most powerful organizations in Ireland, the Catholic Church, opposed any interference with the status quo. A bitter campaign ensued from pulpits right throughout the country, and a solemn novena was called upon to aid those who opposed any greater state involvement in Irish education.

The controversy and the bitterness dragged on into 1920. Then MacPherson resigned, while the Catholic hierarchy denounced the Bill in an outright fashion. Perhaps, the bishops understood that following a political settlement, they would gain greater favouritism under a Free State native regime. If one single item in the whole debate can be extracted it is the proposal to establish a central department of education. This caused the most angst among the bishops.

One result from the whole debacle was the insurance that in future any tampering by the state in educational affairs would not succeed without the support of the Catholic Church. The foregoing twenty-year period was fraught with the usual difficulties, namely the relationship between the state and the Catholic hierarchy. One wonders what the outcome would have had common sense prevailed in the light of the introduction of a policy document such as the Revised Programme.

As the results programme in national schools terminated it found few to sing its praises publicly, whatever some people may have thought about it privately. It no longer fitted the spirit of the times, and, as thirty years previously it was in fashion to extol it, it was no longer fashionable to see merit in it. As the new century dawned, there was a confidence in the new arrangements affecting national education of which the Report of the Commissioners for the year 1900 felt they 'will, we trust lead to a great educational advancement and mark the commencement of a new era in the history of National Education'.[9]

The application of a payment by results policy in Irish education led to many grave and injurious effects on education in this country. It was seen by many as an administrative and political ploy rather than as an educational measure. The formulators of the policy drew a false distinction between the role of the educationists and that of the state. It was held that the educationists carried out their task and it was the distinct role of the state to ascertain whether the money it gave in support was in fact being earned. Keenan was very blunt when he stated:

9 *Sixty-Seventh Report of the Commissioners, for 1900*, H.C. 1901 XXI, 569.

> The function of the educationalists is to discover methods of instruction, the function of Government is to discover tests of efficiency. In respect of the latter function, the great discovery of modern times is the system of payment for ascertained results.[10]

Apart from the fact that the crudity of the method actually employed could not have ascertained the results of the educational process, there is a false dichotomy involved. When a monetary reward system is invoked on such testing procedures it becomes clear that the examination 'tail' wags the educational 'dog' in no uncertain terms.

A highly centralized bureaucracy monitored and controlled the general working of the educational system. To avoid complications no flexibility whatever was allowed for situations and conditions which differed widely from one another. With an apparent virtue of impartiality the rules were applied regardless of any mitigating or extenuating circumstances which might have pertained to individual cases.

One of the dangers of such centralized power in the hands of bureaucracies is that, once the system is put in motion, it assumes a life of its own, and it is more likely to be an extenuated life rather than one that is frequently re-assessed. Major Dease, who had long experience with the Education Boards in Ireland, expressed this aspect in a telling manner:

> When regulations are once drafted and printed by a body of officials, the work of these gentlemen is in their own eyes complete: the possibility of their rules being disobeyed or inappropriate or impracticable does not enter into their reckoning, and nothing short of serious trouble will open official eyes to the fact that anything is wrong. Discontent, incongruity, and incompetence may simmer officially unnoticed for years because the machine is far too large and unwieldy to risk upsetting for anything but a grave defect: yet the pretence that such things do not exist will not remove them – least of all in Ireland.[11]

Payment by results took little or no account of the sensitive, delicate features of the teacher-pupil interaction in genuine educational encounter.

10 Report of Keenan's Speech to the Social Science Congress, 1881 in *Freeman's Journal*, 6 October 1881.

11 Major Gerald Dease, *A Plea for Educational Reform* (Dublin: Browne and Nolan, 1925), 47.

Its concern was not with education as such but with the running of schools.

Educationally the payment by results policy failed, and it is only with very myopic administrative eyesight that it could be seen as having been either cheap or efficient. In periods of economic stringency, the call for accountability of education systems absorbing increasing amounts of public funds is likely to be raised. It is vital to ensure that the accountability criteria applied on such occasions are enlightened and not injurious to the heart and spirit of true education.

# Bibliography

## Manuscript Papers


Larcom Papers – Mss. 7652–7655.
Mayo Papers – Ms. 11, 217.
Minutes of the Meetings of the Commissioners of National Education 1866–1873: Mss. 5549–5554; 1878: Ms. 5557; 1899–1900: Mss. 5773–5774.
Monsell Papers – Ms. 8317.


## British Parliamentary Reports


*Commission on Manual and Practical Instruction in Primary Schools under the Board of National Education in Ireland. Appendices to the Reports of the Commissioners*, (C.8925).
*Fiftieth Report .... for the Year Ending 31 March 1883* H.C. 1884 [4053], xxv.
*Fifty-Eighth Report .... for the Year Ending 31 March 1891* H.C. 1892 [6788], xxix.
*Fifty-Fifth Report .... for the Year Ending 31 March 1888* H.C. 1889 [5738], xxxi.
*Fifty-First Report .... for the Year Ending 31 March 1884 H.C.* 1884–1885 [4458], xxiv.
*Fifty-Fourth Report .... for the Year Ending 31 March 1887* H.C. 1888 [5406], xl.
*Fifty-Ninth Report .... for the Year Ending 31 March 1892* H.C. 1893–1894 [7124], xxvii.
*Fifty-Second Report .... for the Year Ending 31 March 1885* H.C. 1886 [4800], xxvii.
*Fifty-Seventh Report .... for the Year Ending 31 March 1890* H.C. 1890–1891 [6411], xxix.
*Fifty-Sixth Report .... for the Year Ending 31 March 1889* H.C. 1890 [6074], xxx.
*Fifty-Third Report .... for the Year Ending 31 March 1886* H.C. 1887 [5082], xxxi.
*Final Report, (Cd. 8923)*, 1898, xiiv.

*First Report of the Commissioners appointed by the Lord Lieutenant to administer Funds Voted by Parliament for the Education of the Poor of Ireland* H.C. 1834 [70], xl.
*Fortieth Report ... for the Year Ending 31 March 1873* H.C. 1874 [965], xix.
*Forty-Eighth Report .... for the Year Ending 31 March 1881* H.C. 1882 [3243], xxiv.
*Forty-Fifth Report .... for the Year Ending 31 March 1878* H.C. 1878–1879 [2312], xxiv.
*Forty-First Report .... for the Year Ending 31 March 1874* H.C. 1875 [1228], xxv.
*Forty-Fourth Report .... for the Year Ending 31 March 1877* H.C. 1878 [2031], xxix.
*Forty-Ninth Report .... for the Year Ending 31 March 1882* H.C. 1883 [3651], xxvi.
*Forty-Second Report ... for the Year Ending 31 March 1875* H.C. 1876 [1503], xxiv.
*Forty-Seventh Report .... for the Year Ending 31 March 1880* H.C. 1881 [2925], xxxiv.
*Forty-Sixth Report .... for the Year Ending 31 March 1879* H.C. 1880 [2592], xxiii.
*Forty-Third Report .... for the Year Ending 31 March 1876* H.C. 1877 [1757], xxxiv.
*Minutes of the Commissioners of National Education*, Ms., 5550, 17 July 1866. National Library of Ireland.
*Report from the Select Committee on Foundation Schools and Education in Ireland*, H.C. 1837–1838, vii, (701), 345–437.
Reports of the Commissioners of National Education in Ireland:
*Royal Commission of Inquiry into Primary Education (Ireland)*, vol. 1, pt 1 *Report of the Commissioners*, (C.6), H.C. 1870, xxviii, pt 1.
*Royal Commission on Manual and Practical Instruction in Primary Schools under the Board of National Education*, 1898.
*Royal Commission ...*, vol. III, Minutes of Evidence, (C.6–11), H.C. 1870, xxviii, pt III.
*Second Report of the Commissioners of National Education in Ireland for the Year Ending, 31 March 1835* H.C. 1835 [300], xxxv.
*Second Report of the Commissioners of Public Instruction, Ireland* H.C. 1835.
*Second Report*, (Cd.8531), 1897, xiiii.
*Sixtieth Report .... for the Year Ending 31 March 1893* H.C. 1894 [7457], xxx, pt ii.
*Sixty-Eighth Report .... For the Year Ending 31 March 1901* H.C. 1902 [Cd.1198], xxx.
*Sixty-Fifth Report .... For the Year Ending 31 March 1898–1899* H.C. 1899 [9446], xxiv.
*Sixty-First Report .... For the Year Ending 31 March 1894* H.C. 1895 [7796], xxiv.
*Sixty-Fourth Report .... for the Year Ending 31 March 1897* H.C. 1898 [9038], xxvii.
*Sixty-Ninth Report .... For the Year Ending 31 March 1902* H.C. 1903 [Cd.1679], xxi.
*Sixty-Second Report .... For the Year Ending 31 March 1895* H.C. 1896 [8142], xxviii.
*Sixty-Seventh Report .... For the Year Ending 31 March 1900* H.C. 1901 [Cd. 704], xxi.
*Sixty-Sixth Report .... For the Year Ending 31 March 1899–1900* H.C. 1900 [Cd. 285], xxiii.
*Sixty-Third Report .... For the Year Ending 31 March 1896* H.C. 1897 [8600], xxviii.
*Third Report*, (Cd.8618), 1897, xiiii.

*Third Report .... for the Year Ending 31 March 1836* [44], 1836, xxxvi.
*Thirty-Eighth Report ... for the Year Ending 31 March 1871* H.C. 1872 [599], xxiii.
*Thirty-Ninth Report ... for the Year Ending 31 March 1872* H.C. 1873 [805], xxv.
*Thirty-Seventh Report .... for the Year Ending 31 March 1870* H.C. 1871 [360], xxiii.
*Vice-Regal Committee of Inquiry into Primary Education (Ireland), 1918: Report of the Committee, vol. 2, Summaries of Evidence, Memoranda, and Returns* (Cd. 178), H.C. 1919, XXI.

## Books

Adamson, John William, *A Short History of Education* (Cambridge: Cambridge University Press, 1930). Republished by Cambridge University Press, 2013.
Akenson, D. H., *Education and Enmity* (Newton Abbot: David and Charles, 1973).
Akenson, D. H., *The Irish Education Experiment: The National System of Education in the Nineteenth Century* (London: Routledge and Kegan Paul, 1970).
Akenson, Donald Harman, *A Mirror to Kathleen's Face: Education in Independent Ireland, 1922–1960* (London and Montreal: McGill-Queen's University Press, 1975).
Altick, Richard D., *The English Common Reader: A Social History of the Mass Reading Public, 1800–1900* (Chicago: University of Chicago Press, 1957).
Arnold, M., 'Irish Catholic and British Liberalism', in R. H. Super, ed., *Religious and Mixed Essays – 1878* (Ann Arbor: University of Michigan Press, 1972).
Atkinson, N., *Irish Education: A History of Educational Institutions* (Dublin: Allen Figgis, 1969).
Atkinson, Norman, *Irish Education: A History of Educational Institutions* (Dublin: Allen Figgis, 1969).
Balfour, Graham, *The Educational Systems of Great Britain and Ireland* (Oxford: Clarendon Press, 1903).
Barnard, H. C., *A History of English Education from 1760* (London: University of London Press, 1961).
Bartlett, T., *The Fall and Rise of the Irish Nation: The Catholic Question 1690–1830* (Dublin: Gill and MacMillan, 1992).
Bentham, Jeremy, *A Fragment on Government and an Introduction to the Principles of Morals and Legislation*. Ed. By Wilfrid Harrison (Oxford: Blackwell, 1948).
Berlin, I. and H. Hardy, ed., *The Power of Ideas* (London: Chatto and Windus, 2000).

Black, R. D. Collison, *Economic Thought and the Irish Question 1817–1870* (1st ed. 1960. Republished Cambridge University Press, 2015).

Bowen, J., *A History of Western Education: The Modern West, Europe and the New World* (London: Methuen, 1985). E-Book, 2013.

Boyce, D. G., *Nineteenth-Century Ireland: The Search for Stability* (Dublin: Gill and MacMillan, 1990).

Bull, Philip, *Land, Politics and Nationalism: A Study of the Irish Land Question* (Dublin: Gill and Macmillan, 1996).

Butt, Isaac, *Irish National Education: The Liberty of Teaching Vindicated* (Dublin, 1865). Republished as Isaac Butt, *The Liberty of Teaching Vindicated; Reflections and Proposals on the Subject of Irish National Education with an Introductory Letter to the Right Honourable Wm. E. Gladstone, M. P.* (London: Forgotten Books, 2018), or General Books, 2012.

Butt, Issac, *The Liberty of Teaching Vindicated: Reflections and Proposals on the Subject of Irish National Education with an Introductory Letter to the Right Honourable Wm. Gladstone, M.P.* (London: Forgotten Books, 2018).

Cannan, Ed., ed., *Wealth of Nations* (London: Methuen, vol. 2, 1904). Smith, Adam, *Wealth of Nations* (Chichester: Capstone, 2010).

Castle, Edgar Bradshaw, *The Teacher* (Oxford: Oxford University Press, 1970).

Clarke, D. M., *Church and State: Essays in Political Philosophy* (Cork: Cork University Press, 1985).

Collison Black, R. D., *Economic Thought and the Irish Question, 1817–1870* (Cambridge: Cambridge University Press, 1960). Published online by CUP, 2011.

Cook, T. G., ed., *The History of Education in Europe* (London: Methuen, 1974).

Coolahan, J. and O'Donovan, P., *A History of Ireland's School Inspectorate, 1831–2008* (Dublin: Four Courts Press, 2009).

Coolahan, John, *Towards the Era of Lifelong Learning: A History of Irish Education, 1800–2016* (Dublin: Institute of Public Administration, 2017).

Corish, Patrick J., ed., *A History of Irish Catholicism*, vol. v: Catholic Education (Dublin: Gill and MacMillan, 1971).

Cunningham, J. and Ó Cíosáin, N., eds, *Culture and Society in Ireland since 1750: Essays in Honour of Gearóid Ó Tuathaigh* (Dublin: Lilliput Press, 2015).

Curtis, S. J. and Boultwood, M. E. A., *An Introductory History of English Education since 1800* (London: University Tutorial Press, 1970).

Curtis, Stanley James, *An Introductory History of English Education since 1800* (London: University Tutorial Press, 1967). Republished by Harper Collins, 1976.

De Montmorency, J. D. G., *State Intervention in English Education* (Cambridge: Cambridge University Press, 1902).

Doyle, J., *Model Schools – Model Teachers?: A Nineteenth Century Irish Teacher Training Initiative* (Kilkenny: Geata Buidhe Books, 2020).
Drudy, Sheelagh, ed., *Education in Ireland: Challenge and Change* (Dublin: Gill and Macmillan, 2009).
Edgeworth, R. L. and Maria, *Practical Education* (London: Johnson, 1798).
Edgeworth, R. L., *Memoirs of Richard Lovell Edgeworth* (Shannon: Irish University Press, 1969); Republished by Cambridge University Press, 2011. Original work concluded by his daughter (1820).
Farren, Seán, *The Politics of Irish Education, 1920–1965* (Belfast: Queen's University of Belfast, 1995).
Fenton, S., *It All Happened – Reminiscences* (Dublin: Gill, 1948).
Fitzpatrick, D., 'The Futility of History: A Failed Experiment in Irish Education', in Ciaran Brady, ed., *Ideology and the Historians, Historical Studies XVII* (Dublin: Lilliput Press, 1991), 168–183.
Foucault, Michel, *Security, Territory, Population: Lectures at the College de France, 1977–1978*, translated by G. Burchell (London: Palgrave Macmillan, 2007).
Garvin, Tom, *Preventing the Future: Why Was Ireland So Poor for So Long?* (Dublin: Gill and Macmillan, 2004).
Glendenning, D., *Education and the Law*. 3rd ed. (Dublin: Bloomsbury Professional, 2022).
Goldstrom, J. M., *Education: Elementary Education, 1780–1900* (Newton Abbot: David and Charles, 1972).
Goldstrom, Joachim Max, *The Social Content of Education, 1808–1870* (Shannon: Irish University Press, 1972). Published by Rowan and Littlefield, 1978.
Grenham, Thomas G. and Kieran, Patricia, eds, *New Educational Horizons in Contemporary Ireland: Trends and Challenges* (Oxford: Peter Lang, 2012).
Hawkins, A., *The Forgotten Prime Minister: The 14th Earl of Derby* (Oxford: Oxford University Press, 2007).
Hobsbawn, Eric J., *Industry and Empire: From 1750 – the Present Day* (Hammondsworth: Penguin, 1987).
Hodgson, W. B., *Exaggerated Estimates of Reading and Writing as a Means of Education* (1867). This essay was published online by Cambridge University Press, 2017.
Hunter, Sandy Leslie, *The Scottish Education System* (Oxford: Pergamon Press, 1972).
Hyland, Áine and Milne, Kenneth, eds, *Irish Educational Documents*, vol. 1 (Dublin: Church of Ireland College of Education, 1987).
Jarman, T. L., *Landmarks in the History of Education: English Education as Part of the European Tradition* (London: John Murray, 1970).
Joyce, P. W., *A Handbook of School Management and Methods of Teaching* (Dublin: Gill, 1892). First Pub., 1863.

Joyce, Patrick Weston, *The Teaching of Manual Work in Schools* (Dublin: Gill and Sons, 1892).

Kaestle, C. F., *Joseph Lancaster and the Monitorial School Movement: A Documentary History* (London: Teachers' College Press, 1973).

Kelly, James and Hegarty, Susan, eds, *Schools and Schooling, 1650–2000: New Perspectives on the History of Education* (Dublin: Four Courts Press, 2017).

Kingsmill-More, H., *An Unwritten Chapter in the History of Education* (London: Macmillan, 1904).

Lawson, J. and Silver, H., *A Social History of Education in England* (London: Methuen, 1973). E-Book imprint by Routledge in 2013.

Lee, J., *The Modernisation of Irish Society 1848–1918* (Dublin: Gill and MacMillan, 1981).

Logan, John, ed., *Teachers' Union: The TUI and Its forerunners, 1899–1994* (Dublin: A. and A. Farmar, 1999).

Lowe, Robert, *Middle Class Education: Endowment or Free Trade* (London: n.p., 1868).

Lowe, Robert, *Primary and Classical Education* (Edinburgh: Edmonston and Douglas, 1867).

Lowe, Robert, *The Revised Code of Regulations of the Privy Council on Education* (London: Ridgeway, 1862).

Lowndes, G. A., *The Silent Social Revolution* (Oxford: Oxford University Press, 1969). First Pub., 1937.

Lyons, Tony, *The Education Work of Richard Lovell Edgeworth, Irish Educator and Inventor, 1744–1817* (Lewiston: Mellen Press, 2003).

McCallister, W. J., *The Growth of Freedom in Education: A Critical Interpretation of some Historical Views* (London: Constable and Co., 1931).

McDowell, R. B., *The Irish Administration 1801–1914* (Connecticut: Greenwood Press, 1964).

McDowell, Robert Brendan (R. B.), *Ireland in the Age of Imperialism and Revolution 1760–1801* (Oxford: Clarendon Press, 1979).

McElligott, T. J., *Education in Ireland* (Dublin: Institute of Public Administration, 1966).

McElligott, T. J., *Secondary Education in Ireland, 1870–1921* (Dublin: Irish Academic Press, 1981).

Maclure, J. S., *Educational Documents: England and Wales, 1816–1967* (London: Chapman and Hall, 1968).

McMillan, N., ed., *Prometheus's Fire: A History of Scientific and Technological Education in Ireland* (Kilkenny: Tyndall Books, 2000).

MacNeill, M., *Vere Foster: An Irish Benefactor* (Newton Abbott: David and Charles, 1971).

Maltby, S. E., *Manchester and the Movement for National Elementary Education, 1800–1870* (London: Longmans, 1918). Reprinted and published by Ulan Press, 2012.

Mill, James, *On Education*. Ed. by W. H. Burston (Cambridge: Cambridge University Press, 1969).

Mill, John Stuart, *Principles of Political Economy*. Ed. by David Winch (Harmondsworth: Penguin, 1970).

Miller, David W., *Church, State and Nation in Ireland* (Dublin: Gill and Macmillan, 1973).

Moroney, M., *National Teachers' Salaries and Pensions 1831–2000: A Historical Chronology and Review of the Role of the INTO* (Dublin: Institute of Public Administration, 2007).

Morrish, Ivor, *Education since 1800* (London: George Allen and Unwin, 1973).

Morrissey, Thomas J., *Bishop Edward Thomas O'Dwyer of Limerick, 1842–1917* (Dublin: Four Courts Press, 2003).

Murphy, A., ed., *Economists and the Irish Economy from the Eighteenth Century to the Present Day* (Dublin: Irish Academic Press, 1984).

Neuburg, V. E., ed., *The Social History of Education, First Publication* (Central Society of Education, Taylor and Walton, 1837). Reprint Woburn Press, 1968.

Norman, Andrew, *Charles Darwin: Destroyer of Myths* (New York: Skyhorse Publishing, 2014).

Norman, E. R., *The Catholic Church and Ireland in the Age of Rebellion, 1859–1873* (London: Longmans, 1965).

Ó Buachalla, Séamus, *Education Policy in Twentieth-Century Ireland* (Dublin: Wolfhound Press, 1988).

Ó Glaisne, Risteárd, *Dúghglás de h-Íde, 1860–1949* (BÁC: Conradh na Gaeilge, 1993).

Ó hÉideáin, E., *National School Inspection in Ireland: The Beginnings* (Dublin: Scepter, 1967). Published online by Cambridge University Press, 2016.

Ó hEochaidh, Marcus, ed., *Modhscoil Luimnigh, 1855–1986* (An Bórd Bainistíochta, Modhscoil Luimnigh, nd).

Ó hUallacháin, Seán Breandán, *Pobal an Stáit agus an Ghaeilge, 1920–1939* (BÁC: Coiscéim, 2010).

O' Donoghue, Tom and O'Doherty, Teresa *Radical Reform in Irish schools, 1900–1922: The 'New Education' Turn* (London: Palgrave MacMillan, 2021).

O'Brien, G., *Anglo-Irish Politics in the Age of Grattan and Pitt* (Dublin: Irish Academic Press, 1987).

O'Connell, T. J., *History of the Irish National Teachers' Organisation 1868–1968* (Published by the INTO, 1968).

O'Connor, Joseph, *Hostage to Fortune* (Dublin: M.F. Moynihan Books, 1955).

O'Donoghue, Tom and Harford, Judith *Piety and Privilege: Catholic Secondary Schooling in Ireland and the Theocratic State, 1922–1967* (Oxford: Oxford University Press, 2021).

O'Donovan, P., *Stanley's Letter: The National School System and Inspectors, 1831–1922* (Galway: Galway Education Centre, 2017).

Parkes, Susan, *A Guide to Sources for the History of Irish Education, 1780–1922* (Dublin: Four Courts Press, 2010).

Paz, D. G., *The Politics of Working-Class Education in Britain, 1830–1850* (Manchester: Manchester University Press, 1980).

Plamenatz, John P., *The English Utilitarians* (Oxford: Basil Blackwell, 1966).

Pollard, H. M., *Pioneers of Popular Education, 1760–1850* (London: John Murray, 1956).

Raftery, Deirdre and Fischer, Karin, eds, *Educating Ireland: Schooling and Social Change, 1700–2000* (Dublin: Irish Academic Press, 2014).

Silver, Harold, *English Education and the Radicals, 1780–1850* (London: Routledge and Kegan Paul, 1975).

Silver, Harold, *The Concept of Popular Education* (London: MacGibbon Kee, 1965). Republished by Routledge 2013.

Simon, B., *Education and the Labour Market 1870–1920* (London: Lawrence and Wishart, 1965).

Simon, Brian, *The State and Educational Change: Essays in the History of Education and Pedagogy* (London: Lawrence and Wishart, 1994).

Simon, Brian, *The Two Nations and the Educational Structure* (London: Lawrence and Wishart, 1960).

Smith, Adam, *An Inquiry into the Nature and Causes of the Wealth of Nations*, vol. 1. Ed. by Edwin Cannon (London: Methuen, 1904).

Somervell, D. C., *English Thought in the Nineteenth Century* (London: Methuen, 1964).

Spencer, Herbert *Essays on Education* (London: J. M. Dent and Sons, 1963).

Stephens, W. B., *Education in Britain, 1750–1914* (London: Macmillan Press, 1998).

Stephens, W. B., *Education, Literacy and Society, 1830–1870: The Geography of Diversity in Provincial England* (Manchester: Manchester University Press, 1987).

*Supplement to the Encyclopaedia Britannica* (1818).

Sutherland, G., ed., *Arnold on Education* (London: Penguin, 1973).

Sylvester, D. W., *Robert Lowe and Education* (Cambridge: Cambridge University Press, 1974).

Taylor, John, *Amalgamation of Unions, and Pauper and National Education in Ireland* (Dublin: John Falconer, 1857). Reprinted by Bibliolife, n.d.

Walsh, B., ed., *Education Studies in Ireland: The Key Disciplines* (Dublin: Gill and MacMillan, 2011).

Walsh, Brendan, ed., *Essays in the History of Irish Education* (Basingstoke: Palgrave Macmillan, 2016).
Wardle, David, *English Popular Education 1780–1970* (Cambridge: Cambridge University Press, 1970).
Warnock, M., ed., *Utilitarianism – Selections of Writings of J. S. Mill, Jeremy Bentham, John Austin* (Fontana, 1972).
Willey, Basil, *Nineteenth-Century Studies: Coleridge to Matthew Arnold* (Cambridge: Cambridge University Press, 1980). First Pub., Chatto and Windus, 1949.
Williams, R., *Culture and Society, 1780–1950* (Harmondsworth: Penguin, 1971).
Williams, Raymond, *The Long Revolution* (London: Chatto and Windus, 1961).
Wiseman, S., ed., *Examinations and English Education* (Manchester: Manchester University Press, 1986).

## Articles

Bane, L., 'John MacHale and John MacEvilly: Conflict in the Nineteenth Century Catholic Hierarchy', *Archivium Hibernicum* XXXIX (1984).
Breathnach, M., 'The Infancy of School Inspection', *Irish School Weekly* Nov. 7, 14(1953).
Burton, E. F., 'Richard Lovell Edgeworth's Education Bill of 1799: A Missing Chapter in the History of Irish Education', *The Irish Journal of Education* 8/1 (1979), 24–33.
Coolahan, J., 'Fear of the Imagination: Roots of the Tradition', Paper Read at the European Conference on Reading in St. Patrick's College, Dublin, 15 July 1985.
Coolahan, J., 'The Ideological Framework of the Payment by Results Policy in Nineteenth Century Education', *Proceedings of the Education Conference, University College, Cork, 24–26 March 1977*, 166–171.
Dalton, M., 'Irish Education', *Westminster Review*, September (1897), 306–315.
Hogan, P., 'Teacher Education and Higher Learning', *Studies* Summer (1982), 109–120.
Hyland, Áine, 'The Treasury and Irish Education: 1850–1922: The Myth and the Reality', *Irish Educational Studies* 3/2 (1983), 57–82.
*Journal of Statistical and Social Enquiry Society of Ireland* III (1863), 82–93. See F. W. Connor, 'Competitive Examination and the Civil Service'.
Magee, J., 'The Master', *An Múinteoir Náisiúnta* 27/2 (1983), 17–23.

Marcham, A. J., 'The Revised Code of Education, 1862: Reinterpretations and Misinterpretations', *History of Education* 10/2 (1981), 81–89.

Murdoch, J. and Ward, N., 'Governmentality and Territoriality Statistical Manufacture of Britain's 'National Farm', *Political Geography* 16/4 (1997), 307–324.

O' Doherty, T., 'William Starkie: The Teachers' Adversary', *Irish Educational Studies* 18/1 (1999), 248–260.

O'Donoghue, Thomas, 'Teacher-Based Curriculum Development: The Case of the Bilingual Programme of Instruction, 1904–1922', *Oideas* 33/3 (1988), 82–94.

O'Donovan, Patrick, 'Archbishop Walsh and the Commission on Manual and Practical Instruction', *Irish Educational Studies* 6/2 (1986–1987), 76–87.

Raftery, D., '"Among School Children": The Churches, Politics and Irish Schooling, 1830–1930', *A Century of Studies* 100/400 (2011), 433–440.

Rogers, N, 'Class and Popular Education in Nineteenth-Century Britain', *History of Education Quarterly* Spring (1978), 476–488.

Taylor, B. W., 'Jeremy Bentham and the Education of the Irish People', *The Irish Journal of Education* XIV/1(1980), 19–32.

Walsh, T., 'The Revised Programme of Instruction, 1900–1922', *Irish Educational Studies* 26/2 (2007), 127–143.

Ward, M. H., 'The Irish Language Movement', *Irish Educational Review* 1/10 (July 1908), 610–615. Larkin, E., 'The Devotional Revolution in Ireland 1850–1875', *American Historical Review* 77 (1972), 625–652.

*Westminster Review* 1 (1824), 43–79.

## Unpublished Theses

Carton, J. J., *The Development of Technical Education in Ireland 1889–1930* (M.Ed., Trinity College, Dublin, 1972).

Coolahan, John M., *The Origins of the Payment by Results Policy in Education and the Experience of It in the National and Intermediate Schools of Ireland* (M.Ed., thesis, Trinity College, Dublin, 1975).

Cremin, Peadar, *The Irish Language as a Medium of Instruction and as a School Subject, 1800–1921* (M.Ed., University College, Cork, 1977).

Galway, Síle, *Towards Bilingualism in Ireland* (MA, UUC, 1988).

Hayes, J. C., *Bilingualism as an Objective in Education in Ireland, 1893–1941* (M.Ed., Trinity College, Dublin, 1982).

Hyland, Áine, *Educational Innovation: A Case History. An Analysis of Events Leading up to and Following the Introduction to the Revised Programme of 1900 for National Schools in Ireland* (M.Ed., Trinity College, Dublin, 1975).

Jacques, William, *The Chief Factors Determining Developments in Primary Education, Ireland 1831–1947* (Doctoral thesis, Queen's University, Belfast, 1952).

Kelly, Mary, *The Organisation and Control of Educational Knowledge in Irish National Schools, 1831–1900* (Unpublished Doctoral Thesis, Sociology Department, University College Dublin, 1978).

Keogh, Helen, *The Starkie Era – the System of National Education in Ireland, 1899–1922* (MA, University College Galway, 1974).

McBride, Joseph, *A Study of the Contribution of Chief-Secretary Augustine Birrell to Primary and Post-Primary Education in Ireland, 1907–1916* (Maynooth: M. Ed., 1997).

McElligott, T. J., *Intermediate Education and the Work of the Commissioners, 1870–1922* (M.Litt., Thesis, Trinity College, Dublin, 1969).

Nic an Ríogh, M., *The Working Conditions of the Irish National Teacher, 1831–1868* (Unpublished M.Ed., thesis submitted to the Education Department, University College, Dublin, 1986).

Ó hAodha, C., *Bilingualism as an Objective in Ireland, 1893–1941* (Unpublished M.Ed., Thesis, 1982. Submitted to Trinity College, Dublin).

O' Dubhthaigh, F. S., *A Review of the Contribution of Sir Patrick Keenan to the Development of Irish and British Colonial Education* (M.Ed., Thesis, Trinity College, Dublin, 1974).

O'Connor, D., *Secondary Education in Ireland 1878–1968* (MA thesis, Maynooth College, 1971).

O'Donoghue, Tom, *An Analysis of the Origin, Development and Implementation of the Bilingual Programme of Instruction, 1906–1922* (M.Ed., University College, Dublin, 1986).

O'Sullivan, D. M., *Catholic Schooling in Mid-Victorian Ireland* (M.Ed., University College, Dublin, 1996).

Rudd, Ann, *The Introduction of the Payment by Results Policy in England and Ireland, 1850–1879: A Comparative Case Study* (M.Ed., Trinity College, Dublin).

Spallen, R. A., *Dr W. J. M. Starkie and the Inspection System in National Education in Ireland, 1889–1922* (M.Ed., Queen's University, Belfast, 1976).

## Newspapers

Belfast Irish News
Daily Independent
Freeman's Journal
Irish Independent
Irish School Weekly (various)
Irish Times
Northern Whig

# Index

www.ingramcontent.com/pod-product-compliance
Ingram Content Group UK Ltd.
Pitfield, Milton Keynes, MK11 3LW, UK
UKHW020200290926
15471UKWH00005B/973

9 781803 741796